MR. ELBRIDGE T. GERRY

FOUNDER OF THE SOCIETY FOR THE PREVENTION OF CRUELTY TO CHILDREN

The Child

in

Human Progress

By

George Henry Payne

With a Foreword by

A. Jacobi, M.D., LL.D.

With 40 Illustrations

G. P. Putnam's Sons

New York and London

The Knickerbocker Press

1916

Copyright, 1916
BY
GEORGE HENRY PAYNE

The Knickerbocker Press, New York

FOREWORD

THIS is a new sort of book, and unique. That is why I look upon the permission to write a brief preface for it as a rare privilege. Writings on children are frequent. When, in 1875, I contributed, for Karl Gerhardt's immense *Handbuch*, my *Hygiene of the Child*, I quoted seven hundred treatises or pamphlets on that subject. There are now at least seven thousand of the kind, and the number of text-books on the diseases of children and infants do no longer lead a pardonable, rarely a laudable, existence. A few monographs on special subjects, or modern publications, as Erich Wulffen's *The Child: His Nature and Degeneration* (Berlin, 1913), or the two large anthropological volumes by H. Ploss, *The Child in the Customs and Morals of Nations* (third edition by B. Renz, 1911), are praiseworthy examples of useful books. But while these are instructive they do not rouse historical interest.

Indeed, the history of the child has been grossly neglected. The epoch-making works of Rosenstein, Charles West, Rilliet and Barthez, and Karl Gerhardt contain no history. The work of Puschmann (Neuberger and Pagel) fills twenty pages with the history of the child in a text of

three thousand pages relating to the history of
medicine. Altogether our country has been dis-
respectful to its best possessions, viz., the children.
There was until a few decades ago not even a
professional teaching of the children's diseases
in our medical schools. A regular chair was
established in 1860 (New York Medical College),
—it lasted for a few years only. The second was
in 1898 (Harvard). There were few child's
hospitals or wards in hospitals until a few years
ago, even in the largest cities. Society, law,
humanitarianism did not mind children. It is
only a few months that an official publication in our
democratic country carried the title; "Is There a
Need of a Child Labour Law?" and our civilization
was humbled by medical discussion of the ad-
visability of killing the deformed or unpromising
newborn. It seems to take a long time before
this republic of ours begins to work out of the ruts
of semi-barbarism. And now, at last, there is a
book to supply our wants.

Laymen have advanced ahead of the medical
profession. Christ and the Stoics, the clergy and
the public opinion of the Crusades and the Christian sentiments of the Mediæval Church, aye, the
great slaughterer and revolutionary reformer,
Napoleon, have called the children under their
protection and benefactions.

A vast amount of study relating to primary
populaces and nations in gradual development
was required to learn the history of the child.

Foreword v

Without the history of the child there cannot be a scientific knowledge of the thousands of years of child life. Nobody has given it until the author of this book afforded us the wealth of his vast studies. This book furnishes what no other work presents to us. I know of none which acquaints us with the position of the child in his social, political, and humanitarian existence in all nations and in all eras. Adults and adult life have long been served by the endeavours of historians, philosophers, and psychologists. We do not believe in completeness of our knowledge unless all that have been perfected. Medical men do not believe in possessing a scientific grasp of any of their subjects without an embryological basis. Statesmen, aye, even politicians, of the better class, insist upon an ample knowledge of the history of their countries, their institutions, and their laws. That is how the last years of our medical and professional life in this country have developed amongst us physicians the taste for history and such books as Fielding Garrison has been able to prepare for us within the last year.

When I said the book before us was unique, I meant to say that it is a special monograph of the life through thousands of years of slow physical, domestic, economic, social existence of the child. No historian, no medical practitioner or teacher, surely no existing pediatrist will be without it.

A. JACOBI.

NEW YORK CITY, *December 21, 1915.*

PREFACE

THE introduction of Dr. Jacobi has saved the author from the onerous task, ofttimes a graceless one, of writing extended prefatory remarks. It was in the course of some researches into the origin of the Child Protection movement in this country that I discovered how little attention had been paid to the historical aspect of this important question. This book represents really a process of elimination, behind which were many fascinating byways, alluring blind alleys, and seeming countless beckoning theories. Toward the last, for a person with human instinct writing on a humane subject, it was hard not to tilt. In the main, however, the author believes that he has hewed to the line.

The author is indebted for many courtesies to the officials of the New York Public Library, likewise to the Congressional Library at Washington, the British Museum at London, and the Bibliothèque Nationale at Paris. His thanks are due also to Dr. C. C. Williamson, formerly Chief of the Economics Division of the New York Public Library, who took a deep and serious interest in the work; to Professor Richard Gottheil of Columbia, for many helpful suggestions in connection with the Semitics studies; to Professor Hiram Bingham of Yale, for some helpful notes on the Incas; to Mr. A. S. Freidus, Chief of the Jewish Division of the New York Public Library; to Professor Adolf Deissmann, of the University of Berlin; to Mr. Elbridge T. Gerry, whose library provided a wealth of material; to the late Thomas D. Walsh, Superintendent of the New York S. P. C. C., a humanitarian of the first water; to Mr. Jesse B. Jackson, Mr. W. J. Yerby, Mr. Charles H. Allbrecht, and Mr. E. A. Wakefield, all of the American Consular Service; to Mr. J. William Davis, for supervision of the Bibliography; to Mr. Gabriel Schlesinger, for assistance in reading the proofs; and, above all, to Mr. Robert E. MacAlarney, of Columbia University, to whose sustaining criticism and deep personal interest the author owes more than can be here set down.

GEORGE HENRY PAYNE.

KINGSBRIDGE, NEW YORK
January, 1916

CONTENTS

ix

CHAPTER XVII

CHAPTER XVIII

CHAPTER XIX

CHAPTER XX

CHAPTER XXI

Contents

ILLUSTRATIONS

Illustrations

Illustrations

History of the Child

CHAPTER I

MATERNAL AFFECTION THE BEGINNING OF HUMAN
ALTRUISM—SYMPATHY AND PARENTAL LOVE THE
BASIS OF OTHER VIRTUES—THE WEAKEST SACRI-
FICED IN ALL PRIMITIVE SOCIETY—NEGLECTED
CHAPTERS IN THE HISTORY OF THE ATTITUDE OF
SOCIETY TOWARD CHILDREN.

IF it were possible to postulate the first definite
concept of the first family that crossed the
vague and age-consuming frontier between
animality and humanity, it would be safe to say
that this primitive and almost animal mind would
reach for an approximation, on the part of the
male, to the maternal affection.

In the gathering of food and the making of
protective war, many animals are the rivals in
instinct and intelligence of primitive man. Continued development in that regard might have
produced a race of men "formidable among animals through sheer force of sharp-wittedness,"
but not *homo sapiens*. In the passage from animality to humanity, there was not only mental

evolution, but moral, and the developing mind would naturally exercise itself for days and years, and perhaps for long periods around that one emotion—the love of the female for its young—an emotion he was incapable of understanding, but the outward manifestations of which he would be bound to imitate.

Whether man was led to an understanding of the maternal affections by the "sensuous aspects of the newly-born progeny" appealing to man himself,[1] or through pity and sympathy, as Spencer suggests, or still more through imitation of the maternal delight, he undoubtedly would be led to a higher mental plane as he slowly came to understand that the maternal affection was not self-gratifying in the sense that marked the entire gamut of his own emotions up to that time.

Even in recent times tribes have been found so low in the social scale that coition and child-birth have been assumed to have no relation, the latter phenomenon being explained by ascribing to certain trees the power to make women fructile. In a society as low in mentality as this, it would be easy to conceive that the woman's unselfishness—her lack of the self-gratifying impulse—in protecting, nursing, and rearing a burden superimposed on her with no pleasurable antecedents, would be even more amazing than it would be to the male living in a state sufficiently advanced to understand the reproductive function.

[1] Alex. Bain, *The Emotions and the Will.*

In either state of society, there then begins in the human consciousness a disturbance "which is significant of something having another value than that of mere pleasure, and which is pregnant with the promise of another than the merely sensuous or merely intellectual life."[1]   The words quoted are Prof. Ladd's, discussing the philosophy of conduct of civilized man—but here, even in the primitive man, the rule applies—the moral idea is born, legitimately enough, out of the altruistic maternal affection.

Not infrequently one comes across such expressions as "when man became civilized," starting always the baffling inquiry—what civilized man? The mystery of life, as Bergson suggests, may be its solution, for in the acquired tendency of looking on the world as containing one emotion at least that was not purely self-gratifying, man was preparing himself for the virtues that followed in the wake of his own first altruistic concept.   The loyalty without which there could be no sociality has, on the one hand, a reasoned basis—the selfish and protecting one that may also explain the gregariousness of animals—but it differs from gregariousness by subordinating to the good of another one's own pleasure, just as the mother subordinates her wishes to the pleasure and good of the infant.   It is, in fact, the developed emotion that the male acquires through imitation and sympathy from the female, for, "when a tendency splits up

[1] George Trumbull Ladd, *Philosophy of Conduct.*

in the course of its development, each of the special
tendencies which thus arise, tries to preserve and
develop everything in the primitive tendency that
is not incompatible with the work for which it is
specialized."[1]

Back of this sociological "leap" is Nature's
long preparation. "The stability of animal marriage," says Wundt,[2] "seems in general to be
proportional to affection for the young," and yet
the primitive instincts are sometimes so powerful
that even among those animals in whom the
maternal instinct is strongly developed, they will,
even after facing great danger for their young,
desert them when the time comes to migrate.
This Darwin says is true of swallows, house mar-
tins, and swifts.[3]

But even in the lowest animals the "chief
source of altrusim" is the family group as it re-
volves round the care of the young,[4] while with
the increase in the representative capacity that
differentiates man from the brute, and the pro-
longation of the period of human infancy, there
is born real altruism, the germ of morality, through
the "knitting together of permanent relations
between mother and infant, and the approximation toward steady relations on the part of the
male parent."

[1] Bergson, *Creative Evolution*, p. 119.
[2] William Wundt, *Human and Animal Psychology*, p. 143.
[3] Darwin, *Descent of Man*, p. 120.
[4] Chas. Ellwood, *Sociology and Modern Social Problems*, p. 39.

How then does it happen that an instinct that has been productive of so much for humanity, an instinct that has given birth to most of those virtues that mark civilized from savage man,[1] served apparently so little as a safeguard for the offspring that generated the moral evolution? Studying the cross currents and the ever-present struggle for existence of the various nations that worked out of barbarism to civilization, we see that after all it is by and through the very virtues, tenderness, sympathy, and humanity, that were first aroused by the helpless offspring, that the infant comes in turn to be protected, though the path is frequently a tortuous one.

The society that was able to exist in primitive times was always the one that sacrificed the individual,[2] and the infant was naturally low in the scale of value. That very sacrifice of the weakest, stratified into a national characteristic, produced in the greatest civilization of ancient times, a narrow and egoistical morality, with little conception of what we call humanity. "No Greek ever

---

[1] Ellen Key, *The Renaissance of Motherhood*, p. 27: "Because of her motherhood, woman's sexual nature gradually became purer than man's. The child became more and more the centre of her thoughts and her deeds. Thus the strength of her erotic instincts diminished. The tenderness awakened in her by her children also benefited the father. Out of this tenderness—as also out of the admiration for the manly qualities which the father developed in the defence of herself and her children—gradually arose the erotic feeling directed to this man alone. Thus love began."

[2] Kidd, *Social Evolution*, p. 138.

attained the sublimity of such a point of view,"
says George Henry Lewes.[1]

In this, the "century of the child," there is a
great conception of humanity, and even of children's rights. Little attempt, however, has been
made to trace in consecutive and co-ordinate
fashion the development among races and nations
of the progress of the human race in its attitude
toward children. We who are so much interested
in the betterment of the race and who are so much
moved by humanitarian considerations that almost
the first consideration of the state is to provide
for the children, have reached this point of view
only after a long struggle against blind ignorance
and reckless selfishness.

The fact that less than fifty years have passed
since we began a definite policy concerning the
rights of children shows how rapidly the human
race moves. The race may be, let us say, something like 240,000 years old; of that time civilized
man—accepting the most generous figures on
Egyptian and Mesopotamian civilization—has
existed only 10,000 years, or $\frac{1}{240}$ of the life of
the human species.

Humanized man has existed not more than a
few hundred years, and it is within only fifty
years that the race has been concerned with the
protection of the child. How deeply ingrained
are the habits of barbarity and darkness, may
be seen from the fact that cannibalism broke

[1] Lewes, *History of Philosophy*, vol. i., p. 338.

out in Japan not more than a hundred years ago.

Unquestionably, this is the century of the child. Undoubtedly, more serious thought is being given in the present generation to the subject than has ever been given before in the entire history of the world. More has been written about the child in the last fifty years than had been written in the world in all civilized times up to the beginning of this half-century. In order to appreciate this statement one must remember that the best friends of the child—Jesus, the Jewish Prophets, and Mohammed—lived centuries before the human theories that they preached had really a living existence.

In this connection, it is germane to state that the theory that philosophy and religion go hand in hand with humanity, is shattered by the fact that Plato, Aristotle, Confucius, and Gautama affected, apparently, not a single jot, the ancient attitude of insufferance toward the undesired children.

There has ever been, on the question of his children, a struggle between man and nature. Endowed with the possibilities of a large offspring man has fought the burdens that nature has thrust upon him. On first view, it seems that parental affection never develops to great degree unless the economic conditions are favourable; yet the various artifices and "laws" used by tribes to get rid of children would show that parental affection kept struggling with the inclinations of men. In other words, if we find, as we do, female children sacrificed in one place because they are useless, and all first-born children sacrificed in another place because the gods must be propitiated, it is evident that parental affection (as represented by the women) was strong enough to force the male sovereigns to invent plausible excuses and taboos in order to have the women give up their offspring.

Considering all that is being done, said, and written on the subject of the child and the relation of the state and citizen toward the child, it would seem safe to assume that there would be some interest in the attitude of our predecessors toward children.

From the regulation of Romulus, as set forth by Dionysius Halicarnassus, to the story of Mary Ellen, as set forth by a settlement worker on the East Side of New York City, is a far cry, but the progress from the first to the second is steady. The Roman General, Agathocles, who made as a part of the terms of peace with the Carthaginians an agreement on the part of that branch of the Semitic race that they would cease to sacrifice children, was a legitimate sociological progenitor of the representative of the arm of the law that stops a drunken father from beating his child and creates a Children's Court where the child gets gentleness with justice, not contamination and corruption.

"Every historian ought to be a jurist; every jurist ought to be a historian," says Ortolan, and

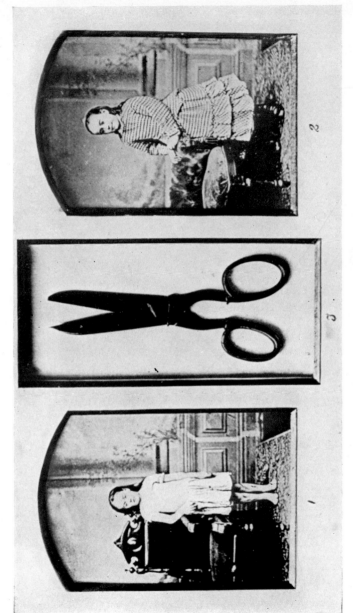

MARY ELLEN AND THE SCISSORS WITH WHICH SHE WAS BEATEN

the historian of child progress feels not only the truth of that statement but the added necessity of meeting the various economic theories that have dealt with the care of the child, from those of Lycurgus to the latter-day essay of Malthus.

The law of primogeniture and the varying laws of inheritance have occasionally led to the study of children as children, but generally the main interest in them of historian and jurist has been as a channel for the transmission of property.

Theories about population and the fascinating pursuit of unravelling tangled economic laws, have obscured the fact that the attitude of a state toward children has been, with few variations, an index to its social progress. The same thing has been said of women, but while the Greeks treated women well, yet with the exception of the single *dema*[1] of Thebes, infanticide was common in all the Greek States.

The Chinese are kind to their women and yet there is no country today where infanticide is more common. The oldest civilization in the world, the Babylonian, was not one in which women were

---

[1] Ælian: the second book, chapter vii.

"This is a Theban law most just and humane: that no Theban might expose his child or leave it in a wilderness, upon pain of death. But if the father were extremely poor, whether it were male or female, the law requires that as soon as it is born it be brought in the swaddling clouts to the magistrate, who, receiving it, delivers it to some other for some small reward, conditioning with him that he shall bring up the child, and when it is grown up take it into his service, man or maid, and have the benefit of its labour in requital for its education."

ill-treated, yet all the indications are that infanticide was practised in the shape of human sacrifice.

The Rajputs of India pleaded for their privilege of destroying infant children when theirs had been the highest civilization in the world.

In other words, disinterested affection for the infant is not necessarily coincident with civilization, or the kind treatment of women a sure sign that the lives of children are safe.

Various writers, including Walt Whitman, Nietzsche, and Edward Carpenter, have taken the attitude that our much vaunted civilization does not really represent progress, and one vivacious author[1] has even undertaken to show in a clever and lively way that there is no such thing as progress, pointing to Greek civilization, in which children were killed at will and public men were confessed degenerates, as the ideal from which we of modern times have fallen away.

What is undoubtedly true is that civilization does not always indicate social progress, and what is truer is that civilization does not necessarily indicate the *humanization* of the people.

Chremes, the very character in Terence[2] who says "Nothing human is alien to me," is the one who reproves his wife for not having gotten rid of their child. The advance over Homer as

---

[1] Mrs. John Martin.

[2] Heaut., I., i., 23: Homo sum; humani nihil a me alienum puto.

shown by Virgil is that of a great gentleness, a great humaneness,—a difference in their times,—and yet Cicero, who represents the stoical and gentler sentiments of the Virgilian times toward the helpless and powerless victims of force as did no man up to his day, speaks tolerantly of the inhuman practices of his time. But there is a growth of humaneness from Homer to Virgil, there is advance from Plato to Cicero, humanely speaking of course; there was greater advance in the teachings of Christ, and there was further advance in the course of the long-drawn-out struggle between the nominal acceptance of those teachings and their incorporation into the daily philosophy. So, too, progress in the care of the rights of infancy and childhood has been made very little by very little.

It is the fact that, until 1874, there was no organized movement to defend the "rights" of children that led the author to investigate the conditions that had existed previous to that time. The first Child's Protective Movement began in New York in the year mentioned, and the rapidity with which this spread throughout the world indicated that some general law, or as Brinton says, psychological process was at work. Today there are protecting societies in every country where there are Caucasian peoples. To go to the sources of the Child Protection Movement, it was necessary to understand the industrial conditions which arose in the nineteenth century, the eighteenth century, and the latter part of the seventeenth, when the boast was made that children were at last being made useful.

Back of the misuse of children in factories is the interesting story of the rise of modern industrialism with the early attempts of the guilds to protect children, not so much out of any development of the human feelings as from the guild's desire to protect the male labourer from unfair competition.

The Decree of Napoleon in 1811,[1] declaring that the unprotected infant was a charge on the state, marked another advance in humanitarianism; back of this advance was the long and interesting story of the endeavours of the religious orders and the charitably disposed persons of the Middle Ages to save the lives of children, the most conspicuous benefactor of childhood being the noble St. Vincent de Paul. It was he who gave to the golden glories of France's golden age a touch of humanity that would otherwise have been lacking in the epoch ruled over by Mazarin and later the Great Louis.

Leading up to the efforts of St. Vincent de Paul was that complex and interesting chapter of the mixing of the old German laws with the Roman laws, as the barbarians found them.

That the semi-barbarous tribes that descended on Rome were better qualified to take up the humane side of the Christian work than was the decadent Roman, we can assume from the statement

[1] See Appendix A.

of Tacitus, that among the Germans children were treated more kindly than they were by the then ruling lords of the earth.

Satire there may have been, as Guizot and Voltaire suggest, in much that Tacitus wrote about the superior morality of the Germans, but later history demonstrated their ethical superiority over the nation that was then on the verge of moral decay.

In any case, as the Christian religion spread among the tribes that had enfiladed Rome, there are evidences of more humane consideration for children until we find Bishop Datheus as early as 787 A.D. founding an asylum for children in a spirit strangely in advance of his time, though the bitter protests of the Christian fathers in the second century against the slaughter and misuse of children put the mark of infamy on the persecutors of children for all time.

The Roman laws, as the barbarians found them, were the result of a slow growth of a thousand years from the time when the founder attempted to check the slaughter of young children by what must have been, in those primitive times, more or less drastic legislation. That the teachings of Christ and the teachings of the Stoics led to the same result does not detract from the credit due to Christianity for first putting on its proper basis, as we see things now, the standing of the child in the matter of its *rights*.

Back of the Roman developments is the Greek

attitude toward children, disappointing, if we look
for the perfection that we find in art and in philosophy, doubly disappointing when we find that
both Plato and Aristotle saw the child only as a
possibility—only as something of which we must
await developments—only as a human *ovum*.

When we come to trace the attitude of other
races, of other civilizations, toward children, we
find much the same story: out of barbarism, civilization; out of civilization, humanity, though it has
been usually the great Semitic religions—Judaism,
Christianity, and Mohammedanism—that have
awakened the humane instinct the world over. The
humane teachings of the Stoics were not unlike
those of the great religious teachers, but, lacking
the intense driving power of religious fervour, it
is doubtful if they could have accomplished the
revolutions that these three religions did.

That all the great nations, the historical divisions of the races, or those that passed out of
barbarism into civilization, carried with them some
trace of early cannibalistic days or child-murder
days, seems a safe conclusion; and while occasional
followers and interpreters of the Malthusian
philosophy have at times attempted to defend
indirectly these practices as part of the checks and
balances by which over-population is defeated,
the fact remains that the development of the
parental instinct, the greatest of civilizing forces,
has slowly, but surely, tended to put an end to
these "checking" and "balancing" practices.

CHAPTER II

HUMAN MARRIAGE—EVOLUTION OF THE PARENTAL
INSTINCT—SOCIAL CONDITIONS AMONG PAPUANS
—CHILD'S PLACE IN THE TRIBE.

IT is now believed by many scientists that the
cradle of the human race was the Indo-
Malaysian intertropical lands.

The discovery of the remains of the *Pithecanthropus erectus* in 1892 by Dr. Eugene Dubois in
the pliocene beds of East Java, established as a
strong probability what was up to that time regarded as a mere speculation. Keane[1] and Sir
John Evans[2] now assert that man originated in
the East in this vicinity and migrated thence to
Europe.

In this semi-glacial period, man, having taken
on much of his human character and being now an
erect animal (although in physical and mental
respects he still resembled his nearest kin), had
little difficulty in migrating.

During the immensely long old Stone Age to
which Peroché assigns a period of some three

[1] A. H. Keane, *Man Past and Present*, p. 9.
[2] Sir John Evans, Inaugural Address, British Association
Meeting, Toronto, 1897.

15

hundred thousand years since the beginning of the
Ghellian epoch, the pleistocene precursors underwent very few or slight specializations or developments, a fact due mainly to the moderate and
unchanging character of the climate during this
long period. Progress in the arts, however, there
was, to such an extent that in some things the
period has not been equalled. Of this character
are the exquisitely wrought flints of the Silurian
period, which cannot be reproduced now.

Primitive man as he existed in the Stone Age
had very little in common with the "primitive
men" of today. There are savages today who
represent, in a way, a degree of savagery and a
remoteness from civilization that in some respects
takes them farther down the social ladder than
any of the Aryan race of the Stone Age. "No
pure primitive race exists in any part of the world
today."[1] Contact with more advanced races
has invariably produced, sometimes a good and
sometimes an evil effect. Races are what climate,
soil, diet, pursuits, and inherited character make
them,[2] and the Aryan savages of the Stone Age
had a different set of these conditions to face from
the Negro savages of today.

It is not surprising to find today a race that in

[1] A. Featherman, *Social History of the Races of Mankind*, vol.
ii., p. 22.
[2] "Man is affected by these four physical agents: climate, food,
soil, and the general aspect of Nature."—Buckle, *History of
Civilization*, vol. i., p. 29.

NATIVE EAST AFRICAN MOTHER AND INFANT
(COURTESY OF THE MUSEUM OF NATURAL HISTORY, NEW YORK)

A WELL-CARED FOR ESKIMO INFANT
(COURTESY OF MUSEUM OF NATURAL HISTORY, NEW YORK)

many respects represents the Stone Age period of civilization, displaying, together with the most barbarous customs, a wide knowledge of the arts, indicating that there had been contact with some higher race or its representatives.

Tribes grade into one another in the matter of culture so that it is hard to classify them.[1] A struggle for existence may leave its mark on an advanced tribe so that while it may in general retain prominent barbaric or primitive characteristics, it will, in every other regard but these, seem an advanced tribe. The Nigritans, for instance,[2] have learned from their neighbours, the Abyssinians and the Arabs, the use of iron; yet they have not arrived at the Stone and Bronze ages in culture, and show in their social relations and domestic habits none of the characteristics of the more advanced tribes.

So in the treatment of children. Wherever the treatment of the child is at variance with the other customs or conditions of the race, it will almost invariably be discovered that the change is due to economic reasons or to contact with a stronger race. That it is this contact with higher races that has helped undeveloped races to advance, is the opinion of Sir H. H. Johnson.[3]

"In some respects I think the tendency of the Negro for several centuries past has been an actual

---

[1] *Current Anthropological Literature*, vol. ii., No. 1, p. 11.

[2] Featherman, vol. ii., preface.

[3] *British Central Africa*, p. 472.

2

retrograde one.   As we come to read the unwritten
history of Africa by researches into languages,
manners, customs, traditions, we seem to see a
backward rather than a forward movement going
on for some thousand years past—a return towards
the savage and even the brute.   I can believe it
possible that, had Africa been more isolated from
contact with the rest of the world, and cut off from
the immigration of the Arab and the European,
the purely Negroid races, left to themselves, so far
from advancing towards a higher type of humanity, might have actually reverted by degrees to a
type no longer human."

On the other hand, G. Stanley Hall says that
our intercourse with the African races "had been
a curse and not a blessing.   Our own Indians are
men of the Stone Age whom Bishop Whipple
thought originally the noblest men on earth.
Look at them now!"[1]

Up to a short time ago men of authority asserted
that marriage had sprung up from a "state of
promiscuity," the believers in this theory forget-
ting that even "among animals the most akin to
man, this state of promiscuity is rather exceptional."

Most of the people cited as following this practice
have been shown to have individual marriage to
the exclusion of other forms.   Undoubtedly in
many cases what are called group marriages have

[1] G. Stanley Hall, *The Relations between the Lower and the Higher Races.*

been mistaken for promiscuity. Almost equally low in the social scale is polyandry, where one woman may have several husbands.

Whatever the origin of marriage, the fact is, however, that the idea of marriage comes after the idea of the child—as in the animal world, the family is established for the purpose of taking care of the children that have been brought into the world.[1]

In *Mahabharata*, the Indian poem, we are told that marriage was founded by Swetaketu, son of the Rishi Uddalaka; according to the Chinese annals, the Emperor Fou-hi established the custom; the Egyptians ascribed its introduction to Menes, and the Greeks to Kerops. Nowhere is it assumed as a condition of the race of all time. Its origin, growth, and development are really the origin, growth, and development of the idea of protecting human offspring.

A convincing scientific explanation of marriage, however, has been set forth by Westermarck.[2] Among the great sub-kingdom of the Invertebrata not even the female parent exhibits any anxiety about the offspring. The heat of the sun hatches the eggs of the highest order, the insects, and in most cases the mother does not even see her young.[3]

[1] J. Deneker, *The Races of Man*, p. 239.

[2] Westermarck, *History of Human Marriage*, p. 9.

[3] D. G. Brinton, *Races and Peoples*, p. 55. "The sequel of the sexual impulse is the formation of the family through the development of parental affection. This instinct is as strong in many of the lower animals as in human beings. In primitive

Parental care is rare among the lowest vertebrata. Among fishes the young are generally
hatched without the assistance of the parents.
There are exceptions to this among the Teleostei,
where the male assumes the usual maternal functions of constructing a nest and jealously guarding
the ova deposited there by the female. The
male of certain species of the Arius, carries the
ova in his pharynx. Nearly all of the reptiles,
having placed their eggs in a convenient sunny
spot, pay no more attention to them.

With few exceptions, the relations of the sexes
of the lower vertebrata can be described as fickle;
they meet in the pairing time, part again, and have
little more to do with one another.

"The Chelonia form," says Westermarck, "with
regard to their domestic habits, transition to the
birds, as they do also from a zoölogical and particularly from an embryological point of view."
He then goes on to show that parental affection
in the latter class, not only on the side of the
mother but on that of the father, has come to high
development. Members of the two sexes aid
each other in nest-building, the females bringing
the materials and the males doing the work. Other
duties which come with the mating season are

conditions it is largely confined to the female parent, the father
paying but slight attention to the welfare of his offspring. To
this, rather than to doubt of paternity, should we attribute the
very common habit in such communities of reckoning ancestry
in the female line only."

FAMILY LIFE AMONG BIRDS.   GROUP OF AMERICAN EGRET
(COURTESY OF MUSEUM OF NATURAL HISTORY, NEW YORK)

shared by both, the mother being concerned with incubation and the father aiding her by taking her position when she leaves the nest for intervals, providing her with food which he gathers, and protecting her from dangers.   When the breeding season is over and the young have come, a new set of duties is evolved.   Young birds are not left alone by their parents, absences being necessitated only by searches for food for all members of the nest.   When dangers threaten the nest both father and mother defend it bravely.

All efforts are made to have the young shift for themselves as soon as they have grown strong enough to make it feasible.   Independence and self-dependence come only after they are in all ways capable of meeting their needs.

On the other hand, there are some species whose young, from the beginning of their ultra-oval existence, require and receive no care from the parents.   The duck is one of a species which leaves all parental care to the female.   In general it may be said that both parents share the parental duties, the chief duties, such as hatching and rearing of the young, falling to the mother, while the father gathers food and keeps off enemies.[1]

The relations of the two sexes are, therefore, very intimate, and association lasts even after the

---

[1] The ostrich forms, however, a curious exception.   The male sits on the eggs, and brings up the young birds, the female never troubling herself about either of these duties.—Brehm, *Bird-Life*, p. 324.

breeding season has passed. And only the birds of the Gallinaceous family are an exception to the rule of making such association permanent once it has been started, death alone ending it.

Real marriage is to be found only among birds.[1] For mammals the same cannot be said, for though the mother generally gives much attention to the young, the father does not always have as much concern. He even, in some cases, is the enemy of his own offspring. Yet even in the cases of mammals there are durable associations between the sexes. Very often these last only during the rutting season, but among whales, seals, hippopotami, the *Cervus campestris*,[2] gazelles,[3] the *Neotragus Hemprichii* and other small antelopes, reindeer, the *Hydromus coypus*, squirrels, moles, the ichneumon, and certain carnivorous animals, among the latter cats, martens, the yaguarundi of South America, and the *Canis Brasiliensis* and perhaps the wolf, there are durable matings. Association between the sexes is common among all of these animals for periods after the young have been born. And in all cases the male is the family's protector.

What is an exception among the lower mammals is, however, a rule among the Quadrumana. According to the natives of Madagascar some species

[1] Brehm, *Bird-Life*, p. 285, and Herman Müller's *Am Neste*.

[2] Rengger, *Naturgeschichte der Saugethiere von Paraguay*, p. 354.

[3] Brehm, vol. iii., p. 206.

of Prosimii are nursed by both male and female in common. Among the *Arctopitheci* the female is always assisted by the male in taking care of the young.

Coming to the man-like apes, we are told by Lieutenant de Crespigny that "in the northern part of Borneo they live in families—the male, female, and young one. On one occasion," he says, "I found a family in which were two young ones, one of them much larger than the other, and I took this as a proof that the family tie had existed for at least two seasons. They build commodious nests in the trees which form their feeding-ground, and, so far as I could observe, the nests, which are well lined with dry leaves, are occupied only by the female and young, the male passing the night in the fork of the same or another tree in the vicinity. The nests are very numerous all over the forest, for they are not occupied above a few nights, the mias (or orang-utan) leading a roving life."

Dr. Savage says that the gorillas live in bands and that but one male is seen in every band. M. du Chaillu says that the male gorilla is always accompanied by the female.

It is among the Negritians of Africa that we find today the at-hand evidence of the attitude of man toward his progeny in the first stages of culture, or perhaps the last stages of savagery. It must be remembered that in Africa, however, habits of other races will be found grafted on the

negro stock, thereby causing them to appear sometimes unusually gentle or again unusually advanced.   In Africa the Semitic and the Hamitic
grafts on negro stock provide many varieties of
mankind, just as in Oceania, the Mongol (Malay)
and the Caucasian (Indonesian) grafts on the
negro stock have produced many varieties there.
As an example of the methods of the lowest of
savage tribes, there is, however, no better example than the Papuans of New Guinea of whom
the ethnologist, Keane, says: "They stand in
some respects on the lowest rung of the social
ladder."

As an example of the low state of culture in
which part of them exist it is said that those near
Astrolabe Bay on the north-west coast of New
Guinea had no knowledge of the metals, all their
implements being of stone, wood, or bones; neither
had they knowledge of fire, the grandfathers of
the present generation being able to recall the
time when they had no fire at all, but ate their
food raw.   In the study of these people we are
studying contemporaries of our own neolithic
ancestors.

According to their most popular myth, a crocodile named Nugu was responsible for the frequent
disappearance of children until the tribe made an
agreement to supply him with pig's fat instead.
Here we have the beginning of the theory of
sacrifice.

"In their treatment of children they are often

A FAMILY OF ANTHROPOID APES, FROM A DRAWING BY DAN BEARD

(COURTESY OF THE MUSEUM OF NATURAL HISTORY, NEW YORK)

FAMILY OF POLAR BEARS

(COURTESY OF MUSEUM OF NATURAL HISTORY, NEW YORK CITY)

violent and cruel," says Alfred Russell Wallace,[1]
and an example of their idea of kindness may be
gathered from the following description of the
"ornamentation" of a young Papuan:

"The faces of both men and women are frequently ornamented all over with cicatrices either
circular or chevron-shaped. The operation is a
painful and costly one, as the professional tattooer
has to be highly paid for his trouble, and not every
child's friends can afford the fee demanded. The
instrument used is the claw of the flying-fox.
The unfortunate patient is not allowed to sleep
for two or three nights before the operation is
performed, and then, when he is ready to drop from
weariness, the tattooer begins his work, and com-
pletes it at one sitting. I never saw the actual
process, but a child was brought for my inspection
whose face had just been finished off. It was in a
painful state of nervous irritation, and the face
swelled to an enormous size."[2]

Of the condition of these people no one is better
able to speak than Lieutenant Governor J. H. P.
Murray,[3] who describes tribes where the savages
have only weapons of wood, know nothing of the
bow and arrow, and are noted for their immorality.

"It is very often the case that the best of the

[1] Wallace, *The Malay Archipelago*, vol. ii., p. 447.
[2] Charles Morris Woodford, *A Naturalist among the Head-
Hunters*, p. 31.
[3] *Report to the Parliament of the Commonwealth of Australia
on Papua*, for 1909, Appendix D, p. 107.

young girls are sold by their parents as courtesans,
the native name being Jelibo.   I came across men
married, and possessing, in addition, these women.
Young fellows, not having reached puberty, had
clubbed together in parties of three and four, and
bought young girls from the parents to make
courtesans.   At feasts, these girls are used for
the purpose of enriching themselves and their
owners."[1]

As to the attitude of the children, we gain some
idea of the aboriginal point of view by this statement:

"There are some villages in which children
absolutely swarm, but there are few large families;
practically every one is married, but there are
many couples who have no children, or only one
or two.   In many parts of the territory it is considered a disgrace for a woman to have a child
until she has been married at least two years;
infanticide and abortion, though rarely proved,
are said to be common, and a medical expert would
probably discover the existence of other checks
to population.   The result of all this is that in
some districts the population is increasing while
in others it is not; such investigations as we have
been able to make lead, in the absence of definite
statistics, to the conclusion that the population
in that part of the territory which is under control
is certainly not diminishing, though the increase,
if any, is probably very small.   The reason why

[1] J. H. P. Murray, *Papua or British New Guinea*, 1912.

the population does not increase as one would expect now that village warfare has ceased is, as far as I can see, simply that neither men nor women want children, which I take to be the chief cause that limits population elsewhere. The reason why they do not want them is, I think, partly because they find them a nuisance (which is a consideration that was probably effective even before the white man came) and partly that, in their present state of transition from one stage of development to another, they do not exactly see what there will be for their children to do."

Another custom of these people is to bury children alive, when the parents or some person of importance dies; the excuse given for this practice is that the child will be needed to wait on the parent in the other world, a practice that lasted long among the civilized Egyptians.

Cannibalism is rife among these people. Mr. Murray reports that on one occasion a young man was brought before him for having murdered a man in order to please a married woman with whom he was in love—a lover who has not "killed his man" being considered lukewarm.

"On my remonstrating with him on the impropriety of paying attention to a married woman he informed me that there were no girls in the village, as they had all been killed and eaten in a recent raid. The position of a young man who found himself in a village where all the women were either married or eaten was no doubt a difficult one, and I hope that I took it into consideration in passing sentence."[1]

How little is the feeling among these people over the murder of children, is shown from the fact that murder is the only outlet for their feelings!

"I have known cases where a man, grieving over the loss of a relative or over some slight that has been put upon him, has set fire to his house, quite regardless of whether any one was inside, with the result, occasionally, that a child is burnt to death, and I recently tried a case of murder which was the direct outcome of grief over the death of a pig. The prisoners were brothers, and their pig bore the pretty name of Mehboma; but Mehboma died, and the brothers in their unquenchable grief went forth and killed the first man they saw. The victim had nothing to do with Mehboma's death, but the mourning brothers did not care for that—somebody had got to be killed over it. The prisoners told me that it was the custom of the village to show their grief in this way, so that their neighbours must occasionally have suffered rather severely."[2]

As the Australians are closely allied to the Papuans and represent about the same period of culture, we may postulate their attitude toward woman and a marriage from the description of an early Victorian tribe-marriage given by Brough Smith and quoted by A. H. Keane, the latter au-

[1] Murray, *Papua or British New Guinea*, p. 211.
[2] *Ibid.*, p. 214.

PRIMITIVE FAMILY LIFE AMONG THE HOPI INDIANS

(COURTESY OF THE MUSEUM OF NATURAL HISTORY, NEW YORK)

thor remarking that "a common test of a people's culture is the treatment of their women, and in this respect the Australians must, as Prof. R. Semon shows, be ranked below the Bushman and on a level with the Fuegians."

"A man having a daughter of thirteen or fourteen years of age," says Mr. Smith in his description of the marriage customs in vogue among the Victorian tribes, "arranges with some elderly person for the disposal of her; and, when all are agreed, she is brought out and told that her husband wants her. Perhaps she has never seen him but to loathe him. The father carries a spear and a waddy, or tomahawk, and, anticipating resistance, is thus prepared for it. The poor girl, sobbing and sighing, and muttering words of complaint, claims pity from those who will show none. If she resists the mandates of her father, he strikes her with his spear; if she rebels and screams, the blows are repeated; and if she attempts to run away, a stroke on the head from the waddy or tomahawk quiets her. The mother screams and scolds and beats the ground with her *kan-nan* (fighting-stick); the dogs bark and whine; but nothing interrupts the father, who, in the performance of his duty, is strict and mindful of the necessity of not only enforcing his authority, but of showing to all that he has the means to enforce it. Seizing the bride by her long hair he drags her to the home prepared for her by her new owner. Further resistance often subjects her to brutal treatment. If she attempts to abscond, the bridegroom does not hesitate to strike her savagely on the head with his waddy, and the bridal screams and yells make the night hideous."[1]

[1] *Op. cit.*, i., p. 76.

CHAPTER III

IT has seemed necessary to dwell thus at length on the conditions among the Papuans and allied tribes as it appeared to me important that the very beginnings of the family should be understood. The general agreement of ethnologists as to the low standing of the Papuans justifies, I believe, our assuming them to be as near the point of culture of our neolithic (or paleolithic) ancestors as it is possible to come.

From now on the course is upward. Strange as it may seem, the lowest tribes are less "human," both in the matter of offspring and in the matter of sentiment of love for women, than some of the beasts and birds,[1] but having touched that depth, the next step brings us in contact with feelings that, in a way, begin to approximate our own.

In the stages above the Papuans there is some affection for the woman; her position is nearer to that of wife and less that of captive. In consequence there is a more kindly regard for the child-

---

[1] D. G. Brinton, *Races and Peoples*, pp. 53 and 54.

31

ren that she bears. Now begins the development of
the parental *affection*. It is, however, confined to
the female at first; "to this fact, rather than to
doubt of paternity, should we attribute the very
common habit in such communities of reckoning
ancestry in the female line only."[1]

Man, no longer relying on his own cannibalistic
brute force to do with his progeny as he wishes,
invents reasons for doing away with his burdensome offspring.

We have already seen that the Papuans restricted their families to two children, when it
was possible. As late as the middle of the seventeenth century, Dapper reported that in Benin
no twins were found, as it was regarded as a sign
of dishonour for a woman to have twins.[2]

Among the Arunta tribes in Central Australia,
twins are "immediately killed as something which
is unnatural."[3] Among northern tribes they
"are usually destroyed as something uncanny."[4]
With the Kaffirs, it was found that "when twins
are born, one is usually neglected and allowed to
die."[5] Of the western Victorian tribes we learn
that "twins are as common among them as among
Europeans; but as food is occasionally very scarce
and a large family troublesome to move about,

[1] D. G. Brinton, *Races and Peoples*, p. 55.

[2] Dapper, *L'Afrique*, p. 309.

[3] Spencer and Gillen, *Native Tribes of Central Australia*, p. 52.

[4] Spencer and Gillen, *Northern Tribes of Central Australia*, p.
609.

[5] Joseph Shooter, *Kafirs of Natal*, p. 88.

it is lawful and customary to destroy the weaker twin child, irrespective of sex."[1]

In some parts of the Benin territory, according to a contemporary of Dapper, the twin-bearing women are treated very badly.

According to Nyendael, they actually kill both mother and infants, and sacrifice them to a certain devil, which they fondly imagine harbours in a wood near the village. "But if," says this authority, "the man happens to be more than ordinarily tender, he generally buys off his wife, by sacrificing a female slave in her place; but the children are without possibility of redemption obliged to be made the satisfactory offerings which this savage law requires. In the year 1699, a merchant's wife, commonly called *ellaroe* or *mof*, lay-in of two children, and her husband redeemed her with a slave, but sacrificed his children. After which I had frequent opportunities of seeing and talking with the disconsolate mother, who never could see an infant without a very melancholy reflection on the fate of her own, which always extorted briny tears from her. The following year the like event happened to a priest's wife. She was delivered of two children, which, with a slave, instead of his wife, he was obliged to kill and sacrifice with his own hands, by reason of his sacerdotal function; and exactly one year after, as though it had been a punishment inflicted from heaven, the same woman was the second time delivered of two child-

[1] James Dawson, *Australian Aborigines.*

3

ren, but how the priest managed himself on this occasion I have not been informed, but am apt to think that this poor woman was forced to atone for her fertility by death. These dismal events have in process of time made such impressions on men, that when the time of their wives' delivery approaches, they send them to another country; which makes me believe that for the future they will correct these inhumanities."[1]

On the west coast of Africa "twins are killed among all the Niger Delta tribes, and in districts out of English control the mother is killed too,"[2] which shows the fanatic point to which a belief, or rather an excuse, founded on the economic desire to keep down the size of a family, may be carried.

All Kaffir children are neglected, according to Kidd,[3] but on the birth of twins, "one frequently is killed by the father, for the natives think that unless the father places a lump of earth in the mouth of one of the babies, he will lose his strength."

The next provision to keep down the "cost of living" is directed against children with blemishes, a practice that was not easy to check even among civilized peoples. Among the Australian aborigines "it is usual to destroy those that are malformed."[4]

[1] Nyendael, Ulricht, 1688, quoted by H. Ling Roth in *Great Benin*, pp. 35-36.
[2] Mary H. Kingsley, *Travels in West Africa*, p. 472.
[3] Dudley Kidd, *The Essential Kafir*, p. 202.
[4] Slaughter, *Australian Aborigines*, p. 39.

Among certain tribes on the west coast, children whose mothers have died are thrown into the bush, "as are all children who have not arrived in this world in the way considered orthodox or who cut their teeth in an improper way." A child born with teeth is put to death, in some parts of Africa; children born in stormy weather are destroyed in Kamchatka.[1] In Madagascar "the superstition of lucky and unlucky days prevailed throughout all the tribes, and the unfortunate infants that came into the world on one of these unlucky days were immediately destroyed."[2]

How obvious are the so-called reasons for killing the children may be seen from the fact that according to another authority, the proscribed or unlucky periods and days include all children born in March and April, or in the last week of each month, or on Wednesdays and Fridays.[3] Among the Antankarana tribes of the Amber Mountains in Madagascar, a child that sneezes at or shortly after its birth is exposed. Among the Basuto, when a child is born with its feet first, it is killed,[4] whereas among the Bondei it is killed if it is born head first.[5]

Among the Bondei, the excuses found for killing children are many. If the child is born head

[1] M. Kracheninnikow, *Histoire du Kamchatka*, chap. xii.

[2] Henry W. Little, *Madagascar*, p. 60.

[3] H. H. Ploss, *Das Kind in Brauch und Sitte der Völker*, vol. ii., p. 257.

[4] *Ibid.*, vol. ii., p. 258.

[5] Dale, *Journal, Anthrop. Inst.*, vol. xxv., p. 183.

first, it is a *kigego* (unlucky child) and is strangled; if it cries, it is a *kigego* and is strangled. If the father has not been in the *galo* (kekutoigwa), or the mother has not been in the *kiwanga* (kekuviniwa) (initiated), the child is a *tumbwi* (offence) and is strangled."[1]

Mental processes the world over are much the same. The American legislator raising the tariff to keep out competitors is not employing a system entirely dissimilar from that of the barbarians who, finding the first proscriptions fail to keep down the birth-rate, widen the scope of the proscription. And so the customary law grows to include female children among the proscribed. Writing in the latter part of the eighteenth century, Don Felix de Azara declared he had found that among the Guanas in South America it was the custom for the women to bury alive the majority of the female children, and that they never brought up more than one boy and one girl.[2]

Rude attempts to regulate the number of children next appeared. It has been suggested that this phase of primitive development argues mentality sufficient to foresee destruction of the tribe that does not provide for the future. Doubtless, in the mind of some savage Malthus, the idea that the tribe must allow at least a given

[1] Godfrey Dale, *Journal of the Anthropological Institute*, vol. xxv., p. 182.

[2] Felix de Azara, *Voyages dans l'Amérique Méridionale*, vol. ii., pp. 93 and 115.

number of children to live, was conceived with the warm glow of discovery.

Among the Tokelaus, or Line Islanders, "no married pair are allowed by their law to have or bear more than four children; that is, only four get the chance of life. The woman has a right to rear, or endeavour to rear, one child. It rests with the husband to decide how many more shall live, and this depends on how much land there is to divide."[1]

On Radack Island a woman "is allowed to bring up only three children; her fourth and every succeeding one she is obliged to bury alive herself."[2]

Two boys and one girl were all that the Australian mother brought up, according to Curr, although the women bore an average of six children.[3]

Economic ingenuity—and trepidity—could go no further than the practice in the Solomon Islands, where "a small portion of the Ugi natives have been born on the island, three-fourths of them having been brought as youths to supply the place of offspring killed in infancy. When a man needs support in his declining years, his props are not his own sons, but youths obtained by purchases from the St. Christoval natives."[4] Another author says of the same islands that when "it

[1] Tutila, *Journal of the Polynesian Society*, vol. i., p. 267.

[2] Otto von Kotzebue, *A Voyage of Discovery into the South Sea and Beering's Straits*, London, 1821, vol. iii., p. 173.

[3] Edward M. Curr, *The Australian Race*, vol. i., p. 70.

[4] H. B. Guppy, *The Solomon Islands*, p. 42.

becomes necessary to buy other children from other tribes good care is taken not to buy them too young."[1]

At Vaitupu, of the Ellice Islands, "only two children are allowed to a family, as they are afraid of a scarcity of food.[2] It is on these coral islands that Robert Louis Stevenson says the fear of famine is greatest. He bears out the statement that only two children were allowed to a marriage on Vaitupu Island, and adds that on Nukufetu only one child was permitted; "on the latter the punishment was by fine, and it is related that the fine was sometimes paid and the child spared."[3]

In the Dieyerie tribe, of Australia, "thirty per cent. are murdered by their mothers at their birth, simply for the reasons—firstly, that many of them, marrying very young, their first-born is considered immature and not worth preserving; and secondly, because they do not wish to be at the trouble of rearing them, especially if weakly. Indeed all sickly and deformed children are made away with in fear of their becoming a burthen to the tribe."[4]

With the coming of ritual, man assumes to pacify his voracious deities by the sacrifices of children, thereby propitiating the gods and reducing the economic burden. The people of the Sen-

[1] H. H. Romilly, *The Western Pacific*, p. 68.
[2] George Turner, *Samoa*, p. 284.
[3] R. L. Stevenson, *In the South Seas*, p. 38.
[4] Samuel Gason, "The Dieyerie Tribe," in vol. ii. of Curr's *Australia*.

jero offer up their "first-born sons as sacrifices,
because, once upon a time, when summer and
winter were jumbled together in bad season, and
the fruits of the field would not ripen, the sooth-
sayers enjoined it."[1]

After telling an almost unprintable tale, Dr.
Brinton says of the Australian blacks that "among
several tribes it was an established custom for
a mother to kill and eat her first child, as it
was believed to strengthen her for later births.

"In the Luritcha tribe, young children are
sometimes killed and eaten, and it is not an infrequent custom, when a child is in weak health, to
kill a younger and healthy one and then to feed
the weakling on its flesh, the idea being that this
will give to the weak child the strength of the
stronger one."[2]

Frank admission that the children are in the
way and are a burden, may be regarded either as
a sign that the tribe has progressed, or that it has
not yet reached the point of shame where it
cloaks the evil practice under the guise of religious
sacrifices, hygienic or customary regulations.

In this regard it is not possible to say that the
father, as opposed to the mother, is more inclined
to do away with offspring, or is more frequently
entrusted with that grewsome duty, although I
would venture to say that an exhaustive research

[1] J. L. Krapf, *Travels, Researches, and Missionary Labours in
Eastern Africa*, p. 69.
[2] Brinton, *Religions of Primitive Peoples*, p. 17.

on this one aspect of the study would probably show that the mother at first opposed and gradually accepted, under the force of man's will, the idea that the destruction of her offspring was good; first for herself and her lord and master, and secondly for the tribe.

Should investigation uphold such an hypothesis, it would be easily understood how the frank acknowledgment represented an advanced stage, when the woman, no longer satisfied with the various trivial excuses offered for the destruction of her young, insisted on keeping them alive, and was met with, not the many invented reasons that we have seen, but the plain truth, that their continued existence endangered the food supply.

"Urgent want and sterility of the niggardly earth" were the reasons given by the natives of the island of Radnack for the law limiting the number of children.[1] A second child is killed among the natives of Central Australia "only when the mother is, or thinks she is, unable to rear it"[2] and yet the same authors say that "an Australian native never looks far enough ahead to consider what will be the effect on the food supply in future years, if he allows a particular child to live; what affects him is simply the question of how it will interfere with the work of his wife so far as their own camp is concerned; while,

[1] Kotzebue, *A Voyage of Discovery into the South Sea and Bering's Straits*, vol. iii., p. 173.

[2] Spencer and Gillen, *Central Australia*, p. 51.

from the woman's side, the question is, can she provide food enough for the new-born infant and the next youngest?"[1]

The long suckling time, that these authors and other travellers have noted, and that is here given as a reason, as *opposed* to the economic one, for the frequent killing of children, is due "chiefly to want of soft food and animal milk.[2]

Among the members of the Areoi society, a peculiar and somewhat "secret" society[3] of the islands of the Pacific, "a man with three or four children, and this was a rare occurrence, was said to be a *taata taubuubuu*, a man with an unwieldy or cumbrous burden; and there is reason to believe that, simply to avoid the trifling care and effort necessary to provide for their offspring during the helpless period of infancy and childhood, multitudes were consigned to an untimely grave." A Malthusian motive has sometimes been adduced, and the natives have been heard to say, that if all the children born were allowed to live, there would not be food enough produced in the islands to support them.[4]

From many authorities comes direct evidence of a clash between the man and the woman in the Polynesian Islands. "As the burden of the plantation and other work devolves on the woman, she

[1] *Central Australia*, p. 264.
[2] Westermarck, *History of Human Marriage*, p. 484.
[3] Its secrecy is insured by its indecency.
[4] William Ellis, *Polynesian Researches*, p. 257.

thinks that she cannot attend to more than two or three children, and the rest must be buried as soon as they are born. There are exceptions to this want of maternal affection. At times the husband urges the thing contrary to the wishes of the wife. If he thinks the infant will interfere with her work, he forcibly takes the little innocent and buries it, and she, poor woman, cries for months after her child."[1]

Among the nomadic tribes it is frankly admitted that the children are a hindrance. The Lenguas, of the Paraguayan Chaco, make journeys of from ten to twenty miles, the women doing most of the hard work. The consequence is that children are not desirable. So with the Abipones, of whom Charlevoix says: "They seldom rear but one child of each sex, murdering the rest as fast as they come into the world, till the eldest are strong enough to walk alone. They think to justify this cruelty by saying that, as they are almost constantly travelling from one place to another, it is impossible for them to take care of more infants than two at a time; one to be carried by the father, and the other by the mother."[2]

The explanation offered by the Kurnai was that "it was often difficult to carry about young children, particularly where there were several. Their wandering life rendered this very difficult."[3]   In

[1] George Turner, *Nineteen Years in Polynesia*, p. 394.

[2] Charlevoix, *History of Paraguay*, vol. i., p. 405.

[3] Fison and Howitt, *The Kamilario and Kurnai*, p. 190.

A HINDU CHILD-MOTHER, WHOSE CARES WILL MAKE HER OLD AT THIRTY

ZULU GIRL WITH BABY. THE PRACTICE OF EXPOSURE ENDED AMONG THE ZULUS ONLY WITHIN THE PRESENT GENERATION

the struggle with nature, man descends as well as ascends. The unfavourable conditions into which nomadic tribes frequently come produce not infrequently, a perverted type that is lower than the animals to which our semi-human progenitors of the extremely remote past belonged. "The instincts of the lower animals," says Darwin, "are never so perverted as to lead them to regularly destroy their own offspring or to be quite devoid of jealousy."[1]

In parts of New South Wales, such as Bathurst, Goulburn, and the Lachlan, or Macquarie, "it was customary long ago for the first-born of every lubra to be eaten by the tribe, as part of a religious ceremony; and I recollect," says J. M. Davis, "a black fellow who had, in compliance with the custom, been thrown when an infant on the fire, but was rescued and brought up by some stock-keepers who happened accidentally to be passing at the time."[2]

Ellis declares that among the Marquesans who inhabit a group of islands to the south-east of Hawaii, children are sometimes, during "seasons of extreme scarcity, killed and eaten by their parents to satisfy hunger."[3]

It has been said that the social, moral, and intellectual condition of woman indicates, in an ascending scale, the degree of civilization of every tribe

[1] Darwin, *Descent of Man*, p. 46.
[2] John Moore Davis, "Aborigines of Australia," in Brough Smyth, vol. ii., p. 311, *Aborigines of Victoria*.
[3] William Ellis, *Tour through Hawaii*, p. 300.

and nation. It might with equal force be said
that the attitude of the tribe or nation toward its
young is also a barometer of progress. Behind
the harsh measure and savage customs, underneath the cruelty and at times ferocious indifference to pain, there is in general among the lowest
of the tribes an affection for their young, once it
has been decided that they are allowed to live.

In that too frequently suppressed affection,
stunted as it is by customary law and the unequal
struggle with nature, there is the beginning of
humanitarian progress. Given reasonable security that there will be a sufficiency of food supply
and a surcease of neighbourhood wars, this affection will pass from precept to concept and protect
even the unborn.[1]

"No people in the world are so fond of, or so
long-suffering with, children," Stevenson says of
the same South Sea Islanders among whom he has
just said infanticide is common.[2]   But even after
it has been decided to bring up the child, and it
has become an object of great affection, it is still in
danger should famine conditions seem imminent,[3]
or should the cupidity and avarice of the parents
be aroused, with the consequence that children
are readily sold into slavery.[4]

[1] Sir John Lubbock, *The Origin of Civilization*, p. 3.
[2] Stevenson, *In the South Seas*, p. 38.
[3] Lucien Young, U. S. N., *The Real Hawaii*, p. 78.
[4] John Foreman, *The Philippine Islands*, p. 206.   Dean C.
Worcester, *The Philippine Islands*, p. 208.

Nature's methods are stern, and her progress slow; despite perplexing examples of reactionary forces, the primitive move is steadily toward an understanding of one's duties as a human being—or he dies. For the civilized man, pain is nature's warning that he has violated the rules of his own body, and for the primitive man, decay and despair are the warnings that the path of progress lies the other way.

Looking over this vast field, including not only blacks, Mongols, and Indians, but even the Europeans, as we shall come to see later, we gather that those that have struggled upward have been only those who have taken nature's lesson of lessons to themselves. Horrible as is the story of these stationary and degenerate peoples that we get, what must be the whole story, with its full picture of anguish?

CHAPTER IV

THE DROWNING OF DAUGHTERS—EARLY MONGOLIAN
CIVILIZATION MARKED BY ANCESTOR WORSHIP—
SEVERE CHARACTER OF CONFUCIUS—"BEGINNING"
OF INFANTICIDE, 200 B.C.—REFORMS OF THE
EMPEROR CHOENTCHE AND THE MANCHUS IN THE
SEVENTEENTH CENTURY—DECREES REDUCING
THE COST OF WEDDING GIFTS IN ORDER TO STOP
PARENTS FROM KILLING FEMALE CHILDREN

ASSUMING that the human cradle was in the Eastern Archipelago, and more particularly in the Island of Java where Dr. Dubois discovered his *Pithecanthropus erectus*, the primeval home of the Mongolian division of the human race was the Tibetan plateau. From this central plateau the early Mongol groups spread during the Stone Age over the Asiatic continent, in one place developing into the Akkado-Sumerians of Babylonia, the almost extinct Hyperboreans of Siberia in another, the Mongolo-Tartars stretching across Central Asia from Japan to Europe, the Tibeto-Indo-Chinese of Tibet, Indo-China, and China, and the Oceanic Mongols of Malaysia, Madagascar, and the Philippines.

In Tibet even today, polyandrous customs are

still strong and the nomadic tendencies of the
people show that the years of civilization or near-
civilization have not changed the primitive roving
inclinations, inclinations that partly account for
the indifference to child life among the Chinese.

Our knowledge of ancient China rests principally on two authorities, the *Chou King* of
Confucius, written 484 B.C., and the *Sse Ki* of Tsse
Ma Thsein, written at the beginning of the first
era before Christ. Confucius was not able to go
further back than seventeen centuries before his
own time, so that we can safely say that we know
something about Chinese history for about 2200
years before the Christian era. The social and
political life of the Chinese people in the time of
Yao, the first of the emperors named by Confucius,
was that of a pastoral people, but even then most
of the useful arts had been invented, writing was
already known, and the first notions of astronomy
on which they founded their calendar had been
acquired. The successor of Yao was Chun, and
after Chun came Hia, the founder of a dynasty
which lasted from 2205 to 1767 B.C., with which
dynasty began the real history of China.

When Confucius appeared the Chinese Empire
was a highly civilized nation, but of Confucius
it has been said that he, more than any other one
man, went to make China a nation. Born at a
time when his country was torn with discord and
desolated by war, husbandry neglected, peace of
households destroyed, and plunder and rapine

common occurrences, Confucius was nineteen when he married and added to the national woes his own domestic troubles, divorcing the lady after a brief period in captivity, but not however until she had borne him a son.

It is through this son that we learn something of the personal character of Confucius. An inquisitive disciple asked the son if he had learned any more than those who were not related to the great teacher.

"No," replied Le. "He was standing alone once when I was passing through the court below with hasty steps, and said to me:

"'Have you read the Odes?'

"On my replying, 'Not yet,' he added:

"'If you do not learn the Odes, you will not be fit to converse with.'

"Another day in the same way and the same place, he said to me:

"'Have you read the rules of Propriety?'

"On my replying 'Not yet,' he added:

" 'If you do not learn the rules of Propriety, your character cannot be established.'"

"I asked one thing," said the enthusiastic disciple, "and I have learned three things. I have learned about the Odes, I have learned about the rules of Propriety, and I have learned that the Superior Man maintains a distant reserve toward his son."

In this anecdote—and in his works—it is evident that Confucius had the Chinese estimate of the child—the father was sovereign; the child, as long as that sovereign lived, a mere subject. It was this idea and the strongly implanted idea of filial piety that led to the callous attitude toward children among the disciples of Confucius.

The Chinese explanation and defence of this phase of their life is that up to the year 232 B.C. there did not exist in China anything but the most humane system of treatment of children. The Jesuit authors of the *Mémoires* declare that up to that time there is no trace of the drowning of infants, their abandonment, etc. Instead of being a burden, says the missionary chronicler, children were considered an asset and the orphan was generally in the position of having to choose between many would-be adoptive parents. The law is cited to prove this, the Code declaring that in case there were several people anxious to adopt an orphan, preference should be given to those who were childless.[1]

It was under Ts'in Chi Hoang,[2] who reigned about 232 B.C., that the abominable practice grew up, along with many other ills. The greed and avarice of the nobles and the Emperor's immediate following produced much suffering, in the wake of which came famine, causing mothers and fathers to abandon children that they were not able to feed.

[1] *Mémoires sur les Chinois*, tome ii., p. 396.
[2] Ts'in Chi Hoang, Emperor of China, 220–210 B.C., was King of Ts'in, 246–221 B.C.   Hirth, p. 334.

4

Whatever truth there may be in this statement, there is very little doubt that the reign of Ts'in Chi Hoang was one of bloodshed, war, and suffering and that with the end of the Chou (or Chow), dynasty, and the accession of the Prince Ts'in, first as the dominating King and then as Emperor of China, there was much suffering.

"It was a time of extreme severity," says the historian Tsse Ma Thsien, "and all affairs were decided according to the law without either grace or charity." [1]

In addition to his bloodthirsty qualities, the Prince Ts'in, who was known as the Great First Emperor and who insisted that all successors should be known as the Second, Third, and Fourth Emperors, was superbly egotistic. Everything, including literature, was ordained to begin from his reign, to which end he issued an edict that all books should be burned. He put to death so many hundred of the *literati* who refused to obey this edict that the "melons actually grew in winter on the spot beneath which the bodies were buried" [2] —a tribute to the fertile character of the Chinese *literati*.

Even assuming that the ill-treatment of children as we know it today did not extend farther back than the period ascribed to it by the Catholic missionaries, the period of Ts'in Chi Hoang, the

[1] Se Ma Ts'ien, *Traduits et Annotés*, par Edouard Chavannes, tome ii., p. 130.

[2] H. A. Giles, *Chinese Biographical Dictionary*.

earliest records of the Chinese indicate that the family was placed on a plane that, for severity toward children, challenges even the Roman *patria potestas*. To the Emperor Yao or Yau, who is supposed to have reigned about 2300 years before Christ, is ascribed the first step in establishing the Chinese attitude toward parents and the respectful obedience exacted from children. Particular emphasis was laid on the son's obedience. It was apparently taken for granted that a daughter would not be rebellious.

Having occupied the throne a long time, Yao, as it is said, called his ministers about him and, telling them that he had now reigned for more than seventy years, expressed his willingness to abdicate in favour of any one who felt capable of taking the Emperor's place. When no one volunteered —they were wise Chinese—he asked them to suggest someone who was deserving of charity.

"Yu Chun," answered the ministers, "though an aged man, is without a wife and comes from an obscure family. Though his father was blind and of neither talent nor mind, and his mother a wicked woman by whom he was mistreated, and though his brother Siang is full of pride, he has observed the rules of filial obedience and has lived in peace and has gradually improved the condition of his family."

"Then," replied the Emperor, "I shall give him my two daughters in marriage and he shall succeed me on the throne to the exclusion of my

son, Ly, who has shown himself to be unworthy
by his lack of respect for his parents."

And it was this Yu Chun, it is said, who further established the Chinese principles of morality,
by which the family and not the individual shaped
the progress of the nation.

How well established those principles became
may be seen from the *Li Ki*, which was composed
about a thousand years later.   This is a code or
book of ceremonials on the civil life, composed or
put together by or under the patronage of Tscheou
Kong, uncle of the Emperor Tchin Ouang, in
1145 B.C.

"A son," says the *Li Ki*, "possesses nothing
while his parents are living. He cannot even
expose his life for a friend."[1]

"A son has received his life from his father and
his mother," says Confucius in the *Hiao King*,
composed 480 B.C., "and this gives them rights
over him that are above all others."

In the legend of How Tseih, the founder of the
House of Chow, whose mother was Keang Yuen
and whose father was "a toe print made by God,"
the adventures of the child are thus described:

He was placed in a narrow lane,
But the sheep and oxen protected him with loving care.
He was placed in a wide forest,
Where he was met with by the wood-cutters.
He was placed on the cold ice,

[1] *Li-Ki*, chapter i.

And a bird screened and supported him with its wings.
When the bird went away
How Tseih began to wail.
His cry was long and loud
So that his voice filled the whole way.

No indication is given in the ode as to who was responsible for exposing the infant to these dangers, but just as in other mythologies in which the heroes or near-gods survive the dangers of infancy, there is no doubt that this Chinese hero was pictured as having overlived dangers that were the common lot of the average child. The commentators take different views of the person responsible for the dangers to which How Tseih was subjected, Maou believing that it was the father, the Emperor K'uh; Ch'ing on the contrary holding that it was Keang Yuen, the mother, who did it herself but not for the purpose of getting rid of the child so much as to show what a "marvellous gift he was from Heaven."[1]

It is not that there are not occasional tender strains in the ode. Number seven in the Odes of Ts'e, the poet, sings:

How young and tender
Is the child with his two tufts of hair.
When you see him after not so long a time
Lo! He is wearing the cap.[2]

[1] *She-King*, part iii., book ii., ode 1., verse 3, translated by James Legge.
[2] *She-King*, part i., book viii., ode 7, verse 3.

Writing later the Emperor Tai Tsong, the author
of a book called the *Mirror of Gold*, repeated these
ideas on ancestor worship in the following ordinance (627 to 650 A.D.):

"The foundation of all the virtues is filial piety.
It is the first thing to learn and I in my youth have
received the right lessons.   I have done my best
to place at ease all my subjects to the end that
the parents might be in a state to bring their
children up properly and that infants in their
turn might acquit themselves of their duties toward
their parents.

"When the virtue of filial piety flourishes, then
all other virtues will follow.   In order that the
Empire may know that such is my desire and that
it is nearest to my heart, I now order that there
be distributed in my name and my account to all
those who are known for their filial piety, five
large measures of rice.   To those who have passed
their eightieth year, two measures; to those of
ninety years, three measures; . . . Moreover one
shall give, commencing with the first moon, to
each woman who gives birth to a son, a measure
of rice."

But twice is there mention of human sacrifice
in the *Chu'un Ts'ew* but both references indicate
that there was little regard for honour as well as
for human life.   In the account of the reign of
Duke He, who ruled from 658 to 626 B.C., it is
said that when the Viscount Tsang went to covenant with the people of Choo, the Viscount was

sacrificed as an animal might be sacrificed on an altar built on the banks of the Suy in order that the wild tribes of the East might be frightened and "drawn toward him."[1]

In the twelfth year of the reign of Duke Ch'aou, who was Marquis of Loo from B.C. 540 to 509, the army of Ts'oo seized Yew (Yin) and sacrificed him on Mount Kang.[2]

Not until the reign of Choen Tche (1633 to 1662 A.D.) was there any movement to check the slaughter of infants.   Then it was found that infanticide had desolated so many of the provinces that it was necessary for this Emperor, the founder of the Tsing dynasty, to condemn the crime and warn the inhabitants of Hang Hoi, of Kiang Sou, and of Fou-kien that the practice must stop.

The first official document endeavouring to save the children was dated the second day of the third moon, 1659, and was an appeal to the Emperor by an under-official.

"The Supreme King," it begins, "loves to give life and to prevent destruction.   All men have received from Heaven a pitying heart.   But the corruption of morals comes between the father and the child and causes men to be guilty of cruelty.   I, your humble subject, have learned that in the provinces of Kiang Nan, Kiang Si, and Fou Kien there exists the barbarous custom of drowning little girls."

[1] *Chu'un Ts'ew*, book v., year xix., par. 4.
[2] *Ibid.*, book x., year xii., par. 9.

The request of the official for an imperial edict against the practice was approved by Choen Tche, who condemned the murder of female children and ordered the mandarins of the provinces named to use means to check the practice. On the twenty-third day of the third moon in the same year in the presence of his advisers, he issued the following edict:

"We had heard that there were people who drowned their girl children but we had not been able to believe it. Today our censor T'Kiai having addressed to us a petition on this unholy practice, we are led to believe that it must really exist.

"The paternal emotions come from nature and there ought not be any difference in the manner of treating sons and daughters. Why should parents conduct themselves cruelly toward girl babies and condemn them to death? Meng Tse has said:

"'When one sees an infant on the point of falling into a well every man feels in his heart the sentiments of fear and compassion.'

"Here, however, it is not a question of strangers or of passers-by. Since all men are moved at the sight of an infant in danger when that infant is a stranger, what kind of parents must those be who deprive their own children of life? What excesses are they not capable of when they can commit such crimes?

"The Supreme Ruler loves to give life and wishes

SPECIAL REPOSITORY FOR BODIES OF NEGLECTED BABIES, CHINA

(REPRODUCED FROM " CHINA IN DECAY ")

that all beings might enjoy themselves without harm. But if a mother and father destroy the child to which they have given life, how can they help but see in that act a blot in the celestial harmony?

"If flood and famine, war and pestilence, visit their terrors on the people, it is because these misfortunes are the punishments for the crimes spoken of. The ancient Emperors wept bitterly over these faults of the people and pardoned crimes, and by that spirit imitated the Spirit of Heaven, who loves to give life. When one of our officers addresses us a report concerning a great wrong, we first look to save the life; if it is not possible to use clemency, and if it is necessary that we pronounce the sentence of death, such a decision causes us genuine sadness. How great ought to be our sorrow, however, at the sight of an infant that had hardly been born, condemned to death.

"Although the mandarins have prohibited this custom, all people are probably not aware of the prohibition. Measures must therefore be taken to bring this prohibition to the knowledge of all and an end must be put to this custom. Not until then will we be joyous and content.

"Ho Long Tou in his book entitled *On Abstaining from Drowning Little Girls* has written these words:

" 'The Tiger and the Wolf are very cruel but they understand the relations that should exist between the parent and its offspring. Why then should man, gifted as is no animal, show himself to be on a lower plane? Our infants, boys and girls, are equally the fruit of our bodies. I have heard that the sad cry uttered by these girl babies as they are plunged into a vase of water and drowned is inexpressible. Alas! that the heart of a father or a mother should be so cruel.' "

Choen Tche then makes an appeal to his subjects asking them not to tolerate further this barbarous custom, dwelling on the superior and more gentle quality of daughters over sons, citing historical instances of the good fortune that many daughters had brought to their parents, and concluding by promising the benediction of Heaven on those who would protect the lives of the little females.

Choen Tche (or Shun Chih) was the ninth son of T'ien Ts'ung and was left to the care of his uncle as regent. His reign was marked by an endeavour to consolidate the newly acquired empire. His biographers speak of his magnanimity as a ruler and he was much praised by his contemporaries. The fact that he treated the Catholic missionaries with favour may also partially explain his horror over the conditions of which he was apparently ignorant until the protest.

Choen Tche's reign also marked the beginning of many modern things in the history of China. It was during his life that there took place the first diplomatic intercourse between the government of the Middle Kingdom and the European nations, both the Dutch and the Russians having had an embassy resident at Pekin during 1656, but although both were treated most politely, neither achieved the substantial gains they sought.[1] It was during his reign too that tea was first introduced to England and a substitute produced for the quart of ale with which even Lady Jane Grey washed down her morning bacon.

It was, however, under the reign of Kang Hi, the son of Choen Tche, that the modern attitude toward children was approximated. The great works of Kang Hi and his long reign have obscured the wisdom and moderation of Choen Tche. One of Kang Hi's first acts was to abolish for all time the eunuchs, a law being passed and engraven on metals that it might stand the ravages of time, forbidding for all time the employment in public service of this class of person, and the Manchus, until the time they gave up the sceptre a few years ago, held to their word. Thus passed out of Chinese history its most industrious class of trouble makers.

But two years after the death of Choen Tche, a writer named Li Li Ong collected the edicts that were being issued by mandarins to show the spread of vice among the people. Among this collection was the following addressed to the governor of the province of Tche Kiang by the mandarin, Ki Eul Jia, prefect of Yen Tcheou:

[1] Demetrius Charles Boulger, *History of China*, vol. ii., p. 314. Palatre, p. 6.

"The Heaven and the Earth love to shower benefits on man and to conserve life. But alas! the inhabitants of this prefecture of Yen Tcheou have the habit of drowning their girl babies. The rich as well as the poor have been found to be guilty of this crime. The tiger, despite his cruelty, does not devour his young, and it is hard to think that man should be insensible to the cries of his drowning infant. I myself have witnessed such drownings and that is why I ask that you send into my six districts a proclamation strictly prohibiting infanticide. It will be printed on stone. If any one should then be guilty of the crime, his neighbours should be encouraged to notify the magistrates that he might be dealt with according to law. As you are charged to maintain morality among the people, I propose that you use this means."

Whether this suggestion was taken or not, it is known that in that particular province infanticide increased instead of diminished. The particularly interesting part of this document is that it brings to light the fact from an official source that the rich as well as the poor were the offenders and that it was not lack of food alone that made this practice so common in China.

Even in modern times this is so, a midwife who was asked in recent years to become a Christian saying that it was impossible inasmuch as it interfered with her business. She said that frequently she was asked by wealthy people to drown the female children which the parents had not the courage to kill themselves.[1]

In 1720 Father d'Entrcolles translated a manual for the use of mandarins which bore the title *The Perfect Happiness of the People* and which contained a plan for a "House of Pity for homeless infants"[2] and an exhortation to put such a plan into execution, declaring that in times past there had been such institutions for the reception of orphans and homeless children and that nurses had been provided for them when they had been rescued.

The next proclamation of which we have any knowledge was that issued with the approval of the Emperor Kien Long, who reigned from 1736 to 1796. In 1772, Ngeou Yang Yun Ki addressed to the Emperor, in the thirty-seventh year and the twenty-ninth day of the tenth moon of his reign, a communication in which it was stated that the poor families had been obliged to drown their daughters because they had not had enough food. Permission was asked to inflict on the person who committed this crime, the penalty of sixty blows from a cane, and a year in exile. In 1773 the Emperor Kien Long himself issued the following edict against infanticide:

"The statutes fixing the penalty for the murder of a grown-up child or a small child presuppose that the child has not failed to obey the orders of its parents or grandparents, and cover cases

[1] P. G. Palatre, *Annales de la Sainte-Enfance*, tome xii., p. 304.
[2] *Lettres Edif.*, vol. x., p. 363.

where the infants are murdered deliberately and with premeditation. This crime, which violates the laws of nature, should be punished with the whip and with banishment. If the infants that are thus killed are but newly-born and therefore without intelligence and reason, the guilty cannot plead the disobedience of these daughters as an excuse for their crimes. Therefore henceforth whenever any one following the barbarous custom shall drown his infants, he will be prosecuted for murder with premeditation, and when the proof has been properly established before the proper tribunals he will receive a sentence equal to that which is meted out to the parents or grandparents who voluntarily assassinate their children. It is not necessary to issue a special ordinance. Let all respect this decree."

A dozen years later another voice was raised in protest against the drowning of girls. Chen, Treasurer General of the province of Kiang Sou, presented to the governor of that province a proclamation against infanticide and begged him to publish it.

In 1815 a writer named Ou Sing King made an appeal to the officials of China to stop the drowning of infants and the sale of women, and this appeal falling into the hands of the Emperor Kia King, a proclamation was issued against both vices. The writer, Ou Sing King, was given imperial permission to go further in his investigations.

Early in the reign of Tao Kang (1820–1851)

the then governor of the province of Tche Kiang, believing that the expensive wedding gifts were the real cause of the child murder, decreed:

"It is ordered that ornaments of gold, pearls, precious stones, and embroidered gowns are forbidden at all marriages. As for silver ornaments, silks, and other materials, this is the rule that we hereby establish:

"For rich families the sum set out for such purchases must not be over one hundred taels. For people of medium fortune the expense must be limited to from forty to fifty taels. Those of inferior blood must not spend more than twenty or thirty taels and the poorest people must not go beyond two or five.[1]

"As for gifts by the parents to the husband, the quantity is left to their discretion; this being the means to avoid all dispute. After the marriage, on certain occasions, it is permitted to make one or two presents. The celebrations of three and seven days when the grandson is born or when he attains his first year are hereby forbidden and henceforth the people should not have any more difficulties about bringing up daughters. If, in spite of this, the poor are unable to bring up their female children, they must carry them to the orphanage or give them to other families."[2]

On the 19th of February, 1838, the Lieutenant

---

[1] P. Gabriel Palatre, *L'Infanticide et l'Œuvre de la Sainte-Enfance en Chine*, p. 16.

[2] *Te-i-lou*, tome i., 2ᵉ partie, *Tao-yng-hoei-Koei-taio*, p. 16.

General Ki of the province of Koang Tong instituted an investigation to find out what the actual conditions were in his provinces, and after receiving his reports, issued a proclamation in which he said:

"I am convinced that in the province of Koang Tong the custom of drowning and suffocating the girl babies is common and that the rich as well as the poor are guilty. The poor pretend that, not having sufficient means of existence, they are not able to bring up their female children, while the rich declare that there is no object in bringing up children that occupy a purely ornamental position in the household."

Ki then goes on to philosophize on the enormity of the crime and the folly of these reasons. Never, perhaps, did any single individual in China devote himself with more energy to trying to eradicate this evil than did Ki, both by verbal castigation of those who were guilty of the crime and by appealing to the sympathies of the inhabitants of his province. He distributed copies of the works of Ouang Ouan. He sent out advice and instructions to his subordinates that infanticide must be prevented; he enlisted the nobles and educated people in this fight and reiterated that those who were guilty of the crime would be seized, judged, and punished with sixty blows and a year's banishment as the law directed. Throughout the province his efforts were regarded as extremely interesting, his proclamations as delightful literature, and there was no decrease in the number of murders.

In 1845 the Emperor Tao Kang himself published an edict condemning the practice and declaring that the extreme punishment permitted by the law would be meted out to the guilty. The edict had no effect.

In 1848 another endeavour was made by the chief magistrate of Canton, acting on the initiative of Ki, to eliminate the evil in that particular city, but neither in Canton or in the province of Koang Tong was there a cessation of the evil for eighteen years afterward. The Emperor Kong Tche listed both Canton and the province as among the places where infanticide was most common.

During the reign of Hien Fong, 1851–1862, little progress was made. In many parts of China during the following reign, that of Tong Tche, 1862–1875, attempts were made to check the evil.

During the minority of the Emperor the two Empress Regents issued a proclamation in which they appealed to the "nobles and rich of all villages to contribute for the erection of orphanages where there might be received abandoned children so that the poor will not be able to justify their abominable practice on the ground of poverty."

The reign of Koang Siu began in 1875, and was marked with vigorous proclamations and warnings to the people to take their children to the orphan asylums that were being established rather than to throw them into the river.[1]

[1] P. Gabriel Palatre, *L'Infanticide et l'Œuvre de la Sainte-Enfance en Chine*, p. 44, note No. 2, which reads:

5

Of the conditions as they exist in modern times, travellers and writers are of one accord—infanticide is horribly prevalent. The conditions vary with different localities.

"In Fuhkien province," says Williams, "especially in the department of Chang Chau, in-

---

"Foochow—'The Prefect and the local magistrates have within the last few days issued a stringent proclamation against the practice of female infanticide. It provides that all parents guilty of destroying a child shall be punished according to the law against the destruction of descendants, which, it seems, provides sixty blows and a year's imprisonment, as the proper punishment. A midwife, who destroys a child, is to be punished by strangulation. Neighbours who know of the commission, and do not report it, are to be punished as accessories to murder; and the Tepo are to be punished in the same way. A vigorous execution of this proclamation would do much to remedy the evil; but it remains to be seen whether the proclamation is more than a periodical fulmination, with the probability that it is not.' Foochow *Herald*." Also note No. 1, p. 45, which reads: "From the Foochow *Herald*. 'The following proclamation was recently issued by the Prefect of Foochow, and is, we understand, extensively circulated throughout the city and suburban districts.

" '"Weng, acting Prefect of Foochow, issues an emphatic proclamation.

" '"It has been found that the drowning of newly-born female infants is of frequent occurrence in places under this prefectural jurisdiction. As a reason for this cruel and outrageous behaviour towards their children, the poor allege that they are without the means to support them; the rich that they dread the expense of providing them with dowries. The Acting Prefect has repeatedly issued prohibitory proclamations since assuming charge of this post, and has also instructed the magistrates to arrest delinquents. It has been reported of late that in the neighbourhood of Shang Kan, under the jurisdiction of the Min magistrate, the practice of female infanticide still exists; it is further reported

fanticide prevails to a greater extent than in any other part of the Empire yet examined.   Mr. Abeel extended his inquiries to forty different towns and villages lying in the first, and found that the percentage was between seventy and eighty down to ten, giving an average of about

---

that in one spot over ten infants have been found drowned, so that there is every reason to believe that this vicious practice extends to other places too.   It is the Prefect's duty to draw up the most stringent supervisory regulations in order to the re-claiming of people from this rooted habit.   The Prefect has instructed the magistrates to act in this spirit, and has now to issue this proclamation peremptorily forbiddng the practice.

" '"Wherefore now know ye all, gentry, elders, scholars, civil and military, and all persons whatsoever in this prefecture, that it is your duty to act one and all of you in accordance with the spirit of the following Regulations, and exercise a watch upon each other.   If any families are found drowning their female infants, it will assuredly be at once reported to the magistrates, who will severely punish the act in accordance (with law).   If any persons favour or connive at this practice and do not act upon the instructions, on the discovery or report of a case the hundred-men, neighbours, and relatives will be held equally accountable.   No leniency will be shown.   Tremble at this! Obey this!   Do not disobey!   A special proclamation." '

"Rules relating to midwives:

" 'Female infanticide must always be practiced immediately after birth, and is generally committed by the midwife, but even if the parents do it themselves, the midwife must know.   The leading gentry and the hundred-men are hereby charged hence-forward to take notice of midwives in their respective villages who may dare to assist in drowning female infants.   The leading gentry, the hundred-men, members of families, and neighbours are authorized to ascertain and send in the names of such mid-wives, and apply for their punishment as accomplices.'

"Extract from *The Shanghai Courier and China Gazette*, number of the 24th of November, 1877."

forty per cent. of all girls born in those places as
being murdered. In Chang Chau, out of seventeen
towns, the proportion lies between one fourth
and three tenths in some places, occasionally
rising to one third, and in others sinking to one
fifth, making an average of one fourth put to
death. In other departments of the province the
practice is confessed, but the proportion thought
by intelligent natives to be less, since there is less
poverty and fewer people than formerly."

"Infanticide, which until now has gone unpun-
ished," says Dr. Lauterer, "is practised especially
in Pekin and Fuhkien. A large per cent. of female
infants meet with an unnatural death because of
their parents' poverty or their niggardliness. The
unfortunates are simply cast into the nearest
stream and the corpse left until the morning when
the government's wagon collects them, or they are
exposed in the open where, not being protected
from the cold, they soon perish. Lately a decree
has been made to prohibit it."[1]

"The province of Fuhkien," says Douglas, "is
that in which this crime most obtains. Inquiries
show that in many districts as large a portion as
one fourth of the female children born are destroyed
at birth. At Pekin, on the other hand, it cannot
be said to exist at all. But in this as in so many
social offences in China, the sword of the law, which
is alone capable of putting down crime, is allowed
to hang like a rusty weapon on the wall. It is

[1] Dr. Joseph Lauterer, *China. Das Reich der Mitte*, p. 130.

AN OVERBURDENED CHINESE CHILD CARRYING MORE THAN HIS WEIGHT IN TEA
(COPYRIGHT BY UNDERWOOD & UNDERWOOD, N. Y.)

"LITTLE MOTHERS"—THE ONE FIVE, THE OTHER EIGHT, YEARS OLD—CHINA

true that occasionally proclamations are issued in which the heinousness of the evil is explained with all the impressiveness that could be desired, but so long as natural affection finds no support from without it will continue, in China, to yield to the requirements of daily food."[1]

"The custom of infanticide," wrote Professor Krausse, "is one which has obtained in many parts of China for ages. It does not, as a rule, take the form of actual murder, but consists rather in assisting the laws of Nature. Thus an infant will be neglected and permitted to perish, or if it sicken, will be put aside and allowed to take its chance."[2]

"Outside the wall [of Wie Hsien]," writes A. J. Brown, "we saw a 'Baby House,' a small stone building in which dead children of the poor are thrown to be eaten by dogs!

"I wanted to examine it, but was warned not to do so as the Chinese imagine that foreigners make their medicine out of children's eyes and brains, and our crowds of watching Chinese might quickly become an infuriated mob."[3]

In the face of all this one reads with interest in a book by a professor of Chinese in the University of Cambridge that:

"Among other atrocious libels which have fastened upon the fair name of the Chinese people, first and foremost stands the charge of female

[1] Robert K. Douglas, *Society in China*, p. 253.
[2] Alexis Krausse, *China in Decay*, p. 38.
[3] Arthur Judson Brown, *New Forces in Old China*, chap. v.

infanticide, now happily, though still slowly, fading from the calculations of those who seek the truth."[1]

[1] H. A. Giles, *Civilization of China*, p. 96.

CHAPTER V

THE first inhabitants of Japan were a numerous people named Koropok-guru, who
lived in conelike huts built over holes
dug in the earth and who were exterminated by
the Ainu people. The latter were in turn conquered by the race that we speak of today as the
Japanese; these last settlers coming to the islands
of Japan from somewhere in the north of Central Asia, while a second stream of South Asian
immigrants were drifted to Japan by the Japan
current.

In the *Kojiki*, or "Records of Ancient Matters,"
dictated by Hide-no-are and completed in A.D.
711 or 712, we have a record of the mythology,
manners, language, and the traditional history
of Japan; this "history" purports to give the actual story of Japan from the year 660 B.C., when
the first Emperor Jimmu, "having subdued and
pacified the savage deities and extirpated the un-

submissive people, dwelt at the palace of Kashi-
wabara." Modern Japanese scholars as well as
Western scholars are inclined to say that there is
really no authentic history before A.D. 461 but as
a picture of the customs of early Japan, the *Kojiki*
is still the only authentic document that we have.

Inazo Nitobe, in dividing the history of his
country into periods, groups the legendary age
and all that went before the political reforms of
the seventh century as the first period, under the
name of the "ancient period."

These ancient people, the mythical people of
the *Kojiki*, had passed through a genuine Bronze
Age and had in general attained a high level of
barbaric skill. Of their many curious customs, both
in the *Kojiki* and in the equally important *Nihongi* or "Chronicles of Japan," prominent notice
is made of the "parturition house"—"one-roomed
but without windows, which a woman was supposed to build and retire into for the purpose of
being delivered unseen." Here is evidence that the
infant was "taboo" until it had been received by
the head of the house.

Even up to recent times in the island of Hachijo the custom survived according to Ernest
Satow, who visited this island in 1878.

"In Hachijo," wrote Mr. Satow, "women, when
about to become mothers, were formerly driven
out to the huts on the mountainside, and according to the accounts of native writers, left to shift
for themselves, the result not unfrequently being

the death of the new-born infant, or if it survived
the rude circumstances under which it first saw the
light, the seeds of disease were sown which clung
to it throughout its after life. The rule of non-
intercourse was so strictly enforced that the
woman was not allowed to leave the hut even to
visit her own parents at the point of death, and
besides the injurious effects that this solitary
confinement must have had on the wives themselves, their prolonged absence was a serious loss
to households where there were elder children and
large establishments to be superintended. The
rigour of the custom was so far relaxed in modern
times that the huts were no longer built on the
hills, but were constructed inside the homestead.
It was a subject of wonder to people from other
parts of Japan that the senseless practice should
still be kept up, and its abolition was often recom-
mended, but the administration of the Shoguns
was not animated by a reforming spirit, and it
remained for the government of the Mikado to
exhort the islanders to abandon this and the previously mentioned custom. They are therefore
no longer sanctioned by official authority and the
force of social opinion against them is increasing,
so that before long these relics of ancient ceremo-
nial religion will in all probability have disappeared
from the group of islands."

As with most early histories there is little description of custom or manners in either the *Kojiki*
or the *Nihongi*, but we gather what the general

attitude was toward children from the fact that
the conception of marriage was probably limited
to cohabitation, this condition lasting until well
on into the Middle Ages,[1] cohabitation being often
secret at first, but afterward acknowledged.
When the latter conditions had come to prevail,
the young man, instead of going to his mistress
under the cover of the night, brought her back
publicly to his parents' home, and that was the
beginning of his own home.

Little is there in the *Kojiki* about the care of
children but the harshness toward women about to
have children, as shown in the frequent reference
to the parturition houses, shows that unless they
were children of royalty they were left to whatever care their mothers might be able to bestow
on them.

In the account of the making of Japan by the
two Heavenly Deities, known as the Izani-gi-no-
kami and Izana-mi-no-kami, the Man Who Invites and the Female Who Invites, it is stated
that their first child was not retained.

"This child," says the legend,[2] after retailing
the events that led up to its birth, "they placed
in a boat of reeds and let it float away. Next they
gave birth to the island of Aha. This is not reckoned among their children."

Among the gods, therefore, children were rejected or accepted without ceremony, and with

[1] Brinkley, vol. i., p. 61.
[2] *Kojiki*, introduction, p. xl.

such an attitude of rejection or acceptance depicted as the normal condition among the deities, it may easily be imagined what was the attitude of the ordinary beings who modelled their conduct on that of the deities.

It is told of the first Emperor Jimmu, that, meeting a group of seven maidens, he invited one of them to become a wife of his, and on her acceptance the sovereign passed the night at her house. This constituted the only marriage ceremony that the times knew. As far as the woman was concerned, all that the new condition meant was that she was liable to receive a visit at any time from her new lord and master, but on his side there was no obligation, no duty of fidelity, and he was free to form as many similar unions as fancy dictated.

The children were brought up by the mother and one household of a man might be in absolute ignorance of another.[1] Mistress, wife, and concubine were on the same footing and could be discarded at any moment. When the Deity of Eight Thousand Spears, attired in his favourite courting costume, is about to go forth and search for a "better wife" he boldly announces that:

When I take and attire myself so
Carefully in my august garments green
As the kingfisher—
It is with the intention of finding another mate.

[1] Chamberlain, Introduction, p. xi.

To this the Chief Empress, Her Augustness the
Forward Princess, to whom the frank statement
is made, plaintively replies:

"Thou . . . indeed, being a man, probably
hast on the various island-headlands that thou
seest and on every beach-headland that thou
lookest on, a wife like the young herbs. But I,
alas! being a woman have no man except thee;
I have no spouse except thee!" [1]

What became of the children in the cases of
conjugal separation does not appear, a statement
that is made by no less a Japanese authority than
Chamberlain. [2]   In only one instance is there any
reference made to the fate of a child that had been
deserted, but this is an unusual case, where the
father had violated the rules of the parturition
house, with the result that the mother disappears,
leaving the father to take care of the child.   He
pledged himself to look after it until the day of
his death but the sister of the child's mother was
first invoked to act as nurse.

The result of this system of family life was that
where the children of different mothers but of
the same father discovered one another's presence
there were feuds and much fighting, especially as
it was the children of the latest affection who were
generally the recipients of his favour to the chagrin
and anger of the less favoured children and families.   Marriages between half-brothers and half-

[1] *Kojiki*, section xxv.
[2] Chamberlain, Introduction, p. xl.

sisters were another result of the system, the only restriction on marriages of any kind being that children of the same mother should not marry. Sons of the same father were thus incited to be enemies rather than brothers, in the accepted sense, and the annals of the civil wars are replete with tales of treachery and ambition and show almost an entire absence of natural affection. The fact that the children had no claim on the love and the protection of the father and that their mother was condemned under the ancient system to the function of a mere animal, is cited by Brinkley as the reason for this cruelty and treachery.[1]

This was the position of the child in the society that is depicted in the *Kojiki* and the *Nihongi*, although the latter, written about forty years after the *Kojiki* (A.D. 720), and under the influence of the Chinese, is more apt to depict the conditions that sprang up with the spreading Chinese culture.

The fourth century brought to Japan a knowledge of Chinese classics, and Chinese morals, and in 552 A.D., there came a still greater change when the Buddhistic religion was introduced through a copy of the scripture and an image of Buddha being sent to the Yamato Court by the government of one of the Korean kingdoms. Unsuccessful preachments there had been by unofficial missionaries before this, but the arrival of the

[1] Captain F. Brinkley, *Japan*, p. 89.

Korean ambassador served to bring to the attention of the government the new religion in a manner calculated to arouse interest in its doctrines.

Whatever may be the defects of Shintoism, human sacrifice never seems really to have been part of its practice,[1] and to this fact, with the increasing regard for life that came with civilization, is undoubtedly due the little emphasis given to infanticide among the Japanese. Another influence, undoubtedly, and this is said to be the "best point of Shinto,"[2] is that the people were taught that they themselves were sons and daughters of the gods, a belief apt to save the killing of surplus members of society in a time of economic stress.

According to the *Nihongi*, human sacrifice was put an end to in Japan in the year A.D. 3:

"Tenth month, fifth day: Yamato-hiko, the Mikado's younger brother by the mother's side, died.

"Eleventh month, second day: Yamato-hiko was buried at Tsukizaka in Musa. Thereupon his personal attendants were assembled, and were all buried alive upright in the precinct of the tomb. For several days they died not, but wept and wailed day and night. At last they died and rotted. Dogs and crows gathered and ate them.

"The Emperor, hearing the sound of their weeping and wailing, was grieved at heart, and commanded his high officers, saying:

[1] G. Underwood, *Religions of Eastern Asia*, p. 75.
[2] *Ibid.*, p. 83.

"'It is a very painful thing to force these whom one has loved in life to follow him in death. Though it be an ancient custom, why follow it if it is bad? From this time forward, take counsel so as to put a stop to the following of the dead.'

"A.D. 3, seventh month, sixth day: The Empress Hibasuhime no Mikoto died. Sometime before the burial the Emperor commanded his ministers, saying:

"'We have already recognized that the practice of following the dead is not good. What should now be done in performing this burial?'

"Thereupon Nomi no Sukune came forward and said:

"'It is not good to bury living men upright at the tumulus of a prince. How can such a practice be handed down to posterity? I beg leave to propose an expedient which I will submit to your Majesty.'

"So he sent messengers to summon up from the land of Idzumo a hundred men of the clay-workers Be. He himself directed the men of the clay-workers Be to take clay and form therewith shapes of men, horses, and various objects, which he presented to the Emperor, saying:

"'Henceforward, let it be the law for future ages to substitute things of clay for living men, and to set them up at tumuli.'

"Then the Emperor was greatly rejoiced, and commended Nomi no Sukune, saying:

"'Thy expedient hath greatly pleased our heart.'

"So the things of clay were first set up at the tomb of Hibasuhime no Mikoto. And a name was given to those clay objects. They were called *hani-wa* or 'clay rings.'

"Then a decree was issued, saying:

"'Henceforth these clay figures must be set up at tumuli; let no men be harmed.'

"The Emperor bountifully rewarded Nomi no Sukune for this service, and also appointed him to the official charge of the clay-workers Be. His original title was therefore changed, and he was called Hashi no Omi. This was how it came to pass that the Hashi no Muraji superintended the burials of Emperors."[1]

The date ascribed to this incident cannot be depended on. "Chinese accounts speak of the custom of human sacrifices at the burial of a sovereign as in full force in Japan so late as A.D. 247," says Aston. Probably all the events of this part of Japanese history are very much antedated. But of the substantial accuracy of the narrative there can be no doubt. Some of these clay figures (known as *tsuchi-ningio*) are still in existence, and may be seen in the British Museum, where they constitute the chief treasure of the Gowland collection. The Uyeno Museum in Tokio also possessed specimens, both of men and horses. None, however, remain *in situ* at the tombs. The *hani-wa* (clay-rings), cylinders which

[1] *Nihongi.* See *Transactions and Proceedings of the Japan Society, London*, vol. i., translated by W. G. Aston.

CROCK CONTAINING REMAINS OF SACRIFICED CHILD. UNEARTHED AT TELL TA'ANNEK

(REPRODUCED FROM " LIFE IN ANCIENT EGYPT '')

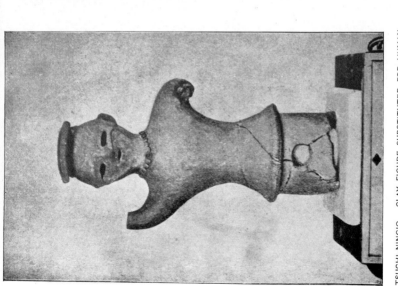

TSUCHI-NINGIO. CLAY FIGURE SUBSTITUTED FOR HUMAN SACRIFICE—JAPAN

(REPRODUCED FROM " TRANSACTIONS AND PROCEEDINGS OF THE JAPAN SOCIETY," VOLUME I)

may now be seen embedded in the earth round all
the principal *misasagi*, are so numerous that they
can hardly have all been surmounted by figures.
But they are of the same workmanship and of the
same date, and no doubt some of them are the
pedestals of images, the above-ground part of
which has been destroyed by the weather or by
accident.

"A similar substitution of straw or wooden
images for living men took place in China in ancient times, though by a curious inversion of ideas,
the former practice is described as leading to the
latter."[1]

While neither the lion or the tiger ever troubled
Japan and her most carnivorous and destructive
animals have been wolves, tradition has ascribed
the sacrifice of human beings in Japan to the desire
to placate the god of wild animals. The victim
was always a girl, and from the earliest ages the
manner of selecting her was to affix to the roof of
a house a bow and arrow. When the householder
arose in the morning and discovered what was
accepted as a divine intimation, the eldest daughter of the family was buried alive, it being supposed
that her flesh served as a meal for the deity.
Later the priests of Buddha found a more profit-
able method of disposing of these girls by selling
them as slaves; thereby following out the fundamental tenet of the Buddhistic religion, which is

[1] *Nihongi.* See *Transactions and Proceedings of the Japan
Society, London*, vol. i., p. 181, by W. G. Aston.

the sanctity of human life, and at the same time increasing their wealth. Some writers refer to this practice as being a sacrifice to an animal in the service of Shakamuni, which would have made it a Buddhistic rite, but the idea is scoffed at by Brinkley.[1] Even up to recent times it is said the habit of sacrificing human beings in order to make the foundation of any great work more stable was common. The corpses of two human beings were said to be under the scarps "of the futile forts hurriedly erected for defence of Yedo [Tokio] in the interval between Commodore Perry's first and second coming."[2]

In the Tokugawa period, extending from about 1615 to 1860, two and a half centuries, Japan was a hermit nation distinguished for its peaceful character. Yet its population for one hundred years remained almost stationary. By some authorities, this has been explained not only on the ground of many famines and devastating diseases but the common practice of abortion and the fact that the Samurai considered it disgraceful to marry until they were thirty, and equally disgraceful to raise a family of more than three children.

"Among the lower classes it was not common to rear all the children born, especially if girls came too frequently." Also, "While there was hardly in the whole country a hospital in our sense of

[1] Capt. F. Brinkley, *Japan*, vol. v., p. 194.
[2] *Id.*, vol. v., p. 195.

the term, there were in the large cities physicians famous for their skill in preventing the birth of living children. They kept private establishments to accommodate calculating patrons. All authorities agreed that sexual morality in the large cities was at a very low ebb among all classes, while luxury and effeminacy prevailed among people high in birth and wealth."[1]

As a picture of what the people were driven to and a terrible example of what attitude famine may lead parents to take toward their children, there is no more important document than the statement of Shirakawa Rakuo, distinguished as the Minister of Finance of the Eleventh Shogun, Iyenari. The trace of cannibalism in semi-civilized peoples is easier to understand after the fearful famine in the third year of Temmei (1783).

"A trustworthy man," says Rakuo,[2] "who had travelled in this district [northern part of country], told me that in a village which had previously contained 800 houses there were only thirty left, the inhabitants of the rest all having died. Having entered a village in which the houses seemed to be larger and more numerous than usual, he proposed to rest there for the night. He soon discovered, however, that not a single house was inhabited, but in all the houses he saw bones and

[1] W. E. Griffis, *Japanese Nation in Evolution*, p. 268.
[2] Quoted by Garrett Droppers in "The Population of Japan in the Tokugawa Period," extract from *Transactions of the Asiatic Society of Japan*, vol. xxi., p. 253.

skulls scattered about the floor. As he went on he saw innumerable bones and skulls by the road-side. He met a man leading a pack-horse on the road, who said that he could survive without eating the flesh of human beings as he was supported by a rich uncle. In some places even those who abandoned themselves to eating human flesh could not find food enough to live. Great numbers starved to death. The price paid for a dog was 500 sen, sometimes even as high as 800 sen, a rat 50 sen. A rare work of art found no purchasers and could not be exchanged for a *go* of rice. If a person died he was of course eaten by the survivors. Those who died of starvation, however, could not be eaten, because their flesh decayed so soon. Some people, therefore, killed those who were certain to starve and put the flesh into brine so as to keep it for a long time. Among other people there was a farmer who went to his neighbour and said, 'My wife and one of my sons have already died from want of food. My remaining son is certain to die within a few days, so I wish to kill him while his flesh is still eatable, but being his father, I do not dare to raise the sword against him, so I beg you to kill the boy for me.' The neighbour agreed to do this, but stipulated that he should get a part of the flesh as a reward for his service. This was agreed to and the neighbour at once killed the boy. As soon as the deed was done, the farmer, who stood by, struck his neighbour with a sword and killed him, saying that he 'was very glad to avenge his son and at the same time have double the quantity of food.' "

Up to the close of the seventeenth century, feudal legislation was very harsh, one of the worst laws of ancient times in force until that time being that by which children were punished for the crime of their parents.[1] If a man or a woman had been sentenced to be crucified or burnt and had male children above fifteen years of age, those children were similarly executed, and if they were under that age they were given over to a relative to be reared until they reached the age of fifteen, when they were banished. When the criminal parent was condemned to the ordinary hanging or beheading it was still within the discretion of the judge to condemn the male children to be executed or exiled. The female children, while exempt from the capital punishment, were liable to be sold as slaves.

In 1721, during the reign of the enlightened Yoshimune, who was Shogun from 1716 to 1746, there were many reforms, and it was then enacted that for all crimes, even those punishable with crucifixion and exposure of the head, only the criminal himself must be punished. In the case of the most heinous of all crimes, according to Japanese standards, parricide or the murder of a teacher, a special tribunal was declared to be the only place where it could be decided whether the children and grandchildren should be implicated.

[1] Brinkley, *Japan*, vol. iv., p. 56.

Interesting too is the fact that this leniency extended to the farmers and merchants only, the Samurai not being included, it being assumed that the crime of a person of nobility and education was a more serious matter than a crime by a person less fortunate—a theory of justice that has never taken root in the minds of the Occidentals except among romancers.

From the time, early in the seventeenth century, when the governing power of Japan fell into the hands of the Buddhist Tokugawa family, through Iyeyasu, the head of the house, there was an endeavour to check the sale of children. No less than eight enactments were issued between 1624 and 1734 declaring the sale of human beings punishable by death.

Progress naturally was slow when the conditions were so flagrant that there were open offices where the sales and purchase of children were effected.[1] In 1649 an absurd compromise was attempted when a law was passed declaring it was lawful to sell a child, providing that the consent of the child was obtained. There was an attempt to regulate, without abolishing, slavery in the law of 1655, which declared that in a dispute between an employer and the employed, the employer, if found to be in the wrong, might be imprisoned or meted out any punishment that the employed might suggest. It is safe to add that the administrative criminal machinery was not in the hands of the

[1] Brinkley, *Japan*, vol. iv., p. 57.

proletariat, nor was there any suffrage that threatened to put the employed in the position of judge.

It was during this period that the law was passed allowing the parent to have his son or daughter imprisoned, a just cause being assumed. A father had the right to punish his son, but the son had the right to appeal to a magistrate for a review of the sentence; but "costs" of the appeal were dangerous inasmuch as if the son lost he had to suffer whatever penalty his father might dole out to him. The Occidental mind will not appreciate so readily the attempts of the Tokugawas, beginning 1627, to regulate the social evil, one of their early laws depriving employers of all authority "to retain the services of a female for immoral purposes outside the appointed quarter."

Modern writers on Japan lay stress on the affection of the Japanese for their children, and yet "during the famine of 1905 many girls who had been sold by the suffering parents were redeemed by the Christians."[1] This sacrifice of the children to the welfare of the parents is traceable to the influence of Confucius. To the same source may be ascribed the fact that, though in ancient times the female sex was prominent in Japan, after the introduction of Confucianism the Samurai considered it beneath him to even converse with his wife and children.[2] "Neither God nor the ladies

---

[1] A. K. Faust, *Christianity as a Social Factor in Modern Japan*, p. 47. [2] E. J. Harrison, *The Fighting Spirit of Japan*, p. 350.

inspired any enthusiasm in the Samurai's heart," says Professor Chamberlain. For is it not written by the great moralist Karbara Ekken in the *Owna Dargaku*, "It was the custom of the ancients, on the birth of a female child, to let it lie on the floor for the space of three days. Even in this may be seen the likening of the man to heaven and of the woman to earth."[1]

Only a few years ago a child, both of whose parents had died of cholera, was on the point of being buried alive by neighbours when it was rescued.[2] "Certain parts of Japan have been notorious from of old for this practice," says Gulick. "In Toas the evil was so rampant that a society for its prevention has been in existence many years. It helps support children of poor parents who might be tempted to dispose of them criminally."

On the other hand, this word from Professor Goodrich, who as a member of the faculty of the Imperial College pictures a nation far from indifferent to the welfare of the child:

"Ever since the beginning of that indefinite period which we call 'modern times' the birth of a child has always been an occasion for rejoicing. To be sure, in Japan that joy was very much greater when it was a boy baby; yet the Japanese have never displayed such intense dislike to girl babies as have the Chinese. One great reason

[1] Karbara Ekken, *Wisdom and Women of Japan*, p. 45.
[2] S. L. Gulick, *Institutions of the Japanese*, p. 100.

for this was that the population of Japan was not
so dense as it is in China. It was easier to provide
for children, and therefore there was no incentive
to put girl babies out of the way. I am sorry to
say that very lately, since the Russo-Japanese
War (1904–5), when the Japanese people are
almost crushed by the weight of taxes to provide
money with which to pay war expenses and to keep
up army and navy, the number of cases of female
infanticide is increasing alarmingly."[1]

[1] J. K. Goodrich, *Our Neighbours: The Japanese*, p. 32.

CHAPTER VI

OUR great grandfathers who accepted the
chronology of the good Bishop Usher,
by which the creation of the world was
placed neatly and exactly at 4004 years before
Christ, would never have dreamed of such periods
of time as those the ethnologist, in his search for
the natural history of man, compasses today in the
annals of a single family, like the so-called, and
at present discredited, Aryan. Nor yet would it
have seemed possible to our grandfathers, that
modern archæology would have made it possible
for our savants and scientists to be today correct-
ing the mistakes of Herodotus, and showing by
their decipherings of new-found inscriptions and
monuments, that before the earliest Greeks, the
Egyptians, and even the Semitic peoples who
inhabited Babylon and Assyria, there was another
people,—a people whose origin it is not possible to
place even now,—the Sumerians and Akkadians,

who in the fourth millennial period B.C. were already a cultured and civilized people.

Recent excavations have changed the entire historical attack. Instead of beginning with the Homeric Age as an age of legend, "civilization may now be traced beyond the Mycenæan epoch, through the different stages of Ægean culture back into the Neolithic Age."[1] In Egypt we can now go back before the pyramid builders to the earliest dynastic kings, even to Neolithic Egyptians of whom there are no written records. Back of the known civilization of Assyria and Babylon, there has been discovered an even older civilization.

"On the northern and eastern confines of the Babylonian culture-system, new nations pass within our ken; Vannic men of Armenia, ruled by powerful kings; Kassites of the Zagros, whose language seems to contain elements which if really Aryan are probably the oldest known monuments of Indo-European speech (c. 1600 B.C.); strange tongued Elamites, also, akin neither to Iranian nor Semite. Nor does it seem to us remarkable that we should read the trilingual proclamations of Darius Hystaspis to his peoples in their original tongues, although an eighteenth century philosopher would have regarded the prospect of our ever being able to do so as the wildest of chimeras!"[2]

[1] Leonard W. King, *History of Sumer and Akkad*, p. 1.
[2] Hall.

Recent excavations have established the fact that the earliest known civilization was in what afterwards came to be known as Mesopotamia, between the Euphrates and the Tigris, and that groups of people living in cities and calling themselves, in the lower section of the country, the Sumerians, and in the upper section, the Akkadians, dwelt in civilized state until they were conquered by the Semitic peoples. The Semites in their conquest of the Greeks, as we now know, took from the conquered the culture of the race that was physically weaker, as indeed the Gauls did from the Romans.

In government, law, literature, and art the Sumerians were the superior people, and though the Semites improved on their models, the impulse, says King, came from the Sumerians.[1] It is now known that Hammurabi's Code of Laws, which influenced in so marked a degree the Mosaic legislation, was of Sumerian origin, and the later religions and mythological literature from which the Hebrews borrowed so freely, was also of Sumerian origin.

Even with the excavations that are now going on and the discoveries that are being made almost daily, our evidence is still too scanty and imperfect, the gaps in it are too numerous,[2] as Professor Sayce says, apropos of the Babylonian religion, to make it possible for us to discuss with any definite-

[1] L. W. King, *History of Sumer and Akkad*, preface, p. ix.
[2] A. H. Sayce, *Religions of Ancient Egypt and Babylonia*, p. 253.

ness the attitude of these first civilized peoples toward children. Years will pass before the tablets already in the museums will have been deciphered, to say nothing of those that are being dug out now. A library of 30,000 tablets was discovered by M. de Srazec at Telloh in Northern Babylonia, at Nippur in the great temple of Bel, and five times as many were discovered later by the American excavators. Once the British Museum was the sole repository of these treasures, containing everything from business contracts to prayers to the gods, but now they are in the Louvre, the Berlin Museum, the Museum of Constantinople, the University of Pennsylvania, and even in private collections.

From these Semitic conquerors of the Sumerians, however, there came the first civilization and the first humanization, for in this rich valley with its abundance of water and its rich soil, the Nomads became an agricultural people; there was plenty for all, and the germ of human tolerance that the world was to show later toward the child, was there in that long ago pre-Semitic civilization of Babylonia.

Traces there are, however, of an earlier attitude, when the first-born was sacrificed.   Speaking of a Babylonian text, that he believed established the fact that there were sacrifices of the first-born among the Sumerians, Professor Sayce said:

"My interpretation of the text has been disputed, but it still appears to me to be the sole legitimate one. The text is bilingual, in both Sumerian and Semitic, and therefore probably goes

back to Sumerian times. Literally rendered, it
is as follows: ' Let the *abgal* proclaim: the offspring who raises his head among men, the offspring for his life he must give; the head of his
head among men, the offspring for the head of the
man he must give, the neck of the offspring for
the neck of the man he must give, the breast of the
offspring for the breast of the man he must give.'"
It is difficult to attach any other meaning to this
than that which makes it refer to the sacrifice of
children.[1]

Further corroboration of this belief of Professor
Sayce was furnished by the recently dug up Stele
of the Vultures, now in the Louvre. Here there
is a representation of a wicker cage, filled with
captives who are waiting to be put to death by
the god Ningirsu, who holds in his hand the
heraldic emblem of the city of Lagash. The Stele
of the Vultures records the triumph of the King
of Lagash, the great Eannatum, over the men of
Umma who are undoubtedly the captives and
are about to be sacrificed.[2] These few examples of human sacrifice indicate, however, that
the practice had disappeared at an early date, but,
as we shall see, it did not entirely disappear, or
rather reappeared among the Semites of Palestine
at a later period.[3]

[1] Sayce, *The Religions of Ancient Egypt and Babylonia*, pp. 466–
469.

[2] E. de Srazec, *Découvertes en Chaldée*, plates 48, and 48 *bis*.

[3] Sayce, *The Religions of Egypt and Babylonia*, p. 466.

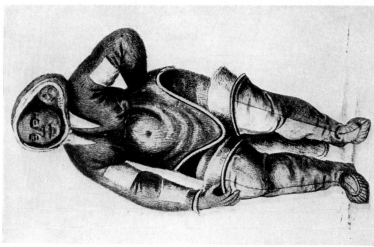

The wyf of an Herowan of Pomeiok

A POMEIOC CHIEFTAIN'S WIFE AND CHILD

(FROM THE ORIGINAL WATER-COLOUR DRAWING IN THE BRITISH
MUSEUM BY JOHN WHITE, GOVERNOR OF VIRGINIA IN 1587)

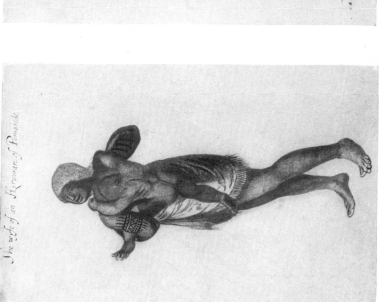

ESKIMO MOTHER CARRYING INFANT IN HER HOOD

(FROM ORIGINAL WATER-COLOUR DRAWING IN BRITISH MUSEUM
BY JOHN WHITE, GOVERNOR OF VIRGINIA, 1587)

More positive knowledge, however, we have of
the Sumerian laws, laws it should be remembered
that tell of a civilization 1000 years before the
Chinese.

That there was a sense of justice in Sumer
and Akkad long before the period of Hammurabi,
is evident from the inscriptions found at Tello
by Gerzec. Inscriptions of the year 3500 B.C.,
according to Cuq, and about the year 2800, according to King, show that Hammurabi was indebted
to the reform king, Urukagina, for many of his
laws. Urukagina declared that the people had
rights, and even went so far as to say that if the
king bought the property of a subject, he must pay
for it. We have many tablets telling of the wonderful things that he did, but the one reform which
indicates that he had a regard for the family, and
consequently, there was probably more care for
children, is that provision of his laws which
deals with divorce.

In telling of his reforms in these inscriptions,
Urukagina records the fact that under the old
régime, if a man put away his wife, he paid the
patesi five shekels of silver and gave one to the
grand vizir.

Undoubtedly in the beginning, the object of
these fees was to prevent the nobles, and through
them by force of example, the plain people, from
putting away their wives too easily. In other
words there was a desire to hold together the old
Sumerian family. In the course of time, however,

this became merely a bribe, for as the economic conditions improved, the money became not so much a deterrent as a bribe. One of the things that Urukagina did was to abolish the fees of divorce, and to attempt to stamp out practices that were growing up.

Tablets of the time of Urukagina and his predecessor, Lugalanda, translated by M. de Genouillac, give some indication of what the family condition was, although we still have to guess as to what was the real attitude toward children. Women were important; they could hold property and they were protected in their property rights by law. This in itself might indicate that there were no such primeval practices as exposing or drowning female children. Among these tablets of Tello, is a series telling what provision was made for the women who were attached to the Temple of Bau, the goddess to whom the great ruler prays, as:

" . . . The one that grantest life unto the land. . . .

"Thou art the Queen, the mother that founded Lagash."[1]   In these tablets the name of each woman is followed with the number of infants belonging to her family, and their sex. In all, two hundred and twenty-nine infants are enumerated, of which ninety-seven are boys and one hundred and thirty-two, girls. Five hundred and fifty-two women are named, but before coming to a conclusion as to the percentage this shows of children

[1] R. W. Rogers, *Religion of Babylonia and Assyria*, p. 162.

to mothers, it is well, as de Genouillac points out,[1]
to remember that among these five hundred and
fifty-two women there were many young girls.
Some idea of the size of the Sumerian family
may be obtained from the fact that the number of
infants charged to a single mother is seldom more
than four. Once the number seven occurs, but
this is in connection with the wife of the king,
and two of these children would seem to have
been adopted.

"The education of a large number of infants,"
concluded de Genouillac, "was encouraged by
the pension for mothers." Here indeed was
progress!—at a time when there was nothing
but barbarism everywhere else in the world.

It is interesting to note in these same tablets
the fact that the wife of the king or the *patesi*
was of great importance, for all documents signed
by Lugalanda bear the name of his wife, Barnam-
tarra, and those under Urukagina have the signature of his wife, Sagsag. It is more than likely
too, that the service mentioned above as being
for the Temple of Bau, was for the goddess's
representative, the Queen Sagsag. Another
tablet, in which are set forth the expenses of the
servants who were apparently more attached to
the queen, speaks of thirty infants to fifty-seven
women,[2] and in this and other tablets the frequent reference to the orphans who were being

[1] H. de Genouillac, *Tablettes Sumériennes Archaïques*, p. xxii.
[2] *Ibid.*, p. xxxii, Tablet 12.

7

taken care of, shows that there was provision for the infant whose immediate protectors had passed away.

In the Imperial Museum at Constantinople two tablets show that parents were free to sell their children and that these sales were frequent matters of legal adjudication four centuries before Hammurabi. Tablet No. 830, excavated at Tello, is imperfect, but there is enough of it to show us that in the month of the fête of the goddess Bau, the daughter of Ab-ba-gi-na was sold by her father, and the sale was confirmed and properly sworn to and then registered. In Tablet No. 925, we have the sale of a daughter to a cook, by a widow who was probably in hard straits. The daughter tries to break the contract and the mother stands by her, but the cook brings two witnesses who prove that the sale took place and was a proper one; as a result of this attempted fraud, the master then inflicts punishment on the slave.[1]

As a further evidence of the humanity of the Sumerians, we have the fact that, like the Egyptians, they had a god who presided over the *accouchements*, a god who corresponded in some ways to the Hera of the Greeks and the Juno of the Latins, but who had other and more kindly functions, and was there to ameliorate pain and apparently to protect the young. Among the Greeks and Romans the young were never thought of except as the property of adults, whose interest always came

[1] H. de Genouillac, *Revue Assyriologie*, vol. viii., p. 18.

first. In fact, among the Babylonians and Egyptians, there was this essential difference, that the goddess was really a midwife. Among the Sumerians, she was known as Belitile, and was afterwards identified with Mama, the goddess of the young; and in two texts translated by P. Dhorme,[1] the two are referred to as one. Later on the two goddesses were absorbed by the all-powerful Istar.

It was in December, 1901, that M. J. de Morgan, Director-General of the expedition sent out by the French Government, while excavating the acropolis of Susa, found three large fragments of a block of black diorite among the debris.[2] When fitted together these three fragments formed a stele eight feet high, on the upper end of the front side of which was a bas-relief showing the sun-god, Shamash, presenting the Code of Laws to the king, Hammurabi.

Under this bas-relief was the longest cuneiform Semitic inscription yet recovered, having sixteen columns of text of which four and a half formed the prologue. On the reverse of the stele there were twenty-eight columns, the entire inscription being estimated by Johns to contain "forty-nine columns four thousand lines, and eight thousand words."[3]

[1] P. Dhorme, *Revue d'Assyriologie*, tome vii., p. 2.
[2] Robt. Wm. Rogers, *Cuneiform Parallels to the Old Testament*, p. 395.
[3] C. H. W. Johns, *Babylonian and Assyrian Laws, Contracts and Letters*.

Hammurabi, identified by Assyriologists as the Amraphael of Genesis xiv., 1, was the sixth King of the dynasty of Babylon, reigning over fifty-five years, about 2250 B.C., and the first king to consolidate the Semitic empire, making Babylon the capital. [1]

There are two periods in the history of humanity: one when the morals make the laws, and one when the laws change the morals. The Code of Hammurabi, the oldest known code in the world, belongs to the second period. [2]

While it appears from the prologue and epilogue of the Code that Hammurabi was deeply devoted to religion and was, in addition to being king, a pious, God-fearing man, one who destroyed his enemies North and South, the Code is strictly devoted to civil and secular affairs. Nevertheless, scarcely anything is known of the laws of the time dealing with crimes, nothing having been discovered to show how murder or theft was treated. [3]

Hammurabi's Code is undoubtedly a compilation and, while he enacted fresh laws, he built for the most part on the foundations of other men.

In the Sumerian days that preceded these Semitic kings, of whom Hammurabi, Sargon I., and Lugalzaggisi were the greatest, there were codes of laws

[1] L. W. King, *Letters and Inscriptions of Hammurabi.*

[2] M. E. Rivellout, "La Femme dans l'Antiquité," *Jour. Asiatique*, tome vii., p. 1.

[3] David Gordon Lyon, *Studies in the History of Religions*, article on "The Consecrated Women of the Hammurabi Code," p. 342.

on which Hammurabi doubtless built. The attitude taken toward children in this period is indicated in extracts from the series called *ana ittisu*, the seven tablets of the series giving the following seven laws:

"I.   If a son has said to his father, 'You are not my father,' he may brand him, lay fetters upon him, and sell him.

"II.   If a son has said to his mother, 'You are not my mother,' one shall brand his forehead, drive him out of the city, and make him go out of the house.

"III.   If a father has said to his son, 'You are not my son,' he shall leave house and yard.

"IV.   If a mother has said to her son, 'You are not my son,' he shall leave house and property.

"V.   If a wife hates her husband and has said, 'You are not my husband,' one shall throw her into the river.

"VI.   If a husband has said to his wife. 'You are not my wife,' he shall pay half a mina of silver.

"VII.   If a man has hired a slave and he dies, is lost, has fled, has been incapacitated, or has fallen sick, he shall measure out 10 *ka* of corn *per diem* as his wages."[1]

From this it will be observed that if the son repudiates his parent, real or adoptive, he meets

---

[1] C. H. W. Johns, *Babylonian and Assyrian Laws, Contracts and Letters*, pp. 41 and 42. *Laws of Hammurabi*, Col. III., i. 22 to Col. IV., i. 22.

with a swift and heavy punishment.   On the other
hand, a father and mother have the power to drive
the child out without any ceremony whatever.
That such laws were the result of the disposition
of foundling children is without question.   We will
see later that the Roman Empire in its endeavour
to save the lives of children, was continually at-
tempting legislative reforms for the purpose of
giving men and women incentive to protect the
helpless infant that had been deserted by its own
parents.

Adoption was an ancient institution, and the
rights of the man who adopted the infant were
protected in order that he might be paid for the
trouble and expense of his charge.[1]

The adoption of children in the Code of Hammurabi is the subject of much minute regulation.
In the Code the endeavour to protect the father
who picks up a child, is shown in paragraphs 185,
186, 187 and 188:

"185.   If a man take in his name a young child
as a son and rear him, one may not bring claim for
that adopted son.

"186.   If a man take a young child as a son, and,
when he takes him, he is rebellious toward his
father and mother (who have adopted him), that
adopted son shall return to the house of his
father.

"187.   One may not bring claim for the son of

[1] M. E. Rivellout, "La Femme dans l'Antiquité," *Jour. Asiatique*, tome viii., p. 74.

a NER. SE. GA, who is a palace guard, or the son
of a devotee.

"188.   If an artisan take a son for adoption and
teach him his handicraft, one may not bring claim
for him."[1]

Coming down to a later period, we may see the
influence of other peoples on the Babylonians in
the *Assyrian Doomsday Book* or *Liber Censualis*,
copied from the cuneiform tablets of the seventh
century, B.C.[2] Sixty-eight families are enumerated
in these tablets, and to these sixty-eight husbands there are allotted ninety-four wives. Seventy-four sons are mentioned and only twenty-six
daughters, a proportion that is extremely suspi-
cious. That there was no such slaughter of the
females as we find in other countries, is shown by
the fact that in some of the families enumerated
there were as many as three daughters to one son,
but the majority of the families were without
female children and had one or two sons, an even-
ness of distribution which would lead one to surmise
that the people of the district of Harran, where this
census was taken, were regulating the birthrate
themselves.

Of this period too, is the story of Sargon the
younger—a legend that is interesting not alone
because of its similarity to that of Moses, but
because it shows that this section of the country

[1] *The Code of Hammurabi, King of Babylon about* 2250 B.C.,
trans. by Robt. F. Harper, p. 71.

[2] C. H. W. Johns, *Assyrian Doomsday Book*, pp. 26, 27, 28.

had also fallen into the ways of the rest of the world. Here, at the time of the legend, it was a common thing for a child to run the risks of exposure and death.

As an indication of the conditions a thousand years later, we may take the certificate of adoption cited by Dr. Rogers, of the time of King Kurigalzu who reigned in Babylon from about 1390 B.C. to 1375.

"Ina-Uruk-rishat, daughter of (mu) shallim, had no daughter and therefore she adopted Etirtu, daughter of Ninib-mushallim, as her daughter. Seven shekels of gold she gave. She may give her to a husband, she may appoint her a temple slave, *but* she may not make her a servant. If she does make her a servant, Etirtu shall go to her father's house. As long as Ina-Uruk-rishat lives, Etirtu shall pay her reverence. When Ina-Uruk-rishat dies, Etirtu, as her daughter, shall offer the water libation. If Ina-Uruk-rishat should say, 'Thou art not my daughter,' she shall lose the gold which she has paid. If Etirtu should say, 'Thou art not my mother,' she shall become a servant. There shall no claim be made. Before Ellil, Ninib, Nusku, and King Kurigalzu they have made oath together.

"Before Damkum, her uncle on the mother's side. Before Rabasha-Ninib. Before Ellil-ibni, son of Ellil-ishu. Before Etel-pi-Azagshug, son of Amel-Marduk; before Rish-Marduk, son of Ba'il-Nusku; before Arad-Belit, the scribe, son of

Ninib-mushallim. The fifth day of Shebat, the twenty-first year of Kurigalzu, king of the world."[1]

From another point of view we may also understand the Babylonian morality. As a characteristic it is interesting to note "that the general modesty of the Babylonian art, in the matter of clothes, is very marked," says Ward, "we never see any display of Phallism."[2] That the influence and importance of the women had much to do with the character of these people is undoubtedly true.

They were a truly remarkable people of whom we are yet to learn a great deal. Future excavations may reveal much, but up to now "the abundant literature of Babylon," says Dussaud, "does not offer a single example of human sacrifice and yet one has the right to suppose that it was common among them."[3]

[1] Dr. Robt. Wm. Rogers, *Cuneiform Parallels to the Old Testament*, p. 393.

[2] William Hays Ward, *Seal Cylinders of Western Asia*, p. 154.

[3] René Dussaud, *Les Sacrifices Humaines chez les Canaanéens*.

CHAPTER VII

MOST ANCIENT NATION WAS KIND TO CHILDREN—
ECONOMIC PRESSURE BROUGHT NO SPECIAL CRU-
ELTY—PICTURE OF THE PROLETARIAT—ABJU-
RATIONS OF THE OLDEST BOOK IN THE WORLD
—EGYPTIANS AS SEEN BY DIODORUS SICULUS—
DEGENERATING EFFECT OF GREEK SUPREMACY.

PLEISTOCENE man wandered from the Indo-
Malaysia region into the northern part of
Africa, and there, in the Nile valley, the
Egyptian Hamites, as a truly autochthonous race,
were evolved.

In a climate particularly favourable, great progress was made by these aboriginal people, especially in the New Stone Age, which was of
unusually long duration, as can be seen from the
beautiful flint knives plated with gold on which
are carved animal figures.[1] That the actual beginnings of Egyptian culture are twice as long as
the historic period is the statement of Keane, and
Oppert claims that there are indications of a thoroughly established social and political organization as far back as 11,500 years B.C.

It is therefore not surprising that we find among

[1] A. H. Keane, *Man, Past and Present*, p. 479.

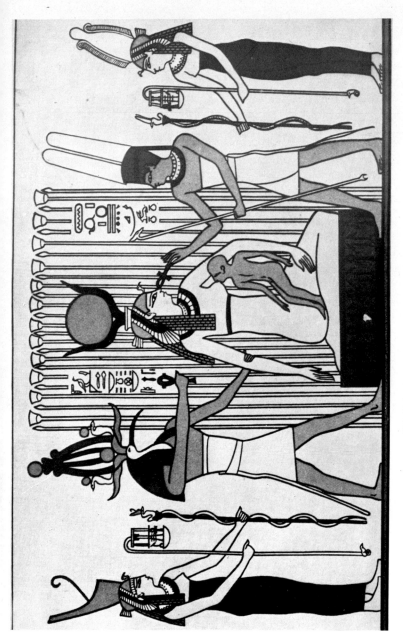

ISIS IN THE PAPYRUS SWAMPS, SUCKLING HORUS

(REPRODUCED FROM " THE GODS OF THE EGYPTIANS, OR STUDIES IN EGYPTIAN MYTHOLOGY ")

the Egyptians, just as we find among the Sumerians and the Akkadians, who were contemporaneous in civilization about four and five thousand years before Christ, that the attitude toward children is settled, and apparently in the child's favour; for aside from occasional sacrificial offerings in which the child is on a par at least with the slave or the servant about to be sacrificed, there is no evidence of the endeavour to do away with the children on the scale that we find in ancient Greece and Rome and later in India and China.

Had there been, however, less positive division of castes in Egypt, the infants of the higher class would not have been as well treated. The lives of the military and priestly castes were almost sacred[1]; it was on them that the king relied for support, and the rest of the population, whether nominally free or slave, were foreordained to a life of incessant toil. Maspero quotes from the Sellier Papyrus, a satiric poem, which goes to show the conditions in the earliest time among these workmen whose lives of hardship were only varied by the irregular visits of the tax-gatherers. These visits, though dreaded, were never prepared for and were always the occasions of several days of protestations, threats, beating, cries of pain from the tax-payers, lamentations from the women and children, the gathering up of the tax, the departure of the tax-collectors and then the calm with the resumption of labour until the next visit of the collectors.

[1] A. H. Keane, *Man, Past and Present*, p. 484.

"I have never seen a blacksmith on an embassy," so runs the complaint of the proletariat 3000 years before Christ,—"nor a smelter sent on a mission—but what I have seen is the metal worker at his toil,—at the mouth of the furnace of his forge,—his fingers as rugged as the crocodile, and stinking more than fish-spawn. The artisan of any kind who handles the chisel, does not employ so much movement as he who handles the hoe; but for him his fields are the timber, his business is the metal, and at night when the other is free,—he, he works with his hands over and above what he has already done, for at night, he works at home by the lamp. The stone-cutter who seeks his living by working in all kinds of durable stone, when at last he has earned something, and his two arms are worn out, he stops; but if at sunrise he remain sitting, his legs are tied to his back. The barber who shaves until the evening, when he falls to and eats, it is without sitting down—while running from street to street to seek custom; if he is constant (at work) his two arms fill his belly, as the bee eats in proportion to its toil. Shall I tell thee of the mason—how he endures misery? Exposed to all the winds—while he builds without any garment but a belt—and while the bunch of lotus-flowers (which is fixed) on the (completed) houses—is still far out of his reach—his two arms are worn out with work; his provisions are placed higgledy piggledy amongst his refuse, he consumes himself, for he has no other bread than his fingers, and he becomes wearied all at once. He is much and dreadfully exhausted—for there is (always) a block (to be dragged) in this or that building, a a block of ten cubits by six,—there is (always) a block (to be dragged) in this or that month (as far as the) scaffolding poles (to which is fixed) the bunch of lotus-flowers on the (completed) houses. When the work is quite finished, if he has bread, he returns home, and his children have been beaten unmercifully (during his absence). The weaver within doors is worse off there than a woman; squatting, his knees against his chest,—he does not breathe. If during the day he slackens weaving, he is bound fast to the lotuses of the lake; and it is by giving bread to the doorkeeper, that the latter permits him to see the light. The dyer, his fingers reeking—and their smell is that of fish-spawn;—his two eyes are oppressed with fatigue, his hand does not stop,—and, as he spends his time in cutting out rags—he has a hatred of garments. The shoemaker is very unfortunate; he moans ceaselessly, his health is the health of the spawning fish, and he gnaws the leather. The baker makes dough, subjects the loaves to the fire; while his head is inside the oven, his son holds him by the legs; if he slips from the hands of his son, he falls there into the flames."[1]

The matriarchal tendencies of the Egyptian Government also account for the fact that children,

---

[1] G. Maspero, *Dawn of Civilization*, pp. 311–314.

as a rule, were not only allowed to live but were
better treated than they were among other peoples.
Even the first Egyptians, although semi-savages
like those inhabiting Africa and America, were
different in their attitude toward women to ƷUCH
an extent that the Greeks were led into believing
that in Egypt the woman was supreme.   The
husband entered the house of the wife instead of
the wife entering his[1] and this led to the children recognizing the parental relation through the
mother alone.

To this matriarchal tendency may also be attributed the activity of Maskonit, the god who appeared at the child's cradle at the very moment of
its birth, and Raninit, who gave him his name and
saw that he was properly nursed.   With two such
deities in the list of gods, obviously the creations
of women and hardly those of semi-savage men,
it was evident that the women were using their best
supernatural means to protect childhood.   Significant, too, may be the fact that these protecting
deities were goddesses, for, as may be seen from the
story of the ill-fated prince,[2]—there was always a
chance that either the crocodile, the serpent, or
the dog, might get the infant.   In the possibility
of death by either of the three, there was the memory of days when mothers were either less careful
or had not much authority.

[1] G. Maspero, *Dawn of Civilization*, p. 52.
[2] Harris Papyrus, No. 500, British Museum; Maspero,
Études Égyptiennes.

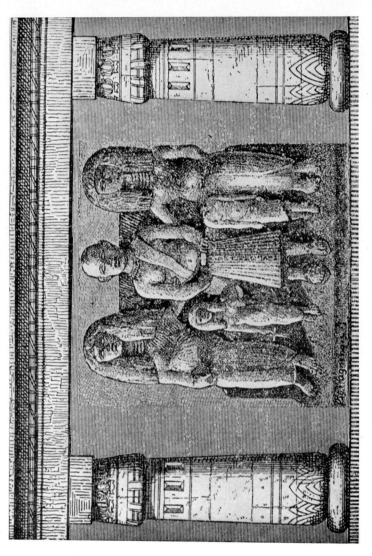

GROUP OF M'AYPTAH, THE PRIEST OF PTAH, WITH HIS FAMILY

(REPRODUCED FROM "LIFE IN ANCIENT EGYPT")

Such knowledge as we have of the kings of the Fifth Dynasty indicates that they were builders, but it was during this dynasty, in the reign of Tetka-Ra (about 3366 B.C.), that what has been described as the oldest book in the world, the *Precepts of Ptah-Hotep*, was written.   In this remarkable document the first care of the author after a stirring picture of old age, for it is evident that Ptah-Hotep wrote in his old age, is to enjoin those who read, that by following in the ways of the fathers, the children will prosper.   All through there are, as M. Chabas pointed out, evidences that it furnished the basis for many of the later injunctions of the Hebrews in regard to filial obedience:

"Bring up your son in obedience."

"The son who receives the word of his father will live to be old because of it."

"Beloved of God is obedience; disobedience is hated by God."

The later injunction of Ecclesiastes, ix., 9, is found in the 18th rubric:

"If you are wise take good care of your house; love your wife and cherish her."[1]

The husband and wife are frequently represented together at this time, and their attitude toward one another is most affectionate.   In the group of M'Ayptah we see the Priest of Ptah in what to our modern understanding is a real family group, not unlike those the photographer of the congested

[1] F. Chabas, *Œuvres Divers*, tome i., pp. 183–214.

districts in large cities is frequently called on to perpetuate. On the left of the Priest is his wife, Ha'tshepest, while on his right is his grown-up daughter. Two smaller figures represent a second daughter and the grandson of M'Ayptah.[1] The prominence of women here in relations so affectionate is unlike anything that we find in other ancient nations, and argues the presence of a spirit different from that of most nations at the same stage of culture.

In the time of the Old Kingdom (from the Third to the Sixth Dynasty), a man had but one wife, who was the mother of his heirs, was in every respect his equal, and shared authority with the father over the children. The natural line of inheritance was through the eldest daughter, and the closest ties were through the mother.[2]

In the *Adventures of Sanehat*, a story written apparently at the time of Amenemhat I., the founder of the Twelfth Dynasty, Sanehat's description of his reception in the court of the king, when the royal children were brought forth to join in the general celebration, would also indicate that there was no desire to show any preference to either sex.[3]

That human sacrifice lasted up to the Eleventh Dynasty[4] is the belief of Messrs. King and Hall,

[1] A. Erman, *Life in Ancient Egypt*, p. 150.

[2] J. H. Breasted, *History of Egypt*, p. 86.

[3] W. M. Flinders Petrie, *Egyptian Tales*.

[4] L. W. King and H. R. Hall, *Egypt and Western Asia in the Light of Recent Discoveries*, p. 71.

who point to the excavations at Thebes, in the precinct of the funerary temple of Nebhapet-Ra-Mentuhetep and about the central pyramid which commemorated his memory. There were buried a number of ladies of his *harim*, who were without doubt killed and buried at the same time, in order that they might accompany their royal master to his new abiding place. With each of these ladies there was buried a little waxen human figure placed in a little coffin, the image being intended to take the place of the slave of the lady of the *harim*. As the ladies were not royal, real slaves were not killed for them, which shows that the idea of sacrifice even then had contracted until it was restricted to personages of the highest rank.

According to Porphyry, who quotes a work of Manetheo on *Antiquity and Piety*,[1] the law permitting or ordering the sacrifice of men was repealed by Amosis. Amosis, it is said, ordered that waxen images be substituted. The excavators have found not only the wax images but those of later days, when wood and glazed *faience* as well as stone were used, the growing humanity of the age seeking in this way to progress from the primitive indifference to the death of others.[2]

Nowhere is there any evidence that among the Egyptians of the Old, and Middle or New period (that is from the Fourth Dynasty up to the

[1] Porphyry, *De Abstin.*, book ii., chapter lv.
[2] King and Hall, *Egypt and Western Asia in the Light of Recent Discoveries*, p. 73.

Twentieth, or from about 2800 to 110 B.C.), children were ill-treated or suffered from any of the usual methods of getting rid of surplus progeny. It is true that the monuments are more given to warlike exploits than to revelations of social manners, but the conditions in early Egypt all seem to point to the fact that, living in a land of plenty, they had early passed beyond the stage when the life of the child was the first sacrifice to the god of necessity.

In this connection it must be said that the only direct evidence we have from the ancients is that of Diodorus Siculus, a contemporary of Cæsar, who visited Egypt in the course of his thirty years' preparation for his historical work. In what he says of the punishment of those who killed their children, he is citing the ancient Egyptians before they came under the influence of the Greeks and Romans:

"Parents that killed their children, were not to die, but were forced for three days and nights together to hug them continually in their arms, and had a guard all the while over them, to see they did it; for they thought it not fit that they should die, who gave life to their children; but rather that men should be deterred from such attempts by a punishment that seemed attended with sorrow and repentance."[1]

In another section of his work, Diodorus is

[1] *The Historical Library of Diodorus, the Sicilian*, vol. i., par. 6, p. 79, trans. by G. Booth.

evidently speaking of the Egyptians of his own
day:

"The Egyptian priests only marry one wife,
but all others may have as many wives as they
please; and all are bound to bring up as many
children as they can, for the further increase of
the inhabitants, which tends much to the well-
being either of a city or country. None of the
sons are ever reputed bastards, though they be
begotten of a bond maid, for they conceive that
the father only begets the child, and that the
mother contributes nothing but place and nourishment. And they call trees that bear fruit, males,
and those that bear none, females; contrary to
what the Grecians name them. They bring up
their children with very little cost and are sparing,
upon that account, to admiration: for they provide them broth, made of any mean and poor
stuff that may be easily had; and feed those that
are of strength able to eat it, with the pith of bul-
rushes, roasted in the embers, and with roots and
herbs got in the fens; sometimes raw, and sometimes boiled; and at other times fried and boiled.
Most of their children go barefooted and naked,
the climate is so warm and temperate. It costs not
the parent to bring up a child to man's estate,
above twenty drachmas; which is the chief reason
why Egypt is so populous, and excels all other
places in magnificent structures. The priests
instruct the youth in two sorts of learning; that
which they call sacred, and other, which is more

common and ordinary. In arithmetic and geometry, they keep them a long time: for in this
regard, as the river every year changes the face
of the soil, the neighbouring inhabitants are at
great difference among themselves concerning the
boundaries of their land, which cannot be easily
known but by the help of geometry."[1]

Strabo also speaks of the Egyptians as exceptions, when he refers to the parents' power of life
and death over children: and others assert that
while they were cruel toward the new-born of the
Hebrews, they were kind toward their own.[2]

The early development of the belief in a hereafter, as it showed itself in the unusual care of the
body of the deceased, also affected, without doubt,
the attitude of the Egyptians toward their own
progeny, if it did not affect it toward that of others;
in dealing with the primitive and early peoples we
must always realize that we can understand them
only by the way in which they dealt with their own.
Their kindness to their own, argued an advanced
civilization—to test their degree of civilization by
the attitude they took to the children of slaves or
the children of servants, is to ask more of them
than we can ask of our contemporaries.

In the desire to look after the future life, the
Egyptians were exceptional, as their embalming
showed. They lived in a salubrious country, they
boasted that they were "the healthiest of mor-

---

[1] *The Historical Library of Diodorus*, trans. by G. Booth, vol. i.,
p. 82.   [2] *Terme et Malfalcon*, p. 34.

tals,"[1] and so great was their horror that any one should mutilate the human form, that the *paraschistes* (παρασχιστής) who made the necessary incisions in the dead when a body was to be embalmed, became an object of execration as soon as his job was over. According to Diodorus Siculus, he was always assaulted by his own assistants, stones being thrown at him with such violence that he had to take to his heels in order to escape with his life.[2]

Perhaps it is a far cry, but it seems as though a people who made such preparations as the Egyptians did for the dead, would have been chary of causing the death of those who had sprung from their own loins. For the care of the dead was not confined to the noble and the wealthy alone—the lower classes were also affected by the desire for a proper kind of funeral, to the extent that enterprising people procured an old empty tomb, enlarged it, and let places out in it. Hither then, came the fisherman, the peasant, and the dancing girl—in death they were the equal of the king, for they were buried with ceremony, their bodies were placed where the tomb equipment might be by them—and thus with the king, the noble, and the wealthy, they waited the time that was to be.[3]

Among such a people it is hard to think that the death of even a child was treated lightly.[4]

[1] Maspero, p. 215.
[2] Diodorus Siculus, i., 90; E. A. W. Budge, *The Mummy*, p. 180.
[3] Maspero, p. 216.
[4] Adolf Erman, *Egyptian Religion*, p. 139.

Of the Egyptians after the conquest of Alexander we must write as of the Greeks; and in the matter of children it is important to note that a recently discovered papyrus, written in Greek in the year 1 B.C., shows how completely the foreign point of view had been absorbed in a land in which four thousand years yielded up not a single evidence of the assassination of children.

The papyrus is a letter from Illarion, whose home is at Oxyrhynchus, and who evidently has gone to Alexandria with other workmen.   He has apparently not sent his wife many messages of affection despite the fact that she is about to have a child.   When the other workmen are going to return home, he plans to stay in Alexandria, but he promises to send home some of his wages.   The part of the letter that is most interesting to us is his injunction that if the child that is expected should turn out to be a female, it should be cast out.   In the salutation, Illarion refers to his wife as his sister, marriages between brother and sister having been common in Egypt, and the term being one of endearment.   The letter follows:

"Illarion to Alis his sister, many Greetings, and to mother Berous and Apollonarion.   Know that I am still even now at Alexandria.   I urge and entreat you to be careful of the child, and if I receive wages soon I will send it to you.   When you bear offspring, if it is a male let it be, if a female expose it.

"You told Aphrodisisa, 'Do not forget me.'

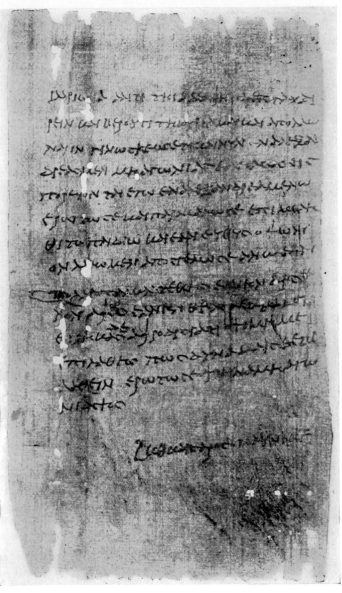

LETTER OF ILLARION, AN EGYPTIAN LABOURER, TO ALIS, HIS WIFE.
PAPYRUS WRITTEN AT ALEXANDRIA, 17 JUNE, 1 B.C.

(REPRODUCED FROM '' LIGHT FROM THE ANCIENT EAST '')

How can I forget you?   I urge you therefore not
to worry.

"Twenty-ninth year of Cæsar, Paune 23 (addressed).   'Deliver from Illarion to Alis.'"[1]

---

[1] *Oxyrhynchus Papyri*, Grenfell & Hunt, vol. iv., p. 244; Adolf
Deissman, *Light from the Ancient East*, p. 154.

CHAPTER VIII

CHILDREN IN INDIA—STORY OF THE MAHABHARATA—
FEMALE CHILD DESPISED—A HUNDRED COWS THE
PRICE OF A SON—RECORDS LEFT BY HISTORIANS
OF ALEXANDER'S CONQUEST — ATTEMPTS BY
BRITISH GOVERNMENT TO CHECK INFANTICIDE—
WORK OF JONATHAN DUNCAN AND COL. ALEXANDER
WALKER.

IN an examination of the attitude of early man toward the child, there could be no more illuminating study than that of the habits of our own ancestry, the so-called Aryan primitives.

Whether the cradle of the race was in India and spread from there throughout Europe, or whether the original habitat was Central Europe, the fact remains that the earliest records of the civilization of all of the races from the Indians and Aryans in Asia to the Celts, Teutons, Hellenes, Goths, and Italians indicate that they were a pastoral rather than an agricultural people and that while the family was the unit, the father was undoubtedly the supreme power that later marked the *pater familias* in Rome.

The mere absence of fish-hooks in the archæ-ological remains and the fact that the Aryans

were for a long time a fish-hating race (the word
fish-eater used as a term of opprobrium by Herodotus, there being no mention of eating fish in
the Vedas and only occasionally in Homer) go to
show how limited was the food of that race.   It
is only as the various branches of the race developed that they came to know the art of fishing
and the value of fish, a fact that is shown in the
lack of a common name for fish in the Aryan
tongues.   The age of Homer was really the beginning of the Iron Age of the Aryan people, the culture
of Italy and Hellas resulting from a "lengthened
process of historical evolution" stimulated and
developed by contact with the high culture of the
Semites, which again was derived from the proto-
Babylonian people.[1]

Up to this time in the struggle for existence of
these semi-savages everything was sacrificed for
war, and infanticide and human sacrifice were
practised, there being reason to believe that even
cannibalism was practised in Britain, if not by the
Celts certainly by the Iberians.

Early Greek myths reveal a condition of society
little different from that which the missionaries in
recent years have found at Dahomey.   Children
were killed when they were not wanted; wives
were bought and sold.   The practice of breaking
a bottle over the bow of a vessel is a survival of a
savage practice of the vikings of binding a human
being to the prow when the war galley was

[1] Isaac Taylor, *The Origin of the Aryans*, p. 182.

launched in order that the keel might be sprinkled with sacrificial blood.

Recent philological research corrected by archæological discovery has established the fact that the members of the Aryan race up to the time of the Homeric legends were nomad herdsmen who had domesticated the dog and wandered over the plains of Europe in wagons drawn by oxen. They knew how to fashion canoes out of the trunks of trees but with the exception of native copper they were ignorant of metals. It is extremely doubtful if they practised any agriculture. They collected and pounded in stone mortars the seed of some wild cereal, either spelt or barley. They recognized the association of marriage but they were polygamous. They practised human sacrifice and they retained after birth only those children that they could conveniently rear, or those male children who were regarded as necessary for the increase of the fighting forces of the tribe.

Upon the Dasyas, the dark-skinned, flat-nosed people who originally inhabited India, the Aryans triumphantly descended, eventually driving the Dasyas out of their lands. From the Rig Vedas we learn the nature of the Aryan conqueror. He was a warrior, but he was a prayerful warrior who prayed for health, a defensive armour, and a comfortable dwelling. There were frequent sacrifices to the gods and at all of the sacrifices interesting philosophical and sphagiological discussions took place. In his prayers he prayed for racy

FLORIDA WOMEN SACRIFICING THEIR FIRST-BORN CHILDREN

(FROM AN OLD PRINT)

and healthy children, but he always prayed for boys and never for girls.   His children were part of his scheme of wealth; they were his body and soul.[1]

The two great epics, the *Mahabharata* and the *Ramayana*, are the two sources of information on this period.   Written down when the art of writing became known about the year 800 B.C., these books mirror the life of the people for centuries further back.   The attitude toward children can only be gleaned from such statements as that Bhishma, one of the heroes of the *Mahabharata*, was the eighth son of his father, and the first to be allowed to live.   The deaths of the previous seven are explained on the ground that his father Shantanu, the King of Hastinapur, was married to Ganga, the river goddess, who had consented to be the wife of the King on condition that, no matter what he might see her do, he would ask no questions.   When she, however, having drowned the seven, attempted to drown the eighth son, he was obliged to cry "enough," thereby saving the son but losing his wife, who departed declaring that the previous seven sons had been seven of the deities, condemned to a fresh life for some venial sin, and had been released by her from their punishment by an early death.

With such a story recited as semi-religious doctrine it can easily be seen why there grew up early the feeling that there was no crime in taking the

[1] M. M. Kunte, *Aryan Civilization*, p. 124.

lives of those children who were regarded as unnecessary.

Bhishma takes a vow not to marry, in accordance with which he refuses the offer of Amva who revenges herself when she is born a second time, as Chikandini, the daughter of a great king. The epic opens up another view of the early Aryan attitude when it is stated that Chikandini, although a daughter, is allowed to live; but in order to accomplish this her mother hides her sex for twenty-one years. [1]

In the Sankhayana-Grihya-Sutra there is a long description of the ceremony of the Pumsavana (the ceremony to secure the birth of a male child) which with its earnest prayer for a male child, not only at the time of coition but again with much ceremony in the third month, shows that the female child was doomed to a most unwelcome reception at the very best. As we shall see later, these ceremonies were bound to produce, in the course of time, not only the practice of killing female infants without remorse but even the disgusting ceremonies that marked female infanticide in some places. [2]

The feeling of these people at all times about women is best expressed in the words of the ordinance of Manu: "Women are born to bear children." [3] The female child that escaped death had

[1] F. A. Steel, *India Through the Ages*, p. 15.
[2] Sankhayana-Grihya-Sutra, Khanda 20.
[3] Manu, ix., 96.

therefore a sharply defined life before it. It is a question, as Professor Gottheil suggests, as to whether it is a degeneracy that brings about the death of these infants in view of the life they would be obliged to lead. Girls were betrothed at three or four years of age and at seven had gone through the ceremony of marriage to boys of whom they knew nothing, and when those boys died they remained virgin widows. At one time it was possible for them to be taken to their boy husbands' homes and in some instances they became mothers before they were eleven. Not until March 19, 1891, was a law passed in India prohibiting cohabitation before twelve.[1]

Vatsyayana, an ancient Hindu sage, author of the Kama-sutra, in which are given rules for the domestic life of the Hindus, mirrors the point of view of his time, about the first century, A.D. According to Vatsyayana parents were to show to their children all indulgence and freedom—until they were five. From five to sixteen they were to be instructed in the fourteen sciences and sixty-four arts, after which time the lord of creation was enjoined to become a householder.[2]

Of this early period there is plenty of evidence of human sacrifice which, even when it did not consist entirely of children, led to the slaughter of children. "There is no evidence," as Professor Wilson says, "that the practice ever prevailed to

[1] Sir Monier-Williams, *Brahmanism and Hinduism*, p. 387.
[2] Anaryan, *Early Ideas*, p. 11.

the extent to which it spread through most of the
ancient nations, or partook in general of the same
character.   They were in the main sacrifices of an
expiatory nature performed in fear and intended
to deprecate the anger of the gods."[1]

Monier-Williams suggests that it is possible that
human sacrifice was at one time part of the
Brahmanical system and adduces the story of
Hariskandra and Sunahsepa as an evidence of
that practice.[2]   In this legend, Hariskandra, being
childless, prays to Varuna to grant him a son, vow-
ing to sacrifice him to the god.   A son is born but
the father does not keep his word, and when the
son reaches the age of discretion he refuses to become a victim.   From a starving Brahman he
purchases a son for one hundred cows, but this
victim escapes by being adopted by the priest
Visvamitra who is a royal sage.[3]

In the Purushamedha, or the section of the
Satapatha-Brahmana dealing with the human sacrifice, a large number of men and women are bound
to eleven sacrificial posts, and after the necessary
rites have been performed on them, they are set
free and eleven animals are killed instead.   That
in times previous to this adoption human beings
had been sacrificed, there is no doubt.

Despite all that can be said in favour of the
Buddhistic religion and the reforms that it wrought,

[1] *Journal of the Asiatic Society,* vol. xiii., p. 104.
[2] Monier-Williams, *Brahmanism and Hinduism*, p. 24.
[3] Satapatha-Brahmana, intro. xxxvi.

it is not possible to find that it made any change
in the attitude of the Hindus toward their children or the practices of the day as did the religion
of Christ and later the religion of Mohammed, one
of which sanctified the child, while the other
expressly forbade infanticide. Laying down the
law that life was a period of suffering and humility,
the Buddhistic religion still declared that Nirwana
was not obtainable by those under seven, so that
the life of the child did not take on any increased
value under the new religion of Gautama.

It was natural that with no forceful check on
infanticide contained in the new religion, the
primitive idea so well planted should spread and
become stronger rather than diminish. It is
therefore not surprising that in the Manava-
dharma-castra ascribed by Burnell[1] to the period
between the year 1 A.D. to the year 500, the daughter is placed very low in the scale of things human:

"184—Children, old people, the poor and sick,
are to be known [to be] lords of the sky; an elder
brother is equal to a father; a wife and son are
one's own body.

"185—And one's own servants are one's own
shadow; a daughter is the chief miserable object.
Therefore offended by these, one should always
bear it without heat."[2]

That infanticide was so common in the time of
Alexander that it attracted the attention even of

---

[1] Manava-dharma-castra, Lect. iv., Nos. 184 and 185.
[2] A. C. Burnell, intro. to the Ordinances of Manu, p. xxiv.

that Greek in his march of conquest through the country, is evident in the records that he brought back.

Q. Curtius Rufus relates,[1] that on entering the kingdom of Sophytes, Alexander was astonished at the wisdom of the laws of this barbarian. According to Curtius and Diodorus, Sophytes was governor of a territory west of the Hyphasis while according to Arrian it lay along the banks of the Hydaspes.

"Here," says Curtius, "they do not acknowledge and rear children according to the will of the parents, but as the officers entrusted with the medical inspection of infants may direct, for if they have remarked anything deformed or defective in the limbs of a child they order it to be killed. In contracting marriages they do not seek an alliance with high birth, but make their choice by the looks, for beauty in the children is a quality highly appreciated."[2]

"These," said Diodorus Siculus, "were governed by laws in the highest degree salutary, for while in other respects their political system was one to admire, beauty was held among them in the highest estimation. For this reason a discrimination between the children born to them is made at the stage of infancy, when those that are perfect in their limbs and features, and have constitutions which promise a combination of strength and beauty, are allowed to be reared, while those that

[1] Q. Curtius Rufus, book 9, chapter i.   [2] *Ibid.*

have any bodily defect are condemned to be destroyed as not worth rearing. They make their marriages also in accordance with this principle, for in selecting a bride they care nothing whether she has a dowry and a handsome fortune besides, but look only to her beauty and other advantages of the outward person."[1]

"A very singular usage," says Strabo, "is related of the high estimation in which the inhabitants of Cathaie hold the quality of beauty, which they extend to horses and dogs. According to Onesicritus, they elect the handsomest person as king. The child [selected], two months after birth, undergoes a public inspection, and is examined. They determine whether it has the amount of beauty required by law, and whether it is worthy to be permitted to live. The presiding magistrate then pronounces whether it is to be allowed to live, or whether it is to be put to death."[2]

As far as I have been able to discover, the first attempt made by the British Government and perhaps the first organized effort in the Eastern world to put an end to the murder of female children was in 1789 when the British resident officer of Benares, Jonathan Duncan, afterwards Governor of Bombay, authenticated from the confessions of a race called the Rajekoomars the existence of the custom. Sir John Shore, afterwards a witness in the trial of Warren Hastings, and later Lord

[1] Diodorus Siculus, book 17, chapter xci.
[2] Strabo, book, xv., c. i. par. 30.

130 History of the Child

Teignmouth, in an address to the Royal Society
of Bengal in 1794 described how, after many
suggestions, it was decided that the only way that
the Rajekoomars could be moved was by getting
them to sign an "engagement" binding them to
desist "in future from the barbarous practice of
causing the death of their female children."

Inasmuch as that engagement was the beginning
of the work in India and was afterwards used as a
model for other engagements and reveals a curious
attitude of mind on both sides, I reprint it in full:

"Whereas it hath become known to the Government of the Honourable English East India
Company, that we, the tribe of *Rajekoomars*, do
not suffer our female children to live; and whereas
this is a great crime, as mentioned in the *Brehma
Bywant Pooran*, where it is said that killing even
a *Fetus* is as criminal as killing a *Brahman*, and
that for killing a female, or woman, the punishment is to suffer in the *nerk*, or hell, called *Kat
Shootul*, for as many years as there are hairs on
that female's body, and that afterwards that person
shall be born again, and successively become a
leper and be afflicted with the *Jukhima;* and
whereas the British Government in India, whose
subjects we are, have an utter detestation of such
murderous practices, and we do ourselves acknowledge, that although customary among us they are
highly sinful, we do therefore hereby agree not to
commit any longer such detestable acts; and any
among us (which God forbid) who shall be here-

"Divine Origin" of Hindus   131

after guilty thereof, or shall not bring up and
get our daughters married to the best of our
abilities among those of our caste, shall be expelled
from our tribe, and shall neither eat, nor keep
society, with us, besides suffering hereafter the
punishments denounced in the above *Pooran* and
Shafter. We have therefore entered into this
agreement.

"Dated the 17th of December, 1789."[1]

On May 27, 1805, Colonel Alexander Walker,
the resident at Baroda, called the attention of the
government at Bombay to the conditions in Guz-
erat, and the government authorized him to go
ahead and use such measures as he deemed wise
to suppress infanticide, sending him a copy of the
engagement of Duncan as a suggestion of lines that
might be profitably employed.[2]

It was while in the course of his investigations
and work in suppressing the practice that Colonel
Walker heard first from the Hindus the supposedly divine origin of the practice of putting female
children to death. It was the supposedly divine
origin and the fact that they acted within the ob-
servance of their religious duties that gave protection against interference from civil authorities.
The Jharejas, a tribe among whom Walker made
his investigations, informed him that the origin of

[1] *Asiatic Researches*, vol. iv., p. 342.
[2] *Selections from the Records of the Bombay Government*, No.
xxxix., part 2, p. 318.

the practice of infanticide came about through the
fact that a powerful Raja of their caste, who had a
daughter of singular beauty and accomplishments,
desired his Rajgor or family Brahmin to affiance
her to a prince of desert and rank equal to her
own.[1]

The Rajgor, after much travelling, returned to
the Raja and informed him that he was not able to
find any one to meet the proper requirements.
The Raja was so dejected over this that, according
to the story, he finally consented to the Rajgor's
putting his daughter to death as the only means out
of the difficulty; and from that time on, according
to the Jharejas, female infanticide was practised
throughout the land.[2]

There is much frankness in this explanation
inasmuch as it was the difficulty of marrying their
daughters in a way they considered properly that
encouraged the practice.   There is no doubt there
had been a persistent warfare in the formative
periods of the tribes, and when the warlike conditions made it impossible to marry the daughters
advantageously, the daughters become a burden
with the result that the practice of infanticide
sprang up.

"The practice which prevailed in Europe," says
Colonel Walker, "and chiefly amongst the princi-

[1] *Selections from the Records of the Bombay Government*, No.
xxxviii., part 1, p. 323.

[2] *Ibid.*, No. xxxix., part 2, p. 324.   Letter of Colonel Walker
to Governor Duncan, dated March 15, 1808.

pal families, of placing their daughters in nunner-
ies, might be traced to the same motives that led
the Jharejas to put theirs to death; and both have
originated in the desire of diminishing the cares
and expense attending a numerous family."[1]

That the practice, no matter how deeply rooted
in the tribe, still leaves the decision with the father,
is shown from the following explanation of putting
the child to death:

"When the wives of the Jhareja are delivered
of daughters, the women who may be with the
mother repair to the oldest man in the house; this
person desires them to go to him who is the father
of the infant, and do as he directs. On this the
women go to the father, who desires them to do as
is customary, and so to inform the mother. The
women then repair to the mother, and tell her to
act in conformity to their usages. The mother
next puts opium on the nipple of her breast, which
the child, inhaling with its milk, dies. The above
is one custom, and the following is another: when
the child is born, they place the navel string on its
mouth, when it expires."[2]

We are further informed that "if a father wishes
to preserve a daughter, he previously apprises his
wife and family, and his commands are obeyed;

[1] *Selections from the Records of the Bombay Government*, No.
xxxix., part 2, p. 327. Letter of Colonel Walker to Governor
Duncan, dated March 15, 1808.

[2] *Ibid.*, No. xxxix., part 2, p. 328, par. 66. Letter of Colonel
Walker to Governor Duncan, dated March 15, 1808.

if a mother entertains the wish of preserving a daughter, and her husband is averse to it, the infant must be put to death."[1]

The heads of the tribes were consulted. Many of them declared that the women and children were well treated and pointed out the fact that the Hindu religion has always protected the female sex from violence and that it was unlawful to put a woman to death for any offence whatsoever. In support of this they quote the following Sloke verse, which is extracted from the Dhurma Shastra:

> "Shut Gao Vudhet Veepra;
> Shut Veepra Vudhet Streeya;
> Shut Streeya Vudhet Bala;
> Shut Bala Vudhet Mroosha."

"To kill 100 cows is equal to killing a Brahmin;
To kill 100 Brahmins is equal to killing a woman;
To kill 100 women is equal to killing a child;
To kill 100 children is equal to telling an untruth."[2]

Walker also came across a tribe of Brahmins called Kurada. Their object of worship was a goddess known as Makalukshmee to whom human sacrifice was acceptable. Another name for their deity was Vishara Bhoot, a spirit of poison, a very

[1] *Selections from the Records of the Bombay Government*, No. xxxix., part 2, p. 329, par. 72. Letter of Colonel Walker to Governor Duncan, dated March 15, 1808.

[2] *Ibid.*, No. xxxix., part 2, p. 340, par. 171. Extract from the letter of Colonel Walker to Governor Duncan, dated March 15, 1808.

amiable ghost inasmuch as it led to the poisoning
of guests as sacrifices for this queen of another
world.

Among these people the following story was told
as giving the origin of the sacrifices of human
beings:

"A certain Raja, having built a spacious and
beautiful tank, found every effort to fill it with
water impracticable.

"This greatly distressed the Raja, and having in
vain exerted every expedient of devotion and labour
the Raja at last vowed to his particular deity the
sacrifice of his own child, provided this precious
offering was accepted by the grant of his prayer.

"Accordingly the Raja directed one of his
children to be placed in the centre of the tank, on
which the deity instantly gave an undeniable
testimony of his assent and gratification; the tank
immediately filled with fine water, and the child
was sacrificed in being drowned."[1]

The records of the correspondence and the engagements for the next eighty years make interesting reading, especially the communications
from the various princes protesting that inasmuch
as they had killed their daughters for 4900 years
it was an unfriendly act for the British Government to interfere with the practice or insist on discussing it. Showing their humanity and their

[1] *Selections from the Records of the Bombay Government*, No.
xxxix., part 2, pp. 361–362. Extract from the letter of Colonel
Walker to Governor Duncan, dated March 15, 1808.

right to be protected from interference in the matter of female infanticide, the Futteh Mahommed Jemadar, writing to Colonel Walker, protests that already "in this country, neither birds nor animals are killed, goats excepted, and but few even eat them; and charitable places for fakirs going and coming from Mecca, and Hindus performing pilgrimages, are so strongly planted that they suffer no annoyance."[1]

In an interesting batch of correspondence, 1835, between the British political agent, J. P. Willoughby, at Kattywar and various Jhallas, Rawuls, Gohuls, and Surwyejas of this section of India, these sub-chiefs reply to the half-cajoling, half-commanding communications of the political agent that they will do their best to see that infanticide is stopped, plaintively informing the representatives of the British Government that in addition they will promise to bring up their own daughters. "Five months since," says the Jhareja Dosajee, Chief of Paal, appealingly, "my brother, Jhareja Hurreebhyee, got a daughter, which he preserved. This I wrote for your information."

In the brief time since 1835 there is evident the great change that has come over the spirit of the once proud sons of the East. The iron of the West has left its mark.

---

[1] *Selections from the Records of the Bombay Government*, No. xxxix., part 2, p. 374. Letter from Futteh Mahommed Jemadar to Lieut.-Col. A. Walker, received on the 21st of October, 1807.

The Infanticide Act, No. 366 A, 14th of March 1871, organized and equalized the work and showed that the government was indeed resolved "to use every means in its power to eradicate the inhuman practice that any relaxation of the repressive measures now to be enforced will depend on the evidence that may be given of a disposition to reform." Copies of the proclamation were affixed in conspicuous places at each *tehseelee*, police station, and village *chopal* in the proclaimed localities and with the employment of the registrar of midwives, the imposition of extra police under certain circumstances, and the fact that midwife and Chowkidar were both obliged to report where the proportion of the girls to the child population falls below twenty-five per cent.,[1] an effectual check was put on the practice of several thousand years.

[1] *Records of Government*, Allahabad, 1871, vol. v., no. 2, p. 116.

CHAPTER IX

IN treating of the Semitic race—a race that gave
to humanity the Bible and the Koran, a race
that founded Judaism, Christianity, and Is-
lamism—its attitude will be better understood if we
approach it through the tribes whose religions and
humanitarian ideas were eventually to become
the religions and humanitarian ideas of the civilized
world.

The beginning of the nation of Israel was the
result of the frequent immigration into Palestine of
Semites who fused with the aborigines and formed
the Phœnician or Canaanitish people. From the
time of Lugalzaggisi (about 4000 B.C.) there were
successive Babylonian immigrations also, and from
1500 B. C. onward there were added to this mixture
the Aramean tribes that had previously inhabited
the highlands between the Mesopotamian Valley
and the Mediterranean Sea. Originally pure

nomads, the Israelites after settling in Canaan
became excellent agriculturists,[1] and there developed the worship of Yahweh—"the worship of no
other god contributing to the sum of humanity's
ethical ideas and spiritual conceptions a tithe of
the value of that contributed by the worshippers
of Yahweh."[2]

These nomadic Semites when they settled in
Palestine about 1000 B.C., after years of wandering,
had many of the characteristics of a highly culti-
vated people but they also had the habits of the
nomadic people that had originally come out of
Arabia. Many too were the lapses into the ways
of primitive people during the four hundred years
of their wandering after their life in Goshen.[3]

If, as has been said, three generations without
education would reduce the civilized peoples of
today to savagery, the proneness of the Semites
to fall back into godless ways may be well understood; so too one may well understand the protests
and lashings of the prophets who saw their people
retrograding.

When the Israelites began to write their own
history they were a highly developed race in which
there were few traces of early savagery, but the
habit of sacrificing the firstling was a remnant of
earlier economic stress that had passed into their
religion. In order to understand the Israelite

[1] Keane, *Man Past and Present*, p. 499.
[2] George Aaron Barton, *A Sketch of Semitic Origins*, p. 269.
[3] Archibald Duff, *The Theology and Ethics of the Hebrews*, p. 17.

branch of the Semitic race and how it was possible for it to produce, on the one hand, the humanitarian ideas that rule the world today, when at practically the same time its leaders were protesting against savage sacrifices, but a step removed from cannibalism, one can do no better than to quote the eloquent and learned Chwolson, though his theory of the innate quality of a race is open to serious objections.

Commenting on the fundamental causes of the peculiarities of a people, one of which he says is the nature of "its heart and nervous system," he thus describes the disposition of the Israelites[1]:

"In reference to the disposition (Gemueth) and organization of the nervous system: the Semite possesses a deep, easily excitable disposition, and is capable of mighty feelings; he is, therefore, lively, mobile, easily excited, passionate, quickly enthused for an idea, active and enterprising, flexible and adapting, easily finding himself at home in strange relations and circumstances, accommodating himself to them without difficulty, without, however, allowing of being absorbed by them."

While, therefore, some of the Israelites developed in humanitarianism and poetry and religion, under the favourable conditions in Canaan, others, under various other influences, reverted to former practices. Among these practices was that of sacrificing the first-born child.

[1] D. Chwolson, *The Semitic Nations*, p. 25.

To understand better how the people who gave to the world the Child's Friend retained so late the habit of sacrificing children, the scope of the custom must be understood.

The sacrifice of human beings to the gods, says Grimm,[1] rested on the supposition that human food was agreeable to the gods and not until man had advanced did the idea come that substitutes might be offered. In the cannibalistic stage of development these sacrifices were eaten by the sacrificers, thus establishing a connecting link between the humans and the invisible gods whom they hoped to appease.

The whole theory of sacrifice will be better understood if we grasp the fact that it was born of fear. When a nation sacrificed out of gratitude or in apparent joyous exultation, it was in memory of days when they suffered and their gratitude was as much a propitiation as anything else. Born in fear, the next step in the development of sacrifice was to economize "without impairing efficiency."[2] The result of this second effort is seen in ingenious devices by which the burden on the worshipper is lightened by his substituting something less valuable than what he is supposed to offer, or what the god is supposed to want, but which the worshipper believes will be acceptable. These substitutions are always made when the forces of nature are treating man more kindly and when his

[1] Grimm, *Teutonic Mythology*, vol. i., p. 43.
[2] Tylor, *Primitive Culture*, vol. ii., p. 362.

attitude toward his gods is less fearful, for the
mind of man in time of plenty and security has
always presupposed that time to be when the gods
are more or less drowsy.

With some primitive peoples, the sacrifice began
as an offering of a meal to the ancestor who had
gone before, but as with all primitive peoples the
determining factor in religion is fear rather than
affection, it became a method of soliciting favours
for the future, and such were the sacrifices among
the Greeks and Romans, the Hebrews, the Aryans,
and the Chinese.[1]

Primitive man, when unwelcome children were
born, found easy excuse for getting rid of them by
offering them as a sacrifice to the impatient and
fearful gods. That at some stage in the development of the parental instinct the excuse that the
gods must be propitiated was needed to quiet the
awakening mother love, is more than likely.
And surely, no more crushing answer could there
be to the request to allow a child to live than that
the gods were angry and had to be propitiated.

Another reason given for offering children was
that, having just come from the other world, they
were nearer to the gods and freer of sin and therefore more acceptable. Such reasoning argues a
stage far in advance of the cannibal who ate his
own children under the idea that he was propitiating an angry god. "The institutions of man de-

[1] M. L. Milloue, *Le Sacrifice, Conférences faites au Musée
Guimet*, p. 3.

velop with considerable uniformity all over the
globe, although as races advance, they naturally
diverge more or less under the influence of different
climate, food, and other conditions."[1] Cannibalism was one of the earliest stages to which we are
able to trace many of the customs even of today,
and the idea of sacrifice of children undoubtedly
had its origin in primitive cannibalistic feasts,
"ceremonies that were softened by the rise of civilization as well as migration to more fertile land
and an abundance of food sufficient to make the
substitution of an animal for a human possible."[2]

Among primitive people the sacrifice of children
is common. In most cases there is some specific
result that is desired when the child is sacrificed.
In the Tonga Islands in the South Pacific, the
sacrifice of the child is called *nawgia* and strangling
is the method adopted, whenever it is found that
the ordinary cures do not affect some sick parent.
It is said that the natives watch the ceremony of
strangling with much pity but that they feel it is
better "to sacrifice a child who is at present of no
use to society, and perhaps may not otherwise live
to be," than to allow a sick chief to die.[3] On one
occasion when the gods had been offended the
native priests decreed that the child of Toobo
Toa, the chief, should be sacrificed, "on such

[1] Lord Avebury, *Marriage, Totemism, and Religion*, preface,
p. vi.
[2] R. Campbell Thompson, *Semitic Magic*, p. xiii.
[3] Wm. Mariner, *The Natives of the Tonga Islands*, vol. ii., p. 220.

occasions the child of a male chief being always chosen as being worthier than others," and a two-year-old child was strangled against the protests of its mother, who tried to conceal it.[1]

That the health of the Ynca also led to sacrifice of children is stated by Acosta:

"They vsed in Peru to sacrifice yong children of foure or six yeares old vnto tenne; and the greatest parte of these sacrifices were for the affaires that did import the Ynca, as in sickness for his health, and when he went to the warres for victory, or when they gave the wreathe to their new Ynca, which is the marke of a King, as heere the Scepter and the Crowne be. In this solemnitie they sacrificed the number of two hundred children, from foure to ten yeares of age, which was a cruell and inhumane spectacle. The manner of the sacrifice was to drowne them and bury them with certaine representations and ceremonies; sometimes they cutte off their heads, annointing themselves with the blood from one eare to another."[2]

Acosta also declared that when an ordinary man was sick and believed he would die, his own son was sacrificed to the Sun or to Virachoca.

Francisco de Jerez says that the Peruvian Indians sacrificed their own children and tinted the doors of their temples and the faces of their idols with the blood.

[1] Mariner, *The Natives of the Tonga Islands*, vol. i., p. 229.
[2] Father Joseph de Acosta, *The Natural and Moral History of the Indies*, vol. ii., p. 344.

THE INCAS OFFERING A HUMAN SACRIFICE TO THEIR CHIEF

(FROM "MOEURS DES SAUVAGES AMERIQUAINS," BY P. LAFITAU, PARIS, 1724)

AMERICAN SAVAGES SUBSTITUTING AN ANIMAL FOR A HUMAN SACRIFICE

(FROM "MOEURS DES SAUVAGES AMERIQUAINS," BY P. LAFITAU, PARIS, 1724)

"They sacrifice each month their own children, and with their blood smear the faces of the idols and the doors of the temples, and sprinkle the blood over the graves of their dead."[1]

It is certain, according to the story of Sieur le Moyne de Mourgues, that "in that part of Florida which is near Virginia,—and where the French are under the leadership of Sieur le Laudonnière—the people of this country regard their chiefs as sons of the Sun and, for this reason, they pay them divine honours, sacrificing to them their first-born."[2]

"Their custom is," according to Le Moyne, "to offer up the first-born son to the chief. When the day for the sacrifice is notified to the chief, he proceeds to a place set apart for the purpose, where there is a bench for him on which he takes his seat. In the middle of the area before him is a wooden stump two feet high and as many thick, before which a mother sits on her heels, her face covered in her hands, lamenting the loss of her child. The principal one of her female relatives or friends now offers the child to the chief in worship, after which the women who have accompanied the mother form a circle and dance around with demonstrations of joy, but without joining hands.

[1] Francisco de Jerez, *Conquista del Peru*, under cover of *Biblioteca ed Aurores Españoles*, vol. xxvi., part 2, p. 327.

[2] P. Lafaitau, quoting Le Moyne in *Mœurs des Sauvages Américains*, vol. i., p. 181.

She who holds the child goes and dances in the middle, singing some praises to the chief. Meanwhile, six Indians, chosen for the purpose, take their stand in a certain place in the open area; and midway among them the sacrificing officer, who is decorated with a sort of magnificence, and holds a club. The ceremony being through, the sacrificer takes the child and slays it in honour of the chief, before them all, upon the wooden stump. This offering was, on one occasion, performed in our presence."[1]

"It was the Custom in Peru, to sacrifice Children from four to ten Years of Age, which was chiefly done when the Inga was sick, or going to War, to pray for Victory, and at the Coronation of those Princes they sacrific'd two hundred Children. Sometimes they strangl'd, and bury'd them, and other times they cut their Throats, and the Priests besmear'd themselves with the Blood from Ear to Ear, which was the Formality of the Sacrifice. Nor were the Virgins (*Mamaconas*) of the Temple exempt from being sacrific'd and, when any Person of Note was sick, and the Priest said he must die, they sacrific'd his son, desiring the Idol to be satisfied with him, and not take away his Father's life. The Ceremonies us'd at this Sacrifice were strange, for they behav'd themselves like mad Men. They believ'd that all Calamities

[1] *Narrative of Le Moyne*, transl. from the Latin of De Bry, p. 13, Boston, 1875.

were occasion'd by Sin, and that Sacrifices were the Remedy."[1]

Further evidence of the attitude of the Indians is given by the first secretary of the Colony of Virginia Brittania, who asserted that the Indians in Florida sacrificed the first-born male child. According to this writer, their Quiyoughquisocks, or prophets to the Indians, persuaded the warriors to resist the settlements of the white people because their Okeus, who was god of the tribe, would not be appeased by the sacrifice of a thousand children if they permitted the white people, who despised their religion, to dwell among them.[2]

In parts of New South Wales[3] such as Bathurst, Goulburn, the Lachlan, or MacQuarie, the first-born of every *lubra* was eaten by the tribe as a part of the religious ceremony. Here, too, it was the male infant that was more desirable as a sacrifice, the female infants being sometimes allowed to live. In this connection, it is interesting to note that where children are killed without any other excuse than that they are a drain on the resources of their parents, it is the female children who are slaughtered. When, however, there is a so-called religious reason for the infanticide, it is the male child that suffers.

[1] Antonio de Herrera, *The General History of the Vast Continent and Islands of America, commonly called the West Indies*, vol. ii., pp. 347-348.

[2] Wm. Strachey, *The History of Travaile into Virginia Britannia*, p. 84.

[3] R. Brough Smyth, *The Aborigines of Victoria*, vol. ii., p. 311.

In India, as we shall see, children were frankly killed for economic reasons; but here too there are evidences of the sacrifice theory. Up to the beginning of the present century, the custom of offering a first-born child to the Ganges was common. A custom akin to this was that of the Ganga Jatra, the murder of sick relatives on the banks of the sacred river. As late as 1812, a mother and sister burned a leper at Katwa near Calcutta, their excuse being that by so doing he would be given a pure body in the next world.

Women, too, who had been long barren dedicated their first child, if one were given them, to Omkar Mandharta.[1]

Bathing in blood, especially the blood of children, in Northern India was regarded as a powerful remedy for disease. In 1870, a Mussulman butcher, losing his child, was told by a Hindu conjurer that in order to make the next child healthy, he should wash his wife in the blood of a boy, with the result that a child was murdered. At Muzaffar Nagar a child was killed and the blood drunk by a barren woman.[2]

In the city of Saugor in India, human sacrifices were offered up in the year 1800, when they were stopped by the local governor, Assa Sahib, although the Brahmin priests objected strenuously to the *innovation*. Outside the city, there was a spot where the young men sacrificed themselves

[1] W. Crooke, *The Popular Religion and Folk-Lore of Northern India*, vol. ii., p. 169.   [2] *Ibid.*, vol., ii., p. 172.

in order to fulfil the vows of their mothers.   The
belief was that when a woman was without a child,
she could overcome barrenness by promising her
first-born, if a male, to the god of destruction,
Mahadea.   If a boy was born after this vow, she
concealed from him the vow until he attained the
age of puberty, when it was his duty to obey his
mother's call and throw himself, at the annual fair
on the sandstone hills, from a perpendicular height
of four or five hundred feet and be dashed to pieces
upon the rocks below. [1]

Among the Banjarilu, a caste of travelling traders
noted in "Bhadrachellam and Rekapalli Taluquas," [2] the custom in former years was, before
starting off on a business journey, to procure a
little child and bury it in the ground up to its
shoulders.   Then the traders would drive their
loaded bullocks over the victim and in proportion
as the bullocks "thoroughly trampled the child to
death" was their belief in a successful journey increased.   Probably very little credence can be
given to their assertions that they have completely
left off such cruelties.

The Chinese philosopher, Mih Tsze, who lived
about the fourth century before Christ, wrote that
there existed at one time in China a state called
Kai-muh, where it was the custom to kill and de-

---

[1] W. H. Sleeman, *Rambles and Recollections of an Indian
Official*, vol. i., p. 133.

[2] R. Cain, "Bhadrachellam and Rekapalli Taluquas," the
Indian Antiquary, vol. viii., p. 219, Bombay, 1879.

vour the eldest brother as an offering to the gods.[1]

We come now to the results of recent excavations in Palestine.

There were discovered at Gezer, the bodies of adults that had been sacrificed at foundation rites and deposited with the corner-stones much as moderns deposit mementoes and newspapers. Mr. MacAlister, who had charge of the excavations at Gezer, says, however, that adult or adolescent victims were rare in comparison with the number of infants or very young children whose remains were found under the corners of houses. Such deposits were found in all the Semitic strata but were very rare in the Hellenistic stratum, showing that the practice died down when the Greeks came into control of the land. The children sacrificed at these foundation rites were deposited in the same manner as those found at the *messobath* or high place, where there was discovered a cemetery of jar-buried infants that went to show how general was the practice of sacrificing their newborn infants among the Canaanites.

"That these sacrificed infants were the first-born, devoted in the Temple, is indicated by the fact that none were over a week old. This seems to show that the sacrifices were not offered under stress or any special calamity, or at the rites attaching to any special season of the year. The special circumstance which led to the selection of

[1] J. J. M. de Groote, *The Religious System of China*, vol. ii., book i., p. 679.

MUSICAL INSTRUMENTS FOUND IN A CHILD'S GRAVE, AT TELL TA'ANNEK

(REPRODUCED FROM '' DENKSCHRIFTEN DER KAISERLICHEN AKADEMIE DER WISSENSCHAFT '')

these infants must have been something inherent
in the victims themselves, which devoted them to
sacrifice from the moment of their birth. Among
various races, various circumstances are regarded
as sufficient reason for infanticide—deformity, the
birth of twins, etc.; but among the Semites the
one cause most likely to have been effective was
primogeniture."[1]

In the vessels in which the infants were placed,
were found by the excavators smaller vessels which
were probably food vessels with a viaticum for the
victim.

At Ta' Annek[2] after the discoveries at Gezer,
a cemetery containing some twenty infants, also
buried in jars, was discovered about a rock altar,
the age of the infants that had been sacrificed
having been as much as five years. At Megiddo[3]
underneath a corner of a temple, there were found
four jars with the bones of children and near them
smaller jars and a bowl, which undoubtedly contained the food that children were supposed to
need in the other world. Professor Sellin suggests that the bones found at Tell Ta' Annek
may have been the bones of children that had
died too young to be buried in the family sepul-
chres, but the burden of evidence suggests a different explanation. Here, then, we have a double

[1] R. A. S. MacAlister, *The Excavation of Gezer*, pp. 405–6, 432.

[2] Ernest Sellin, "Tell Ta' Annek," *Denkschriften der Kaiserlichen Akademie der Wissenschaften*, vols. l.-li., 1904–1906.

[3] Driver, *Modern Research as Illustrating the Bible*, p. 68.

reason for the sacrifice of the children, for the foundation sacrifices were—one might almost say *are*, so recently have there been instances of the practice—of a different order from the sacrifice of the first-born.

On these foundation sacrifices, Dr. Driver has made some interesting notes. We are all familiar with our own foundation ceremonies, which are really nothing more or less than a modification of these primitive ceremonies that consisted almost entirely ot the sacrifice of a human being and in many instances of an infant, inasmuch as the infant, having just come into the world, was purer and nearer to god and therefore more acceptable. Traces of the custom of sacrificing a human life in order that some destructive god or demon might be propitiated and the lives of those about to occupy the building thereby made safer are found in India, New Zealand, China, Japan, Mexico, Germany, and Denmark.

The extent of these foundation sacrifices had been revealed by Dr. Trumbull in his *Threshold Covenant*, all going to show that different branches of the human family, though far removed, mounted much the same steps in their endeavour to achieve the truth about the world in which they lived.

Among the Danes, when the fortifications were first being built around Copenhagen many years ago, the walls, as they were built, kept sinking in, and it did not seem possible that they would ever stand firmly.

"The workmen finally took a little girl, placed her at a table, and gave her play toys and sweetmeats. Then, as she sat there enjoying herself, the masons built an arch over her and in this way the walls were made solid."[1]

A similar story is told[2] of a castle of Liebenstein. It was made fast and impregnable by buying a child from its mother and walling it in.

Slavensk, a Slavonic town on the Danube, had been devastated by the plague and when it was built anew the wise men of the town agreed that there must be a human victim. Messengers were sent out before sunrise to seize the first living creature they met. The victim was a child and it was buried alive under the foundation stone of the citadel, and from that time on, a citadel was called a Dyetinet, from Dyetina[3], a child.

In Africa in Galam, Tylor says[4] that a boy and a girl were buried alive before the gate of the city in order to make it impregnable. In other places, such as Great Bassam and Yarriba, such sacrifices were usual even when the foundation was only that of a house.

In some places, such as among the Tantis of Africa, the sacrifice was made at every new moon. In Sargos, a girl was offered up that there might be good crops. In Bonny, they sacrificed every year

[1] W. K. S. Ralston, *Songs of the Russian People*, p. 128.
[2] H. C. Trumbull, *Threshold Covenant*, p. 49.
[3] Jacob Grimm, *Teutonic Mythology*, vol. iii., p. 1144.
[4] Tylor, *Primitive Culture*, vol. i., p. 96.

a beautiful virgin to Juju that the evil spirits might be kept away.

"The connection between cannibalism and human sacrifice," says Dr. Waitz, "is manifest enough in the festivals of Dahomey."[1]

There were two principal and solemn sacrifices among the Pipiles, a Maya people in Central America—one at the commencement of summer and one at the beginning of winter. Little boys of ten and twelve years of age were the victims, and their blood was sprinkled in the direction of the four cardinal points.[2]

Among the Milanau Dyaks when the largest house was being erected, a deep hole was dug and a slave girl was placed in it. An enormous timber was then allowed to descend on her and crush her to death.[3]

As late as 1843 in Germany, when a new bridge was being built at Halle, the common people fancied that a child was wanted to be walled into the foundations. According to Grimm, the tower called the Reichenfels Castle was built on a live child and a projecting stone marks the place. If that were pulled out, the wall, it is said, would tumble down.[4]

According to a Servian legend, three hundred masons laboured for three years at the foundation

[1] Theodor Waitz, *Anthropologie der Naturvolker*, vol. ii., p. 197.
[2] H. C. Trumbull, *The Threshold Covenant*, p. 146.
[3] Tylor, *Primitive Culture*, vol. i., p. 96.
[4] Jacob Grimm, *Teutonic Mythology*, vol. iii., p. 1142.

stones of Scutari, but what they built by day, the
Vila tore down at night.   At last she made known
to the kings that the place would never be finished
until two brothers or sisters "of like name" were
built into the foundations.   Nowhere could such
be found.   Then the *Vila* required that one of the
wives of the kings should be walled up in the
ground.   The next day the consort of the youngest
king, never dreaming of such a decree, brought out
some dinner to the workmen; thereupon the three
hundred masons dropped their stones around her
and began to wall her in.   At her entreaty, they
left a small opening and there she continued to
suckle her babe who was held up to her once a day.[1]

The foundation sacrifice is well known in India.
At Madras, it has long been a tradition that when
the fort was first built a girl was built into it to
render it impregnable.[2]   A Raja was once building
a bridge over the river Jargo at Chunar and when it
fell down several times, he was advised to sacrifice
a Brahman girl to the local deity.   She has now
become the *Mari* or ghost of the place and is
regularly worshipped in time of trouble.   In
Kumaun, there are professional kidnappers known
as Doqhutiya, or two-legged beasts of prey, who
go about capturing boys that they may be used in
foundation sacrifices.

Up to 1867, when a house was built among the
Tlinkits tribe in Alaska, the relatives and friends

[1] Jacob Grimm, *Teutonic Mythology*, vol. iii., p. 1142.
[2] W. Crooke, *The Religion, etc., Northern India*, vol. ii., p. 174.

of the chief or wealthy man were invited to appear
on the spot that he had chosen for the site. Addressing them at great length, he referred with
pride to the various deeds of his ancestors and
promised to so conduct himself as to shed more lustre on the family name. The space for the house
was then cleared, a spot for the fireplace designated,
and four holes dug wherein the corner posts were
to be set. A slave, or the descendant of a slave
who had been captured in war, was then blind-
folded and compelled to lie down face uppermost
on the spot selected for the fireplace. A sapling
was then cut, laid across the throat of the slave,
and, at a given signal, the two nearest relatives of
the house sat upon the respective ends of the sapling, thereby choking the wretch to death.[1]

[1] *The Journal of American Folk-Lore*, vol. vi., p. 51, Boston,
New York, and London, 1893.

CHAPTER X

HAVING reviewed the ethnological and archæological aspect of the attitude of the Semitic people toward the sacrifice of the first-born, we turn to the written record of the small bands of Semites who gave to the world the humane ideas that dominate it today. From that written record we will learn that nowhere among the civilization of the world was there the same spirit that there was in that outlandish corner of Syria. Israel was never content with the abuses of the world and in this her philosophy differed from Greek, Roman, Egyptian, Mesopotamian, Chinese, and Indian philosophies as we have been able to judge of them in the writing of the civilizations they produced. If, to make one more comparison, the Greeks were wanting in humanity the Israelites were passionately human. "The Israelitish prophets were impetuous writers such as we of the present day should denounce as socialists and anarchists. They were fanatics in the cause of social justice."[1]

Modern Bible criticism has made the period of the writing of the Elohistic part of the Hexateuch about 770 B. C.[2] Whatever the sources that were drawn on and whatever actual historical value they have, we know that the ideas contained therein represent the ideas of the eighth century B. C.[3]

According to these writings, Abraham, the eponymic father of the Israelites, was tested in his loyalty to Yahweh by being told to take his son Isaac into the land of Moriah, a district in Palestine, and there sacrifice him as a burnt offering. In the land of Canaan at the time the Jahvist and the Elohist wrote of this temptation, the ceremony of sacrificing the first-born of a living thing was still practised; among the neighbouring peoples— the Phœnicians on one side and the Sabeans on the south-east—children were still sacrificed. The Elohist therefore was anxious to show that a thousand or more years back, in the time of the founder of their race, it was not the custom of the tribe to sacrifice children and that it was only done when the Lord gave the especial command.

With Abraham the command, while painful, was apparently not surprising. He went about the execution in a businesslike way, only to find when

[1] E. Renan, *History of the People of Israel*, vol. i., preface, p. viii.
[2] J. F. McCurdy, *Jewish Encyclopædia*.
[3] A. Kuenen, *The Religion of Israel*, p. 102.

ABRAHAM AND ISAAC

(FROM A PAINTING BY J. S. COPLEY, R. A.)

he was about to sacrifice the boy, that the Lord was satisfied with his display of zeal and did not intend the command to be carried out. Then "Abraham lifted up his eyes, and behold, behind him a ram caught in the thicket by his horns: and Abraham went and took the ram and offered him up for a burnt offering in the stead of his son."[1]

Here was the first case of substitution, in which the early writer testifies that not only was the substitution satisfactory to the deity, but the human sacrifice was forbidden and an animal providentially provided that the ceremony of sacrifice might be gone through without loss of human blood. However strong the popular inclination to accept the bloody rites of the religion of the surrounding tribes, from that time there was a fixed standard to which the prophets and true believers of Israel held—human sacrifice had been stopped by the Lord himself.

Among the Assyrians also, father Orhan was represented as having substituted an animal for human beings, the Assyrian patriarch being represented as a man of benevolent aspect, seated in an armchair without any sort of military pomp or circumstance.[2]

To make the substitution of an animal for a human being more effective, and more popular, Abraham entered into a covenant with Yahweh by which the deity was still given the blood of

[1] Genesis xxii., 13.
[2] Renan, *History of the People of Israel*, p. 63.

humans without a life being sacrificed.   The rite
of circumcision is the substitution commanded by
Yahweh himself:

"This is my covenant, which ye shall keep, between me and thee, and thy seed after thee;
Every man child among you shall be circumcised."[1]

This rite, mixed as it is with phallic worship
(see Genesis), had its origin in the castration of
prisoners of war,[2] and, as far as the Israelites were
concerned, probably originated in Egypt,[3] although it has been found to be performed among
the tribes of Central Australia with a stone knife
just as is recorded of the Israelites.   With progress
and the fact that use was found for prisoners,
castration gave way to marking the prisoners, until
the original significance passing, as among the
Egyptians according to Herodotus, the practice
became one of purely hygienic value.

That this covenant with Yahweh was kept
when all about them the first-born children of the
Egyptians were sacrificed, the feast of the Pass-
over (from פסח, pesach, meaning "to pass by,
to spare") attests.   Yahweh told Moses that he
was to claim the lives of not only the first-born of
the Egyptians "from the first-born of Pharaoh
that sat on his throne unto the first-born of the
captive that was in the dungeon," but also the

---

[1] Genesis xvii., 10.
[2] P. C. Remondino, *History of Circumcision*, p. 31.   Remondino cites Benjamin—David brought 200 prepuces to Saul to
show the number of slain Philistines.   [3] Remondino, p. 32.

A NOTABLE CASE OF ABANDONMENT—THE FINDING OF MOSES

(AFTER PAINTING BY SCHOPIN)

first-born of all the animals in the land.   That the
chosen people might not suffer in this contemplated
destruction they were instructed, through Moses,
to take the blood of a lamb, "a male of the first
year," and "strike it on the two side-posts and on
the upper door-post of the houses," that it might
be known wherein the faithful dwelt.

Here we see the beginning of the threshold sacrifice or covenant, which became, in time, the
foundation sacrifice.

So complete was this claiming of the first-born
that "there was not a house where there was not
one dead."[1]

From their deliverance from this visitation,
Yahweh instructed Moses to "sanctify unto me
all the first-born, whatsoever openeth the womb
among the children of Israel; both of man and
beast, it is mine."   Already there was the example
of the patriarch Abraham that an animal might be
substituted; now there was the statement from the
One on high that the first-born of the chosen people
might be redeemed.   Of the temper of the people
at this time and their proneness to fall into the
vices of their neighbours, and of idolatry, we need
only the statement of Joshua[2] that while in
Egypt—Renan says that they were not there more
than three hundred years—they acquired the habit
of worshipping false gods.

The speedy fall from grace, as shown by the
worship of the golden calf while Moses was away

---

[1] Exodus, chap. xii.   [2] Joshua, chap. xxiv., v. 14.

11

from them for a short time, is another evidence
of their excitability, although modern scientists
have declared that under adverse circumstances
the entire civilized peoples would revert to barbarity in three generations.

The struggle upward out of barbarism could
have been attended with nothing less than hercu-
lean belief on the part of the leaders of Israel,
when we see this lapse came after their miraculous
escape from Egypt and after the receipt of the ten
commandments. Illuminating too is the fact
that the making of the golden calf was superintended by no less a person than Aaron, the brother
of Moses, his confidant and first lieutenant.

When we come to the period of the Judges, we
find the Israelites falling away from their humanitarianism. While Joshua and his contemporaries
were alive, they held to their religion, but the gods
of Canaan, together with the more easily understood and more deeply ingrained rites of idolatry,
reappeared as soon as the patriarchs had passed
away.

Nothing indeed is more interesting in this study
of the Old Testament than the record of the
difficulty that the leaders and prophets had in
keeping a semi-barbarous people up to their standard of civilization and humanization. Ethnological and archæological data picture the struggle
forward but feebly, when compared to the written
records of the Israelites, especially during the period
of the Judges.

The period of the Judges was the period of the formation of the nation, and had there not been all around them reminders of their own previous nomadic habits, and had they been a less excitable people, there would not have been the recurrence to barbaric traits that we find. Even then, the progress of the Israelites in humanitarianism is unique in the world. From the settlement in Canaan, which was about 1200 B. C., until the birth of Christ, they suffered conquest, disintegration, and many afflictions, but progressed steadily in humanitarianism. In that time the Greeks rose and fell, achieving great intellectual and æsthetic perfection, but failing to even approach the Israelites in humanity. A few hundred years after the settlement in Canaan, the Romans appear as a civilized people and, aided by a transplanted stoicism, developed a great humanitarianism under the Emperors Trajan and Hadrian; the last named, however, despite his greatness, indissolubly linked with the degeneracy that was the mark of Greek self-centredness, or lack of humanity, as Mahaffy calls it.

The transition from idealism to nationalism is never affected with impunity, says Renan, and so the growing nation suffered in its material growth and through the insistence that Yahweh "loved Israel and hated all the rest of the world."[1] Baal and Yahweh were not far apart and at Sechem there was a Baal-berith, or Baal covenant, which

[1] Renan, *History of the People of Israel*, vol. i., p. 149.

the idolators worshipped as Baal, and the Israelites as Yahweh.[1] "If the religion of Israel had not gone beyond this phase, it is certainly the last religion to which the world would have rallied."[2]

It is in this period that we have the story of Jephthah, an outcast, the head of banditti and an illegitimate son, who was asked by the Israelites of Gilead to help them against the Ammonites. Jephthah vowed that if he should be successful he would sacrifice to Yahweh the first thing that met him on his return from the campaign, and the first thing to meet him was his daughter. "And he sent her away for two months and she went with her companions and bewailed her virginity upon the mountains. And it came to pass that at the end of two months that she returned unto her father who did with her according to the vow which he had vowed."[3]

It is suggested by Renan that what probably happened was that Jephthah, before undertaking a difficult war, sacrificed one of his daughters according to the barbarous custom put into practice on solemn occasions when the country was in danger. "Patriarchal deism," he says, "had condemned these immolations; Yahwehism with its exclusively national principle was rather favourable to them. Not many human sacrifices were offered to God nor to the Elohim. The gods

[1] Judges, chap. ix.
[2] Renan, *History of the People of Israel*, vol. i., p. 150.
[3] Judges, chap. xii., v. 38–39.

Triumph of Yahweh 165

whom they thought to propitiate by means of
human sacrifices were the patriot gods, Camos of
the Moabites, Moloch of the Canaanites, Mel-
qarth of Carthage."[1]

The coming of David was the triumph of Yahweh over the contending religions, though, as
modern critics have pointed out, there was little humanitarianism in the semi-barbarous poet.
When there was a three years' famine in the land it
was ascribed to the wrong done the Gibeonites by
Saul and the Gibeonites were allowed to say what
should be the sacrifice to atone for the wrong. The
ancient historian records the fact that they asked
that they might be allowed to hang the seven sons
of Saul, and this was done. The sacrifice was asked
for by the Gibeonites and it was for the purpose of
ending the famine, but, incidentally, it enabled
David to get rid of those who stood in his way.[2]

A few hundred years later, in the ninth century,
we find the effect of the sacrifice of the first-born
telling on the Israelites even though at that time
it is evident that they themselves have given up
human sacrifice. Jehoram, King of Israel, and
Jehosophat, King of Judah, united to defeat the
remarkable King of Moab, Mesha. The combined
forces drove him within his strong fortifications of
Kir-Haraseth and when he found that there was
no way of escape, as a last resort:

"He took his eldest son, that should have reigned

[1] Renan, *History of the People of Israel*, vol. i., p. 278.
[2] 2 Samuel, chap. xxi.

in his stead, and offered him for a burnt offering upon the wall.   And they [the Israelites] departed from him and returned to their own land."

The efficacy of the sacrifice is hereby admitted although it was offered to Camos and not to Yahweh.   The ancient historian says nothing in extenuation of the effect.   Ewald suggests that Yahweh, full of bitterness[1] against Israel for having driven the King of Moab to such a deed of fearful bravery, filled the army full of terror.   Renan, however, suggests that though they did not then offer human sacrifices themselves, the Israelites still had the fullest faith in their efficacy and retired lest they be defeated.

Coming nearer, to a period that is contemporaneous with that which is revealed in the excavations at Gezer and Tell Ta'Annek, we have the direct statement in Kings and Chronicles[2] that Ahaz, the eleventh King of Judah (about 741 to 725 B.C.), "made his son pass through the fire."   To gain the aid of Tiglath-Pileser against the Edomites and the Philistines he became a vassal of the Assyrian monarch and his name appears among the names of those who acknowledged his sovereignty and paid tribute.

Manasseh was another King of Judah (697 to 642 B. C.) who sacrificed his son,[3] emulating Ahaz in this as in other heathenish customs, increasing

[1] Ewald, *History of Israel*, vol. iv., p. 90.
[2] 2 Kings, chap. xvi., v. 3; and 2 Chronicles, chap. xxviii., v. 3.
[3] 2 Kings, chap. xxi., v. 6.

the popularity of the foreign gods and causing the
streets of Jerusalem to run with the blood of
the prophets whom he put to death. In every
way he tried to make the heathen religions more
acceptable and accessible to the whole nation by
providing them with temples and altars. In
addition to sacrificing one of his own sons to Moloch, he revived that religion on a large scale,
building for it a magnificent burning place (To-
phet) in the valley of Hinnom on the southern wall
of Jerusalem. The tortures to which the children
were subjected soon associated themselves in the
minds of the pious with what punishment beyond
the grave must be like, so that the name of hell
itself was taken from this valley, Ge-Hinnom.[1]

With the reforms of Josiah we hear no more of
such treatment of children but we must not suppose that while barbarous practices were going on
the prophets had remained silent. The latter day
writers revolted against the entire idea of sacrifice,
Hosea declaring: "I desired mercy and not sacrifice; and the knowledge of Yahweh more than
burnt offerings."[2] Jeremiah even declared that
the Lord had not commanded the people to sacrifice when they came forth from Egypt:

"For I spake not unto your fathers, nor commanded them in the day that I brought them out
of the land of Egypt, concerning burnt offerings
or sacrifices."[3]

[1] Hosea, chap. vi., v. 6.   [2] *Ibid.*
[3] Jeremiah, chap. vii., v. 21 *et seq.*

To Micah, however, it was reserved to express in those early days the vigorous protest that was to become the ethical keynote of the future religion:

"Wherewith shall I come before the Lord, and bow myself before the high God? Shall I come before him with burnt offerings, with calves of a year old?

"Will the Lord be pleased with thousands of rams, or with ten thousand rivers of oil? Shall I give my first son for my transgression, the fruit of my body for the sin of my soul?

"He hath shewed thee, O man, what is good; and what doth the Lord require of thee but to do justly and to love mercy and to walk humbly with thy God?"[1]

[1] Micah, chap. vi., v. 6 *et seq.*

CHAPTER XI

O F the one remaining tribe of the Semites, a
name that has meant so much to the civilization of the world, it is hardly necessary to
offer a prelude.   Coming, however, in the mouth
of the defenders of the latest religion and as the
youngest of the Semitic languages, it is necessary
to say of the Arabic language that it is nearer akin
than any of the others to the original archetype,
the *Ursemitisch*, from which they are all derived;
"just as the Arabs, by reason of their geographical
situation and the monotonous uniformity of the
desert life, have, in some respects, preserved the
Semitic character more purely and exhibited it
more distinctly than any people of the same
family."[1]

Arabic history divides itself into three periods,
first the Sabean and Himyarite period, from 800
B.C., the date of the oldest south Arabic inscription;

---

[1] R. A. Nicholson, *Literary History of the Arabs*, p. xvi.

second, the Pre-Islamic period, 500 to 622 A.D.; and third, the Mohammedan period, beginning with the Flight, or Hijra (or Hegira). Of the first periods the little that we know except the inscriptions coming to us by tradition is preserved in the Pre-Islamic poems and the Koran.[1]

[1] The Sabeans were inhabitants of the ancient kingdom of Sheba, located in south-western Arabia. According to the records of Mohammed Abu-Taleb Dimeshqi, the Sabeans' sacrifices were made to the planets when they reached their point of culmination. They sacrificed either a man or a woman according to the divinity who was being worshipped. To the Sun, a selected girl was sacrificed; to the Moon, a man with full face. To Jupiter, a boy three days old, the child of the girl who was sacrificed to the Sun. To Mercury they sacrificed a young man of brownish colour who was a scribe and well educated; to Mars, a very red man with a red head; to Venus, a beautiful woman. These sacrifices were connected with various preparations and mysterious ceremonies.

The following passage, showing the extreme of horrible barbarism, describes one of their sacrificial ceremonies; it is from Dr. D. Chwolsohn's *Die Ssabier und der Ssabismus* (vol. ii., pp. 28–29). "On the 8th of August the Sabeans pressed the wine for the gods and called it by many different names. On this day they sacrificed to the gods, in the middle of the forenoon, a new-born male child. First the child was slaughtered, then boiled until it became very soft, when the flesh was taken off (the bones). The flesh was then kneaded with fine flour, oil, saffron, spikenard and other spices, and, according to some, with raisins. It was then made into small cakes of the size of a fig, and baked in a new oven. This was used by the participants in the mystery of Shemal. . . . No woman, no slave or son of a slave, or no idiot was allowed to eat of it. To the killing and the preparation of the child only three priests were admitted. Everything remaining, such as the bones and other things not eatable, the priests offered as a burnt sacrifice to the gods."

[Ab (August) Den 8. dieses Monats pressen sie neuen Wein

The second period is known as the Jahiliyya, or Age of Ignorance or Barbarism, and, in the ample remnant of the poetry of that day, we are enabled "to picture the life of those wild days in its larger aspects, accurately enough."[1]

The pagan Arabs had long been in the habit of burying their infant daughters alive, the excuse offered being that it cost too much to marry them and that their lives were too closely attended with the possibility of disgrace "if they should happen to be made captives or to become scandalous by their behaviour."[2] For these reasons there was never any disguising the fact that the birth of a daughter was considered a great misfortune and the death of one a great happiness.

According to one authority, the method em-

---

für die Götter und legen ihm viele verschiedene Namen bei. An diesem Tage opfern sie in der Mitte des Vormittags den durch Standbilder dargestellten Göttern ein neugeborenes männliches Kind. Zuerst wird der Knabe geschlachtet und dann gesotten, bis er ganz weich wird, dann wird das Fleisch abgenommen und mit feinem Mehl, Safran, Spikenard, Gewürznelken und Oel (nach der andern Lesart: Rosinen) zusammengeknetet, daraus werden kleine Brode, von der Grösse einer Feige, gemacht (oder geknetet) und in einem neuen (oder eisernen) Ofen gebacken. Dies dient den Theilnehmern an dem Mysterion des Schemal (zur Speise) für das ganze Jahr. Es darf aber kein Weib, kein Sklave, kein Sohn einer Sklaven und kein Wahnsinniger etwas davon essen. Zu dem Schlachten und Zurichten dieses Kindes werden blos drei Priester zugelassen. Alles aber, was von seinen Knochen, Gliedmassen, Knorpeln, Arterien und Nerven übrig geblieben ist, verbrennen die Priester den Göttern zum Opfer.]

[1] R. A. Nicholson, *Literary History of the Arabs*, p. xxvii.

[2] George Sale, Introduction to the Koran, p. 93.

ployed by the Arabs to get rid of the female infant was to have the mother who was about to give birth to a child lie down by a pit when she was about to deliver the child, and if it was a daughter, it was thrown into the pit without any more ado.[1]

Another version is that when a daughter was born the father, if he intended to keep her, would have her clothed in a garment of wool or hair as an indication that later he intended to have her keep camels or sheep in the desert. If, on the other hand, he intended to do away with her, he would allow her to live until she was six years of age, and then said to her mother:

"Perfume her and adorn her, that I may carry her to her mothers."

This being done, he led her to a well or pit that had previously been dug for that purpose, pushed her into it, and then, filling the pit, levelled it with the rest of the ground. It does not seem that the latter practice could have been other than rare.

Al Mostatraf is quoted by Sale as saying that these practices were common throughout Arabia, and that the tribes of Koreish and Kendah were particularly notorious in this respect. The members of the former tribe were in the habit of burying their daughters alive in Mount Abu Dalama, near Mccca.

Among the Pre-Islamitic Arabians, the people

[1] George Sale, Introduction to the Koran, p. 93.

of Tamim were noted for their addiction to this practice and claimed, in after years, that it was brought about by the action of their chief, Qays, who was a contemporary of the Prophet. According to this story, Moshamraj the Yashkorite descended on the camp of Qays and carried off, among other women, the daughter of the sister of Qays. This captive was assigned to the son of Moshamraj, and when her uncle appeared to ransom her, she declined to leave her new-found husband. Qays was so incensed over this action that, on returning home, he is said to have killed all of his daughters by burying them alive, and never thereafter allowed another daughter to live.

During his absence some time later, his wife gave birth to a daughter, and knowing the feeling of the father she sent the infant to some relatives to have the child raised in secrecy. When Qays returned home she told him that she had given birth to a dead child.

Years after, when the child had grown up, she came to visit her mother and while the two were together they were discovered by Qays.

"I came in," related Qays himself to Mohammed, "and saw the girl; her mother had plaited her hair, and put rings in the side locks and strung them with sea shells and put on a chain of cowries, and given her a necklace of dried dates. I said:

"'Who is this pretty girl?' and her mother wept and said:

"'She is your daughter'; and told me how she had saved her alive.

"So I waited until the mother ceased to be anxious about her; then I led her out one day, dug a pit and laid her in it, she crying:

"'Father, what are you doing with me?'

"Then I covered her up with the earth and still she cried:

"'Father, are you going to bury me? Are you going to leave me alone and go away?' But I went on filling in the earth till I could hear her cries no longer, and that is the only time that I felt any pity when I buried a daughter."[1]

There were others however before Qays who did not take this attitude toward children. Sa'sa'a, the grandfather of the poet Al-Farazdac, frequently redeemed female children that were about to be buried alive. Inasmuch as he too was of the tribe of Tamim his action would indicate that Qays was not an innovator. In order to save them he was obliged to buy them off and the price he paid every time was two she-camels, big with young, and one he-camel.[2]

Boasting of this humane action on the part of his ancestor (who was the François Villon of his day) Al-Farazdac vauntingly declared one day before the Khalifs of the family of Omayya:

"I am the son of the giver of life to the dead."

[1] Aghani, vii., 150, quoted by W. Robinson Smith, *Kinship and Marriage*, p. 222.

[2] Sale, Introduction to Koran.

When he was reproved for this boasting he justified it by quoting the Koran:

"He who saveth a soul alive shall be as if he had saved the souls of all mankind."[1]

The Aghani explains the practice on the ground of poverty and credits Sa'sa'a with being the first one to attempt to put an end to the practice. Thereafter this humane grandparent of a vagabond poet was known as Muhiyyu'l-Maw'udat, or "He who brings buried girls to life." According to the Kamil he saved as many as one hundred and eighty daughters.[2]

That infanticide was rare in the desert is the claim made by defenders of the faith. The following verses are quoted by Lane as going to show that the Arabs really had a tender feeling toward their women and their children; and that infanticide, which is commonly attributed to the whole Arab nation of every age before Islam, was in reality exceedingly rare in the desert, and after almost dying out only revived about the time of Mohammed. It was probably adopted by poor and weak clans, either from inability to support their children, or in order to protect themselves from the stain of having their children dishonoured by stronger tribes, and the occasional practice of this barbarous and suicidal custom affords no ground for assuming an unnatural hatred and contempt for

[1] Koran, chapter 5, p. 86.
[2] Nicholson, *Literary History of the Arabs*, p. 243.

girls among the ancient Arabs.   These verses of
a father to his daughter tell a different story:

If no Umaymah were there, no want would trouble my
    soul, no labour call me to toil for bread through
    pitchiest night;
What moves my longing to live is but that well do I
    know how low the fatherless lies, how hard the
    kindness of kin.
I quake before loss of wealth lest lacking fall upon
    her, and leave her shieldless and bare as flesh set
    forth on a board.
My life she prays for, and I from mere love pray for her
    death—yea, death, the gentlest and kindest guest
    to visit a maid.
I fear an uncle's rebuke, a brother's harshness for her;
    my chiefest end was to spare her heart the grief of
    a word.

   Once more, the following lines do not breathe
the spirit of infanticide:

Fortune has brought me down (her wonted way)
    from station great and high to low estate;
Fortune has rent away my plenteous store: of all my
    wealth, honour alone is left.
Fortune has turned my joy to tears: how oft did For-
    tune make me laugh with what she gave!
But for these girls, the Kata's downy brood, unkindly
    thrust from door to door as hard,
Far would I roam and wide to seek my bread in earth
    that has no lack of breadth and length;

Nay, but our children in our midst, what else but our
   hearts are they walking on the ground?
If but the wind blow harsh on one of them, mine eye
   says no to slumber all night long.[1]

That the custom was deep-rooted when Mohammed arrived on the scene is evident from the fact
that Ozaim the Fazarite, according to Abu Tamman, when he decided to save his daughter Lacita,
had to conceal that fact from his people, although
she was his only child.[2]

Hunger and famine were undoubtedly the main
causes of the practice of getting rid of the female
children, although according to Porphyry a boy
was sacrificed at Dumat-al Jandal[3] and other
Arabs sacrificed a virgin annually.

The cannibalistic strain is re-occurring.   In the
year 378 A.D. a body of Saracens attacking the
Goths before Constantinople gave an example
of this side of the Arabs.

"Both the Goths and the Saracens were parting
on equal terms," says Ammianus Marcellinus,
when "a strange and unprecedented incident
gave the final advantage to the eastern warriors;
for one of them with long hair, naked—with
the exception of a covering around his waist,—
shouting a hoarse and melancholy cry, drew his

[1] E. W. Lane, *Selections from the Kur-an*, Introduction, p.
xxi.–xix.

[2] Hamasa, quoted by W. Robinson Smith in *Kinship and
Marriage*, p. 293.

[3] Porphyry, book 2, chap. lvi.

dagger and plunged into the middle of the Gothic host, and after he had slain an enemy, put his lips to his throat and sucked his blood.   The barbarians [the Goths] were terrified at this marvellous prodigy and from that time forth when they proceeded on any enterprise, displayed none of their former and usual ferocity, but advanced with hesitating steps."[1]

The last line almost leads one to believe that the wily Arab might have been impelled not so much by the cannibalistic strain as by cunning and generalship.

Procopius, in his account of the wars of Justinian, speaks of the far-off Saracens as anthropophagous,[2] and according to one Arabian authority at Medina they licked the blood of the man who had been killed in blood revenge.   Another custom coming undoubtedly from cannibalistic times is the vow of the mother to drink wine from the skull of the slayer of her son.[3]

These were the conditions that Mohammed undoubtedly ended by his preaching.

"Come, I will rehearse that which your Lord hath forbidden ye; that is to say that ye be not guilty of idolatry and that ye show kindness to your parents and that ye murder not your children for fear lest ye be reduced to poverty: we will provide for you and them; and draw not near

[1] Ammianus, book xxxi., chapter xvi.
[2] Procopius, *Bell. Pers.*, part i., chap. xix.
[3] W. Robinson Smith, *Kinship and Marriage*, p. 296.

unto heinous crimes, neither openly nor in secret slay the soul which God hath forbidden you to slay unless for a just cause."[1]

This, Jalal-ad-din says, was revealed at Medina: "By God, ye shall surely be called to account for that which ye have falsely devised. They attributed daughters unto God but unto themselves children of the sex which they desire. And when any of them is told the news of the birth of a female, his face becometh black, and he is deeply afflicted: he hideth himself from the people, because of the ill tidings which have been told him; considering within himself whether he shall keep it with disgrace, or whether he shall bury it in the dust."[2]

And again he says: "Kill not your children for fear of being brought to want: we will provide for them and for you: verily, killing them is a great sin." And finally he says: "When the sun shall be folded up; and when the stars shall fall; and when the mountains shall be made to pass away; and when the camels ten months gone with young shall be neglected; and when the wild beasts shall be gathered together; and when the seas shall boil; and when the souls shall be joined again to their bodies; and when the girl who hath been buried alive shall be asked for what crime she was put to death."[3]

Wherever the Arab went, he carried his religion

[1] Trans. by George Sale, Al Koran, chap. vi., p. 114.
[2] *Ibid.*, chap. xvi., p. 218.   [3] *Ibid.*, chap. lxxxi., pp. 480–481.

and his law.　And, bloodthirsty as he was in war, it is to his credit that much was done to check infanticide wherever the Mussulman reigned.　The extent to which the law on children was regulated by the Arabs at a time when Europe was in darkness may be seen in "Al Hidaya," by Shaykh Burhan-ad-din Ali, who died A.H. 591 and was, according to his contemporaries, a distinguished author on jurisprudence.

The Hidaya consists of extracts from a number of the great works on Mussulman jurisprudence in which the authorities on different opinions are set forth together with reasons for preferring any one adjudication.[1]　In this work an entire book is devoted to the *Laqeets*, which, it is explained, signified, in the primitive sense, anything lifted from the ground, but later came to mean an abandoned child, and, in the law of the Arab, had come to mean a child that had been cast out from fear of poverty or for other reasons.[2]

Here it is stated that, when the finder sees a *Laqeet* under circumstances which suppose that if it is not taken up it may perish, it is not only praiseworthy to adopt a child, but it is incumbent.

Coming centuries after Christ, it is noteworthy to observe that Mohammed was able to instil into his followers such humane doctrines as the freedom of the foundling and its maintenance from

[1] "Al Hedaya Fil Foroo," by Sheik Burhan-ad-deen Alee, trans. by Charles Hamilton, vol. i., p. xxxiii.
[2] *Id.*, book x., vol. ii.

the funds drawn from the public treasury at a time when the Christians of Europe were groping vainly as to the proper treatment of infants.

"A foundling is free," says the Shaykh Burhan-ad-din Ali, "because freedom is a quality originally inherent in man; and the Mussulman territory in which the infant is found is a territory of freemen, whence it is also free: moreover, freemen, in a Mussulman territory, abound more than slaves, whence the foundling is free, as the smaller number is dependent to the greater."[1]

Christian philosophy offers few more striking mixtures of humanity and democracy. It was also the law when the foundling was to be maintained, the expense of bringing up the child was to be paid out of the public treasury, and in favor of this law the opinion of Omar was cited. A very good reason given for this was that "where the foundling dies without heirs, his estate goes to the public treasury."

The person who took up the foundling was known as a *Multaqit* and it was the law of that day that the *Multaqit* could not exact any return from the foundling on account of maintenance except where he had been ordered by the magistrate to bring up the foundling at its own expense, in which case the maintenance "is a debt upon the foundling, because, the magistrate's authority being absolute, he is empowered to exact the return from the foundling."[2]

[1] "Al Hedaya Fil Foroo," vol ii., book x., par. 3.
[2] *Id.*, vol. ii., book x., par. 6.

According to Al-Quduri,[1] this was the proper
thing to do as the letting out was regarded as con-
ducive to the education of the *Laqeet*. In the Jami
Saghir the hiring out of the foundling was opposed
on the ground that the *Multaqit* had no right to
turn the faculties of his foundling to his own advantage. The opinion of Shaykh Burhan-ad-din
Ali was that Al-Quduri was right and that the
child did gain by being let out.

In Al-Siyar there is given a specific injunction
that children must not be slain:

"It does not become Mussulmans to slay women
or children or men that are aged, bed-ridden, or
blind, because opposition and fighting are the only
occasions which make slaughter allowable (according to our doctors), and such persons are incapable
of these."[2]

In the minute instructions in regard to divorce,
much care is given as to the disposition of a child.
Where the husband and wife separate, the law
was that the child went with the mother, and this
was based on a decision of the Prophet.

"It is recorded that a woman once applied to the
prophet, saying 'O, prophet of God! this is my
son, the fruit of my womb, cherished in my bosom
and suckled at my breast, and his father is desirous

[1] The commentary of Ahmed Ben Mohammed Khadooree,
published A.H. 420 and an authoritative work on the duties of
a magistrate.

[2] The Hidaya, trans. by Charles Hamilton, vol. ii., book ix.,
chap. ii.

of taking him away from me into his own care'; to which the prophet replied, 'Thou hast a right in the child prior to that of thy husband, so long as thou dost not marry with a stranger.'"[1]

If the mother of an infant died, the right of *Hidana*, or infant education, rested with the maternal grandmother. So deeply was this idea imbued that even if the mother were a hated *Zimmi* or female infidel subject, married to a Mussulman, she was still entitled to the *Hidana* of her child until the time when the child was capable of forming a judgment with respect to religion. When such a time arrived the child was generally taken from the mother if she continued to be an infidel, in order that no injury might come to it from imbibing the doctrines of a *Zimmi*.

[1] The Hidaya, trans. by Charles Hamilton, vol. i., book iv., chap. xiv., pp. 385, 386.

CHAPTER XII

THAT the people of the greatest nation of antiquity, with all their intellect, their subtlety,
their productivity in humanity, art, and
moral ideas, were wanting in heart, is the statement
of one of the greatest scholars of modern times, a
scholar who has also earned the right to be classed
among the admirers and defenders of the Greeks.

"Their humanity," says Mahaffy, "was spas-
modic and not constant. Their kindness was
limited to friends and family, and included no
chivalry to foes or to helpless slaves. Antiphon,
in speaking of the danger of conviction on insuffi-
cient evidence, mentions the case of the murder of
his master by a slave boy of twelve,"[1] and had
not the slave-boy murderer revealed by his actions
the fact that he was guilty of the deed, the murdered man's whole family would have been put
to death on the theory that someone in the family
was guilty of the murder, as the real culprit was too
young, under the law, to be suspected of crime.

[1] J. P. Mahaffy, *Social Life of the Greeks.*

184

The Greek's kindness did not extend to his new-born children. We shall see later among the Romans that, from the time of Romulus to the passing of the Roman Empire, there was an upward tendency in the attitude of the Romans toward children. In eight centuries, the Romans changed, from a people indifferent to the fate of the newly-born, to a nation over which the humane Antonines ruled, and ruled successfully.

Among the Greeks, from the time of Homeric legend, which is supposed to be about 1000 B.C., up to the time of the Oxyrhynchus Papyri, a period of over a thousand years, the Greeks changed not at all in callous indifference as to what became of that portion of their population that was daily exposed. Ardent defenders of the Greeks, like Andrew Lang, see in the fact that little mention is made in the Homeric legend of the exposure of female infants, an indication that "Homeric society with its wealth and its tenderness of heart would not be so cruel" as to expose little girl babies.[1]

Homer says little of children and the only child to appear directly in the action of the Iliad is the infant son of Hector and Andromache. "When Andromache meets Hector as he is hurrying to the field of battle, the nurse accompanying her carries in her arms the merry-hearted child, whom Hector called Scamandrius, but the rest called him Astyanax (Defender of the City), for Hector

[1] Andrew Lang, *Homeric Studies.*

alone defended Ilium.'"[1]   It is true that there is no example of exposure in Homer, though Hephaistos says his mother Hera desired to conceal him because he was lame.[2]

But why one should expect a tenderness contrary to the history of the race is difficult to imagine, especially in view of the picture Achilles offers, as he drags the slain Hector about the walls of Troy to the lamentations of the dead man's father and mother.

Wherever there was a Greek colony we have a story of the exposure of some god or hero.   Greek mythology might also be said to have had, as one of its foundations, the right of the parent to reject its offspring.   The Dorians of Crete pictured even mighty Jove as a victim of this practice, and as being suckled by a goat.   He was taken as soon as he was born, to Lystus first, the most ancient city of Crete, and then:

"Hid in a deep cave, 'neath the recesses of the divine earth in the dense and wooded Ægean mount."[3]

Among the Mantineians it was said that when Rhea brought forth Poseidon she delivered him "in a sheep cote to be brought up among the lambs."[4]

[1] Thomas D. Seymour, *Life in the Homeric Age*, p. 139.
[2] *Id.*, p. 139.
[3] Hesiod, *Theogony*, 483-4; Daremberg and Saglio, art. Exposito.
[4] Pausanias, book 8, chap. viii.

Among the Lemnians, Hephaistos was supposed
to have been exposed,[1] as was the Dionysus of the
Etolians and the Thracians.

In Epidaurus it is said that Coronis, when
she gave birth to Æsculapius, "exposed the infant
on that mountain which at present they call Tit-
thion, but which was before denominated Myrtion;
the name of the mountain being changed, because
the infant was suckled by one of those goats which
fed upon the mountain."[2]

In Argos, when Crotopos reigned, a grandson
was born to him, but the infant's mother, fearing
the wrath of her father, "exposed the child to
perish. In consequence of this, it happened that
the infant was torn to pieces by the dogs that
guarded the royal cattle."[3]

In Arcadia, Auge, when she was delivered of
Telephus, "concealed him in the mountain
Parthenion, and he was there suckled by a hind."[4]

In his disappointment at not having a son born
to him, Jasus had the Arcadian Atalanta exposed
on the Parthenian hill[5]; the ancestor of all the
Athenians, Ion, and the founders of Thebes,
Amphion, and Zethus, were exposed on the same
Mount Citharion where Œdipus was exposed.
Amphion afterward married Niobe and their

[1] Apollodorus, *Bibliotheca*, book i., caput 3, par. 5.

[2] Pausanias, book 8, chap. xxviii.

[3] *Ibid.*, book i., chap. xlvi.

[4] Apollodorus, book ii., caput 7, par. 4.   Pausanias, book viii.,
chap. xlviii.

[5] Smith, Dictionary of Greek and Roman Biography.

twelve children, six boys and six girls, were killed by Apollo.[1]

Perhaps we can best judge the attitude of the Homeric Greeks toward children by the later point of view of the flower of Greek intellect. There is not a line in Plato to indicate that the practices we regard as so reprehensible were at all abhorrent to him. In fact, there are passages that would indicate that he not only regarded infanticide as inevitable, but as unobjectionable; and in any case, the incidental references to the practices of his day show that the matter was one that had given him no concern and had not disturbed his philosophic calm. Thus, Plato has Socrates say in the *Theœtetus*[2]:

"Then this child, however he may turn out, which you and I have with difficulty brought into the world. And now that he is born, we must run round the hearth with him, and see whether he is worth rearing, or is only a wind-egg and a sham. Is he to be reared in any case, and not exposed? or will you bear to see him rejected, and not get into a passion if I take away your first-born?"

And in another place, Socrates emphasizes not the sacredness of the life of the child, but the material advantages that accrued to its progenitors[3]:

"Must we not then, first of all, ask whether there is any one of us who has knowledge of that about

[1] Apollodorus, book iii., caput 5.
[2] Plato, B. Jowett, vol. iv., p. 216.
[3] *Ibid.*, vol. i., p. 91.

which we are deliberating? If there is, let us take his advice, though he be one only, and not mind the rest; if there is not, let us seek further counsel. Is this a slight matter about which you and Lysimachus are deliberating? Are you not risking the greatest of your possessions? For children are your riches; and upon their turning out well or ill depends the whole order of their father's house."

Is it true that, aside from the laws of Gortyna, which were excavated in 1884 on the island of Crete,[1] and the injunctions of Lycurgus, as given to us by Plutarch, we have no positive declaration as to the attitude of the legislator in reference to children; but what is lacking in positive legislation is made up by the plethora of literary allusions, going to show a condition singularly heartless. It is interesting to note that the laws of Gortyna, which represent a period of civilization about 500 years before Christ, are not as humane as the law ascribed to Romulus by Dionysius of Halicarnassus, though the Greek laws are those of a people supposedly more civilized than the tribes then beginning their history on the Capitoline Hill. There was a prohibition in the first law ascribed to Romulus: and the extent of the law, as far as we may presume to judge it, was to urge caution on the people who were about to destroy their offspring. Under the Roman law, all children were to be kept for a short time at least, this limiting the power of the father to kill, whereas the law of

[1] Gortyniorum Leges, Daremberg and Saglio.

Gortyna emphasized the power of the father in the matter of the life and death of the child; in one specific instance, it gives the mother direct permission to do away with the infant.

"If a woman bear a child," so ran the Cretan laws, "while living apart from her husband (after divorce), she shall carry it to the husband at his house, in the presence of three witnesses; and if he do not receive the child, it shall be in the power of the mother either to bring up or expose it. If a female serf bear a child while living apart, she shall carry it to the master of the man who married her, in the presence of two witnesses. And if he do not receive it, the child shall be in the power of the master of the female serf. But, if she should marry the same man again before the end of the year, the child shall be in the power of the master of the male serf, and the one who carried it and the witnesses shall have preference in taking the oath. If a woman living apart should put away her child before she has presented it as written, she shall pay, for a free child, fifty staters, for a slave, twenty-five, if she be convicted.

"But if the man have no house, to which she may carry it, or she do not see him, if she put away her child, there shall be no penalty. If a female serf should conceive and bear without being married, the child shall be in the power of the master of the father."[1]

[1] "Law Code of the Cretan Gortyna," *American Journal of Archæology*, vol. i., p. 335.

In prehistoric times, the chief of the *yevos* exercised his right of domain over his own house, by deciding whether children should be brought up or exposed. The reason back of this practice was undoubtedly economic: "the fact of yesterday is the doctrine of today," says Junius.

The Hellenes in their attitude toward children were as all the Aryan people, and, with few exceptions, as most primitive people where moral ideas had little developed; the right of the male parent to kill his child if he so willed is, with variations, a relic of the Stone Age.

Among the Greeks, the practice was well established, for, wherever we find a Greek colony, the traditions of the people show that either a notable human or some mythical god began his history with the story of exposure.

At Athens infanticide was especially common. Aristophanes refers to it in a way that shows it was an accepted practice. The first poet of humanity, Euripides, dwells at great length, in the story of Ion, on the exposure of an infant toward the end of the fifth century; and in "The Phœnician Maidens," he has Jocasta tell the story of the exposure of Œdipus[1]:

Enter Jocasta.

 . . . and when our babe was born,
Ware of his sin, remembering God's word,
He gave the bane to herdmen to cast forth

[1] Euripides, transl. by Arthur S. Way, vol. iii., p. 345.

In Hera's Mead upon Cithæron's ridge,
His ankles pierced clear through with iron spikes,
Whence Hellas named him Swell-foot—Œdipus.

But Polybus' horse-tenders found him there,
And bare him home, and in their mistress' hands
Laid. To my travail's fruit she gave her breast,
Telling her lord herself had borne the babe.
Now, grown to man with golden-bearded cheeks,
My son, divining, or of someone told,
Journeyed, resolved to find his parents, forth
To Phœbus' fane. Now Laius my lord,
Seeking assurance of the babe exposed,
If he were dead, fared thither.

In the fourth century B.C., the favourite figure
in the comedy of the day was the child that had
been exposed and saved, and afterwards found by
its parents. Terence and Plautus afterward used
this theme frequently, and undoubtedly their
comedies were all borrowed from the Greek.
Strange as it may seem in the cultured and refined
city of Athens with its great philosophers and
its wonderful art, the object of jest was a starving
and dying infant. Glotz, in discussing the motives
of this frequent exposure of infants in Athens, ascribed to the shame of young women an initiatory
prominence. Viewing the subject more broadly,
however, we know that shame really plays a minor
part.

More frequently than not, the exposure of the
infant was ordered by the male parent. It was a

live question, current and customary, that the
father was obliged to face every time a child was
born: would he raise it or would he expose it? As
with all primitive peoples, the child was his absolute property.[1] On the fifth day, the Amphidromia
took place. If one interprets literally the passage
in the *Theætetus* of Plato, one must conclude that
this ceremony for receiving an infant into the
house was rigorously followed out in all cases, and
that before the altar of Hestia, the goddess of the
hearth, the father finally decided and proclaimed
whether he intended to keep the child and protect
it, or to abandon it. On the other hand, a father
who did not wish to recognize his child probably
needed no preliminary ceremony for such a decision; if it was decided to abandon it, there was
probably no Amphidromia.

Doubt as to the paternity of the child, to judge
by the history and literature of the times, was of
frequent occurrence and this usually led to exposure.
Agis, King of Sparta, refused to recognize Leo-
tychides, a son born of his wife.[2] In the *Hecyra*
of Terence, the Athenian Pamphile does not wish
to serve as father to an infant of another. Per-
seria, "having viewed at an amorous crisis a statue
of Andromeda," conceals her infant from her husband.[3] At Gortyna, the divorced woman had
to present her son to her former husband; if that
man did not take it, then the woman had her

---

[1] Wm. Botsford, *Development of the Athenian Constitution*, p. 10.
[2] Plutarch, *Life of Alcibiades*.   [3] Heliodorus, *Ethiopica*.

13

choice between nourishing it or exposing it. In most cases, the disavowal of paternity meant the exposure of the infant.

But the mere fact that the legitimacy of the child was incontestable did not save it; many Greeks were discouraged by the thought of the care and trouble children necessitated. Thousands of these little ones seem to have been resented by the Athenians, with what Glotz calls "*singulière vivacité.*"[1] With the intensive and complete education necessary for those reared, some children had to be sacrificed to so complicated and burdensome an enterprise.

"No," says a character in Menander, "there is nothing unfortunate in being a father, unless one is the father of many children."

"Nothing more foolish than to have children," says a Greek proverb. "To raise children is an uncertain thing," said the philosopher Democritus; "success is attained only after a life of battle and disquietude. Their loss is followed by a sorrow which remains above all others."

It was not necessary to have children, reasoned the nimble-minded Athenians; many who wished both tranquillity and posterity adopted a young man whose education was already complete. The greater number of exposures should not be attributed, however, to this excessive love of tranquillity. The principal objection to children was their expense. For the daughter, it was necessary to

[1] G. Glotz, Daremberg and Saglio, art. Exposito.

prepare a *dot:* for boys, there was the expense of
an education prolonged until they were sixteen or
eighteen years of age. The latter imposed the
opening of an account not easy to close.

"I thought my family now large enough," says
the father of Daphnis in explaining to the new-
found son why it was he was exposed.[1]

"Sons of the very rich," said Plato, "who com-
mence to frequent schools at a very early age and
leave them late"—the rich themselves did not wish
to bring up too many sons to such an expensive
life. The rich father of Daphnis considered a son
and a daughter a large family.

At a pinch, the Athenians would undertake to
bring up a first child, but, as a rule, the second was
condemned. It was not for themselves, alone,
that this was done, they claimed: it was also for
their children that the heads of the Greek families
dreaded poverty. The direct transmission and
equal partition of property among the male children was part of the Greek law, and a fair-sized
estate, if broken into many parts, made small
provision for many children. Hesiod wished for a
single son *par famille:* "Let there be only one son to
tend his father's house: for so shall wealth increase
in the dwelling."[2] And Theognis reproached the
citizens for having no other ideal than to bury
away treasures for their children. Even in later
times, Xenophon speaks of the paternal foresight

[1] Longus, *Daphnis and Chloë*, book iv.
[2] Hesiod, *Works and Days*.

that led to continual worrying over the care of children yet to be born.

It was Diphilus, or Menander, who found in the reality of the Greek life and communicated it to the author of the *Adelphi*, this counsel addressed to the father: "Manage, pinch, and save, to leave them (your sons) as much as you can."[1]

But it was not only the poor who found exposure expedient, although they had an excuse; they "had not the heart to leave their misery to their progeny like a grave and dolorous malady."

To a philosopher of the first century after Christ, it appeared as the greatest scandal, however, that a number of fathers "who did not have the excuse of poverty, who were well off and even opulent, should dare to refuse food to the puny infants in order to enrich their elders, should dare to kill their brothers in order that the living might have the greater patrimony."[2]

This was indeed the Greek excuse or explanation—some of the children had to be sacrificed that others might be raised. The head of a Greek family, if asked why he had exposed some of his children, would have probably answered in the words of the Scythian Anacharsis, "Because I love the children I have." This was the principal reason alleged by the Greeks for exposing their progeny on the highways, and the father of Daph-

[1] Terence, *Adelphi*, act v., scene iii.
[2] Musonius, quoted by Glotz.

nis, when he reclaims him, admits this to the son
he had exposed.[1]

In the religious and social ideas of the ancients,
the female child was of little importance—a son
alone perpetuating the race. The daughter was
hardly a member of the family in which she was
born, from the day of her birth until the day she
was married. On that day, she passed into the
possession of her husband and became his, body
and soul. Up to the time she was married, she was
in charge of her parents: after that time, she did
not even exist for them.

On the contrary, it was a sacred duty to bring
up a boy. To raise one, was to provide against
all possible trouble; whereas a girl was an expensive
luxury, a sacrifice for which there was no compensation, and for this reason, in the legend, the
father of Atalanta refused to bring up his daughter.

"Do you remember," asks Sostrata of her
husband in the *Heautontimorumenos*, "me being
pregnant, and yourself declaring to me, most peremptorily, that if I should bring forth a girl, you
would not have it brought up?"[2]   Thus it was that
Antiphili, although of good family, was exposed
by order of her mother.

One has but to read the fragments of the new
comedy to see how the Greeks plainly preferred
boys, and under what various artifices they dis-
closed their dislike to girl children.

[1] Longus, *Daphnis and Chloë*, book iv.
[2] *Heaut.*, Terence., act iv., scene i.

Half of the *Florilegium* of Stobius is composed of extracts under the title—"How much better are male children." In the first rank, he cites Euripides, and after him the authors of the new comedy, Menander at the head. Posidippus indicated crudely the rule of conduct adopted by most Athenians: " The son is brought up even if one is poor: the daughter is exposed, even if one is rich."

CHAPTER XIII

FEMALE CHILDREN NOT DESIRABLE AMONG GREEKS—
PRECAUTIONS FOR SAVING EXPOSED CHILDREN
—ORNAMENTS AS A MEANS OF IDENTIFICATION
—ADOPTION UNDER STRANGE CIRCUMSTANCES.

THE Greeks who exposed their children hoped, as a rule, they might possibly be saved by others and precautions were frequently taken to this end. The gruesome task of doing away with the infant was generally entrusted to a slave or to a midwife, who were willing, apparently, to undertake many services.[1] The time usually chosen was early in the day, inasmuch as the child would perish if it passed the entire night without attracting attention.

The lexicographers and the scholiasts of the time speak of children being left in deserted places. In the "golden days," they were placed where they could be seen. There is evidence that the most frequented places were the most popular— the hippodromes, the entrances to the temples, and the sacred grottoes, where they would be most in evidence. A watch was kept on the place or it

[1] Aristophanes, *Thesmophor.*, act v.

was revisited, in order to be sure of the fate of the infant.

Care was usually taken to wrap the child up carefully. When Laymonde, the shepherd, discovered Daphnis, the child was being suckled by a goat. "Struck with natural astonishment, he advances closer to the spot and discovers a lusty and handsome male child with far richer swathing clothes than suited its fortune in being thus exposed; for its little mantle was of fine purple, and fastened by a golden clasp; and it had a little sword with a hilt of ivory."[1]

The jests of Aristophanes show that more often children were exposed in large copper pots with two handles, called *kutrai* (χυτράι). The Athenians had been in the habit of making sacrifices to some of their divinities in these *kutrai*, and it is likely that when children were first abandoned, they were placed in these receptacles that they might invoke the protection of the immortals. Recent excavations at Gezer and Tell Ta'Andkk show children were sacrificed in a similar way.

Various objects were placed with the child when it was so exposed. Creusa, the daughter of Erectheus, King of Athens, when she exposed Ion, the son whom she had secretly borne to Apollo, "observant of the customs of her great progenitors," in addition to leaving with him what ornaments she had, also added:

[1] Longus, *Daphnis and Chloë*, book i.

BLIND BOYS AT DRILL IN "THE LIGHTHOUSE," NEW YORK CITY

A branch of olive then I wreathed around thee,
Plucked from that tree which from Minerva's rock
First sprung; if it be there it still retains
Its verdure; for the foliage of that olive,
Fresh in immortal beauty, never fades.[1]

This, and the sacred bandelettes, were always
the symbols of inviolability.

This final act of maternal affection, characteristic of both the human and the barbaric side of Greek parents, became, in time, a widespread custom. When the child was exposed, there was generally placed alongside of it a small basket or collection of trinkets. The royal daughter of Erechtheus attached to the neck of her son many precious ornaments, including a serpent of massive gold. The shepherd Laymonde found on Daphnis a clasp of gold and a small ivory sword. Among the very poor, hand-made collars, shoulder straps, with various trinkets of little worth, were used to mark the infant.

In all this, dramatists saw but a means to establish the identity of the hero and heroine and an assistance to the *dénouement*. The ceremony, with its pathos and its strangeness, was, to tragic as well as to comic writers, but a means to end the fifth act. The pity of it all never seems to have occurred to the Greek mind.

It was rare that the father or the child-mother who renounced the infant had any real desire to

[1] Euripides, *Ion*, 1489.

find it when better days came. The real wish was that the child might be taken up by some stranger before death came and the trinkets were an inducement to befriend the child.

If, on the other hand, the child should die, the feeling was that these ornaments would assure for it a happy life on the other side of the Styx.

For this reason the favoured objects of mothers were amulets; and, as in the case of the serpent placed around the neck of Ion, Creusa hoped to invoke the aid of Minerva, who had guarded her ancestor, Erichthonius, with two dragons; the object being to watch over the child's existence. These gewgaws were supposed to give the infant exposed all the rights of a suppliant.

As to how far these ceremonies of supplication were successful, as to how far they commended the unfortunate infant to the public, is a grave question. From the religious and literary myths one might imagine that the greater number of the infants were saved. We read of Hephaistus, nourished by the Sintians or by Thetis; of Atalanta by a bear; of Zeus and Dionysos, nursed by the nymphs; the shepherds found and received Telephus, Amphion, and Œdipus; Ion, by a priestess, and Sirus, by a beggar.

Greek artists frequently show a Satyr holding in his arms a newly-born that he had found on the road.

Poets of the new comedy delight to represent their heroes, or, more frequently, their heroines, as people who had gone through the trial of exposure and were raised by either courtesans, shepherds, or innkeepers. It is in this way that Menander, among others, shows us Silenium growing up in the house of Melænis to whom she has been given by the evil woman who picked her up[1]; Casina treated as a daughter by the brave Cleostrata.[2]

Longus, in this way, brings Daphnis and Chloe into the cabin of a goatherd.

But these examples prove little about the actual conditions, only going to show the facility of the writers of the time, and Glotz suggests that these scenes flattered the Athenians, who liked to think of themselves as a philanthropic people.

Apparently, the first impulse when a child was found was to ignore it, for the attitude of Athenian society was probably well expressed by Longus when he said:

"Those who seek paternity are many."

In fact, the author of *Daphnis and Chloe* says that when Daphnis was first seen by the shepherd being suckled by a goat, "Laymonde (the shepherd) resolved to leave it to its fate, and to carry off only the tokens; but feeling afterward ashamed at the reflection, that in doing so he should be inferior in humanity, even to a goat, he waited for the approach of night and then carried home the infant with the tokens."[3]

Old Megacles, the father of Chloe, in the same

---

[1] Plautus, *Cestellaria*.   [2] Plautus, *Casina*.
[3] Longus, *Daphnis*, book i.

story seeks to excuse himself for having exposed his daughter, by a number of bad reasons: he did not have the means, it was a moment of weakness, he hoped that the nymphs would take pity on the child: and then, there were so many people who did not have children, etc. The most interesting of his reasons, however, is the statement that he had spent his fortune equipping theatrical choruses!

As a rule, when adoption did take place it was not for the benefit of the child. In many instances, those who wished to adopt a son waited and adopted a grown-up one so as not to have the trouble and expense of educating him.

As set forth in the plays, it was apparently not infrequent that a courtesan sought to attach a lover, or a wife a husband who was slipping away from her, by adopting a child and passing it off as her own. It was to this subterfuge that Silenium, in the *Cistellaria* of Plautus, owes her life. Speaking of the incident, the Procuress in the play, says:

"But once upon a time, that girl (Silenium) who has gone hence in tears, from a lane I carried her off a little child exposed. . . . I made a present of her to my friend, this courtesan, who had made mention of it to me that somewhere I must find for her a boy or a girl, just born, that she herself might pass it off as her own.

"As soon as ever the opportunity befell me I immediately granted her request in that which she had asked me. After she had received this female child from me, she at once was brought to bed of the same female child which she had received from me. . . . She said that her lover was a foreigner."[1]

It is hardly likely, however, that many courtesans in real life were willing to be so encumbered, and perhaps, as Demosthenes says, this was only the sort of thing one "sees in tragedies," like the fatal and convenient malady described by Heine as a sort of "fifth act sickness."

That the substitution of foundlings and exposed children was frequent in Greece is evident, however, from the many plays bearing this name. Cratinus the younger was the author of a piece called *The Substituted Child* [ὑποβολιμᾶιος], and the title was also used by Menander. Athenæus quotes from a play by Alexis entitled *The Suppositious Child*[2] and from one by Epinicus called the *Suppositious Damsels* [ὑποβολλομεναῖ] and from[3] another by Crobylus called the *Pseudo-Suppositious Child* (*Falsus suppositus*).[4]

In the Thesmophoriazusæ, Aristophanes depicts the father of Euripides, Mnesilochus, as making a tactless defence of his son-in-law at the festival of Thesmophoria by abusing the very women he would placate.

---

[1] Plautus, *Cistellaria*, act i., scene i.

[2] *Poetarum Comicorum Græcorum Fragmenta.* Ed. Didot, p. 57; *Athenæus*, Trans. C. D. Yonge, vol. ii., p. 804.

[3] *Poet. Comic. Græc. Frag.*, p. 687; *Athenæus*, vol. ii., p. 794.

[4] *Ibid*, p. 710; *Ibid.*, p. 575.

"And I know another woman," he says "who for ten days said she was in labour, till she purchased a little child while her husband went about purchasing drugs for a quick delivery. But the child an old woman brought in a pot with its mouth stopped with honeycomb that it might not squall. Then, when she that carried it nodded, the wife immediately cried out: 'Go away, husband, go away, for methinks that I shall be immediately delivered.' For the child kicked against the bottom of the pot. And he ran off delighted, while she drew out the stoppage from the bottle and it cried out. And then the abominable old woman who brought the child, runs smiling to the husband, and says: 'A lion has been born to you, a lion; your very image, in all other respects whatever, and its nose is like yours, being crooked like an acorn cup.'"[1]

That there was a class of people who looked on children in the light of good or bad bargains we must assume from the certainly serious words of Demosthenes in his oration against Midias. In his attack on his physical assailant, Demosthenes says that the real mother of Midias was a wise woman because she got rid of him as soon as he was born, whereas the woman who adopted him was a foolish woman because she made a bad bargain.

"And why?" asks the orator, "because the one sold him as soon as he was born, while the other,

[1] *Thesmophoriazusæ*, 502, 516.

when she might have obtained a better for the same price, bought Midias."

Ion,[1] when he meets his father for the first time and learns that he had been exposed, congratulates himself on having escaped slavery, indicating that in all probability the majority of children saved after they had been exposed by their parents were saved by the professional slave dealers. The general view, however, was that children were cheap, Xenophon,[2] declaring that "good slaves when they had children generally become still better disposed, but bad ones increase their power to do mischief."

Only in two instances as far as we know did the law of the Greeks reach out to protect the child against the destroying whim of the parent. According to Ælian[3] the Thebans were not allowed to expose their children or leave them in a wilderness under the pain of death. If the father were extremely poor, the child, whether male or female, had to be brought to the magistrate in its swaddling clothes, and there delivered to some person who would agree to bring up the child and when it was grown up, take it into service and have the benefit of its labour in return for its education.

As to the other instance of the law protecting the child it has been truly said that all that Lycur-

---

[1] Euripides, *Ion*, line 144.
[2] Xenophon, *Œconomicus*, chapter iv., par. 5.
[3] *Ælian*, liber ii., caput vii.

gus did was to insist that all "fit" children should be raised.

"If," says Plutarch,[1] "they (the Spartans) found it puny and ill-shaped, they ordered it to be taken to what was called the Apothetæ, a sort of chasm under Taygetus, as thinking it neither for the good of the child itself, nor for the public interest, that it should be brought up, if it did not from the very outset, appear made to be healthy and vigorous."

And this was the most "protecting" move of the ancient Greeks.

[1] Plutarch, *Lycurgus* (Dryden trans.), vol. i., p. 82.

CHAPTER XIV

FIRST RECOGNITION OF RIGHTS OF CHILDREN—LAWS OF
ROMULUS AND OF NUMA POMPILIUS—THE TWELVE
TABLES—ATTITUDE OF PARENTS SHOWN IN TER-
ENCE—PATRIA POTESTAS SPARINGLY USED.

I T is interesting to think that what might be
called the legal movement which fructified
in the United States, in the latter half of the
nineteenth century, had its beginning in the
eighth century B.C. in Rome; it is doubly interesting that legend ascribes to Romulus the first
interest in what can conservatively be called the
child protection movement.

Like all other lawmakers—even legendary ones
—especially those who sought to prepare and
safeguard their states for and against hostile
neighbours, the first concern of the founder of
Rome was a strong nation; and a strong nation
meant necessarily as many adult males in good
health and physical condition as possible. Soldiers were more important than other human
beings; in this the supposed founder followed the
spirit of his time and the standard of his age of
development.

According to the legend, Romulus, having made

peace with the Sabines and become the king of both people on the death of Tatius, was bent on making the new city impregnable, working out a system of government that, in the mind of the historian, was worthy of "a man of great military accomplishments, personal courage and extremely capable of instituting the most perfect sort of government."[1]

To the end that there might be as perfect a fighting machine as possible, Romulus pledged his people to bring up all males except those who were lame or monstrous from birth. To the same end, and according to the same authority, he pledged them to bring up the first-born of the females—and in this he acted purely in the spirit of the time and as the founder of a warlike race. Personal interest may be conceded, inasmuch as he would have been the victim of the practice of exposing children had his uncle Amulius had his way.[2]

In his introduction to the *Institutes of Justinian*,[3] Sandars declares that Roman law will be better understood if those interested will apprehend the distinction between the contribution of Romulus and the tribe of Ramnes, who dwelt on the Palatine Hill, and the contribution of Numa and the Titienses who dwelt on the Capitoline and the Quirinal. The two races combined to make a united society, the Ramnes bringing distinct ideas of public law and, in the dimmest days of history,

[1] *Dionysius Halic.*, bk. ii., par. vii.   [2] Livy, i., 4.
[3] Thos. Collett Sandars, *Institutes of Justinian*, p. 3.

presenting the features of a carefully organized polity. "When the tribe went out to war it did not conquer lands for the benefit of individuals, but for the whole people."[1]

The Titienses, or Quirites, on the other hand, were of Sabine extraction. To them are traceable the private law, and, what is of interest to us, the peculiar notions of the family and of property. The great peculiarity of the Sabine law, or as it was called by the Latin writers, the *jus* Quirium, was the form of the *manus*—the hand. The *manus* was the conqueror's sign of conquest, or rather the insignia of the freebooter; all he laid hand upon became absolutely his; he could deal with it as he pleased. All that his wife and children had, also belonged to him, to be done with as he willed— even their lives. This was the Sabine contribution to what afterward became "Roman Law," when the Sabine tribes of the Capitoline Hill and the Ramnes tribe of the Palatine united to form the city of Rome.

Nowhere in law or history is there so interesting a duality as this origin of Rome and the Roman law, and no single custom arising as it did, has affected civilization as strangely and so widely. To think of a tribe living at Fleet Street super-imposing a law on a tribe living at Westminster, or a clan having its habitat in Wall Street grafting a law upon a people fortressed and buttressed in Madison Square Garden—taking either section of

[1] Sandars, p. 4.

London or New York as an example of the extent
of the Rome of that day—it seems impossible that
such a law, thus accepted, should become the law
of the world, and remain so for centuries.

This power of the Roman father over the very
lives of his children was called the *patria potestas*
and nowhere else in a civilized community was
there anything like it. [1] He had the power to sell
his children, he had the power to mutilate them,
he had the power to kill them; and it is because
there is evident first, in the laws ascribed to
Romulus, an intention to abate that power, not
only for military purposes but for what we would
now call humane reasons, that I have referred to
the first Roman lawmaker as an innovator along
lines which have been historically neglected.

It matters little whether or not the Romulus of
Plutarch and Dionysius existed; it does matter
that the human note was in the laws of his time,
and that citizens of the new city were enjoined
not only to bring up all healthy male children—
and at least one female child—but that all children must be allowed to live *until they were three
years old*, unless they were lame or monstrous.

Surely here was the beginning of some recognition of the rights of children. Even the lame and

[1] Gibbon, vol. iv., p. 341: "The law of nature instructs most
animals to cherish and educate their youthful progeny. The law
of reason inculcates to the human species the returns of filial
piety. But the exclusive, absolute and perpetual dominion of the
father over his children is peculiar to the Roman jurisprudence
and seems to be coeval with the foundation of the city."

the monstrous in the eyes of this early lawgiver had some rights, for it was further decreed that parents in doing away with them must act not entirely on their own judgment.

"These (the lame and monstrous infants) he allowed their parents to expose, provided they first showed them to five of their neighbours and these also approved of it, and besides other penalties he punished those who disobeyed this law with the confiscation of half their fortunes."[1]

It may be contended perhaps that we are giving high attributes to one who is not much more than a mythical person, but no other explanation of the law of Romulus is offered than that already referred to in Dionysius.

Despite the credit given to Numa Pompilius, by both Plutarch and Gibbon, Romulus gains by the comparison, although Numa amended one of the laws of Romulus in the matter of the right of a father to control a son up to the point of being able to sell him as a slave.[2]

"If a father gives his son leave to marry a woman who, by law, is to partake of his sacrifices and fortunes, he shall no longer have power of selling

[1] *Dionysius Halic.*, bk. ii., par. 15.

[2] W. A. Hunter, *Roman Law*, p. 190, calls the conclave of neighbours a "humane and interesting exception." John F. McLennon, in *Primitive Marriage*, says it is a "fine example of good old savage law." According to Hunter, infanticide receives its first customary check when the destruction of males and the eldest female is forbidden: the ancient tribes preferring rather to steal their wives than to rear them.

his son"—such was the amendment of Numa for which Plutarch commends the Sabine lawmaker; but in amending the law of Romulus permitting a father to sell his children, the second king of Rome was actuated by the idea of making it attractive for the young women to marry; doubtless he was having no easy time in eradicating the differences between the two warlike tribes first brought together under his predecessor. Lessening the power of the parents, as he did in the most material degree,[1] it was for the purpose of general polity and the accomplishment of his own harmonious designs, rather than for what I like to call, even in that early day, humanitarian reasons. There was no consideration of the child, or the female as such in Numa's amendment. His object was to make marriages more desirable that there might be more *male* Romans.[2]

As a matter of fact, declaration of the power of the father over the women and children of his family was nothing more on the part of Romulus than the codification of the laws of the past, with the softening provisos to which I have already

[1] *Dionysius Halic.*, bk., ii., par. 26.

[2] "Numa Pompilius," Plutarch, Dryden's Translations, vol. ix., p. 106: "He is also much to be commended for the repeal, or rather amendment, of that law which gives power to fathers to sell their children; he exempted such as were married, conditionally that it had been with the liking and the consent of their parents; for it seems a hard thing that a woman who had given herself in marriage to a man she judged free, should afterwards find herself living with a slave."

referred. The power of the father to imprison, scourge, or sell his son for a slave, or put him to death, was not lessened even when that son had risen to the highest honours of the State, as we shall see later.

Expulsion of the kings and the establishment of the Republic is dated B.C. 509, some two hundred and fifty years after the reputed founding of the city. With this stern period begins a series of thrilling examples of the use made of the *patria potestas*—stories that in themselves show how the power of the father extended over the life of the child, even when the child had become a man, and that man had been honoured by the State as was Cassius Viscellinus. The latter, although a tribune of the people and the author of the first Agrarian Law, was tried in the house of his own father, who, after having him whipped, "commanded him to be put to death and his estate consecrated to Ceres."[1]

That there was little progress made in the next great step in the history of Roman law, by which of course one refers to the adoption of the laws of the Twelve Tables, was because those laws were practically the codification of the ancient customary law of the people, despite the story that the patricians dispatched three commissioners to

[1] *Valerius Maximus*, edition of 1678, lib. v., cap. viii. According to Niebuhr, the story was disbelieved, and the historian himself says it is an invention by those who found it difficult to believe that after three consulships and as many triumphs, Cassius was still in his father's *potestas*. *Hist. of Rome*, vol. ii., p. 167.

Athens to bring home a copy of the laws of Solon. Acrid political fights, uncertain and sometimes corrupt administration of the law, led to the commission empowered to draw up what afterward became the Twelve Tables and the foundation of the whole fabric of the Roman law.

As the laws of the Twelve Tables represented the earliest fight against privilege, it would be too much to expect that they should contain any amelioration of the statute which gave the father the right to sell or kill his children. Even the language of the laws, in the fragments which have come down to us, shows in rugged, concise, and sternly imperative style that the law gained the respect in which it eventually came to be held, by no soft or easy methods. [1]

"If the complainant summon the defendant before the magistrate, he shall go; if he do not go, the plaintiff may call a bystander to witness, and take him by force;" this is the first section of the first paragraph of the laws of the Twelve Tables.

Where there was so much sternness, and where every family was presided over by a parent who had the right to inflict death as a punishment for disobedience, the disciplinary attitude of the Roman mind naturally became such, no matter what it had been in the beginning, that tender or human emotions had but little place. It is not surprising therefore that the one extract of the laws of the Twelve Tables, relating to our subject,

[1] Stephen, *Hist. of the Criminal Law of England*, p. 1.

should deal curiously, abruptly, and sharply with the power of the father to sell his son, a power that was diminished only after the son's spirit must have been entirely extinguished.

Si pater filium ter venum duit, filius a patre liber esto—if a father sells his son three times, let the son then go free of the father. In other words, three times did the father have the right to dispose of his son as a slave; and, while a slave might purchase his freedom, by paying his master, the son of a Roman citizen did not become free until the father had abused his right and misused the *potestas* three times.[1]

One sees the Rome of the Republic in the plays of Terence and Plautus, and the attitude of the parents toward exposure is vividly shown in the *Heautontimoroumenos* of the former.

Nearly always the exposed child died. Occasionally some escaped through the tenderness or cupidity of some passer-by who would pick up an exposed child either out of pity or for the material profit that came with the possession.

Sometimes mothers who were obliged to obey the orders of their husbands, arranged to have their children rescued. The comedy of Terence goes to show what the attitude of the father was under such circumstances. It is indeed, as De Gour says, "a chapter of the morals of the Greeks and Romans seen in action."

Chremes, departing on a long voyage, orders

[1] Ortolan.

his wife, Sostrata, who is about to have a child, to expose the child if it should turn out to be a girl. In obeying this order, she hopefully places a ring with the child.

Years later she meets the child at a bath and is given (by her own daughter) a ring to guard. Sostrata recognizes the ring and when she sees her husband the following dialogue ensues:

Sos. (*turning 'round*). Ha! my husband!

CHREM. Ha! my wife!

Sos. I was looking for you.

CHREM. Tell me what you want.

Sos. In the first place, this I beg of you, not to believe that I have ventured to do anything contrary to your commands.

CHREM. Would you have me believe you in this, although so incredible? Well, I will believe you.

Sos. Do you remember my being pregnant, and yourself declaring to me, most peremptorily, that if I should bring forth a girl, you would not have it brought up?

CHREM. I know what you have done, you have brought it up.

Sos. Not at all; but there was here an elderly woman of Corinth, of no indifferent character; to her I gave it to be exposed.

CHREM. O Jupiter! that there should be such extreme folly in a person's mind.

Sos. Alas! what have I done?

CHREM. And do you ask the question?

Sos. If I have acted wrong, my dear Chremes, I have done so in ignorance.

Chrem. This, indeed, I know for certain, even if you were to deny it, that in everything you both speak and act ignorantly and foolishly: how many blunders you disclose in this single affair! For, in the first place, then, if you had been disposed to obey my orders, the child ought to have been dispatched; you ought not in words to have feigned her death, and in reality to have left hopes of her surviving. But that I pass over; compassion, maternal affection, I allow it. But how finely you did provide for the future! What was your meaning? Do reflect. It's clear, beyond a doubt, that your daughter was betrayed by you to this old woman, either that through you she might make a living by her, or that she might be sold in open market as a slave. I suppose you reasoned thus: "Anything is enough, if only her life is saved." What are you to do with those who understand neither law, nor right and justice? Be it for better or for worse, be it for them or against them, they see nothing except just what they please.

Sos. My dear Chremes, I have done wrong, I own; I am convinced. Now this I beg of you; inasmuch as you are more advanced in years than I, be so much the more ready to forgive; so that your justice may be some protection for my weakness.

Chrem. I'll readily forgive you doing this, of course; but Sostrata, my easy temper prompts you to do amiss. But, whatever this circumstance is, by reason of which this was begun upon, proceed to tell it.

Sos. As we women are all foolishly and wretchedly superstitious, when I delivered the child to her to be exposed, I drew a ring from off my finger and ordered her to expose it, together with the child; that if she should die, she might not be without some portion of our possessions. [1]

CHREM. That was right; thereby you proved the saving of yourself and her. [2]

Sos. (*holding out the ring*). This is the ring.

CHREM. Whence did you get it?

Sos. From the young woman whom Bacchis brought with her.

CHREM. What does she say?

Sos. She gave it to me to keep for her, whilst she went to bathe. At first I paid no attention to

---

[1] Madame Dacier observes upon this passage, that the ancients thought themselves guilty of a heinous offence if they suffered their children to die without having bestowed on them some of their property; it was consequently the custom of the women, before exposing children, to attach to them some jewel or trinket among their clothes, hoping thereby to avoid incurring the guilt above mentioned, and to ease their consciences.

[2] Madame Dacier says that the meaning of this passage is this: Chremes tells his wife that by having given this ring, she has done two good acts instead of one—she has both cleared her conscience and saved the child; for had there been no ring or token exposed with the infant, the finder would not have been at the trouble of taking care of it, but might have left it to perish, never suspecting it would be inquired after, or himself liberally rewarded for having preserved it. (Bohn trans.) See chapters xii. and xiii.

it; but after I looked at it, I at once recognized it, and came running to you.

CHREM. What do you suspect now, or have you discovered, relative to her?

Sos. I don't know; unless you enquire of herself whence she got it, if that can possibly be discovered.

CHREM. Is this woman living to whom you delivered the child?

Sos. I don't know.

CHREM. What account did she bring you at the time?

Sos. That she had done as I had ordered her.

CHREM. Tell me what is the woman's name, that she may be inquired after.

Sos. Philtere.

CHREM. Sostrata follow me this way indoors.

Sos. How much beyond my hopes has this matter turned out! How dreadfully afraid I was, Chremes, that you would now be of feelings as unrelenting as formerly you were on exposing the child.

CHREM. Many a time a man cannot be such as he would be[1] if circumstances do not admit of it. Time has now so brought it about, that I should be glad of a daughter; formerly I wished for nothing less.

There is no evidence that the Romans as a people at any time approved of the sale of children,

---

[1] This he says by way of palliating the cruelty he was guilty of in his orders to have the child put to death.

and while the suggestion is made by Gibbon that early in the days of the kings impoverishing conditions occasionally made it necessary to dispose of members of the family, from the time of the adoption of the Twelve Tables as the codified law of Rome there is not a single indication that the power of the father over grown-up children was used otherwise than sparingly, and with a view to strengthening the stern and military character of the Roman idea of family. The main use of the provision for the sale of children, in time of prosperity at least, was to put the boy out to business, this being in general more a form that took the place of what was later apprenticeship and, still later, the labour contract. As late as Constantine this was permitted, even of new-born children, but only in cases of extreme need (*propter nimiam paupertatem*),[1] and then when it seemed the only way to prevent their parents from murdering them.

[1] Greenidge, *Roman Public Life*.

CHAPTER XV

A STONISHING depravity marked the last
days of the Republic, to the point where it
was even said that annual divorces were
as much the fashion in Rome as voluntary celibacy.[1] Seneca says there were women who
reckoned their years by their husbands. In the
severe, early period of the Republic, celibacy was
considered censurable and even guilty,[2] whereas
later it was not only condoned but wittily approved,
to judge by the quips of the dramatist, Plautus,
whose cynical references to marriage and the
burden of a wife read not unlike our own scoffing
and immoral dramatists of the eighteenth century.[3]

Civil wars and proscriptions had left great voids
in Roman families; more prolific foreigners, freed-

[1] Becker's *Gallus*, p. 178.
[2] According to Festus (*De Verborum Significatione*), there was a
celibate fine. Cicero, *De Leg.*, iii., 3, and Val. Max., ii., 9, i.
[3] Becker's *Gallus*, p. 179.
Apæcides—"I' faith, money's a handsome dowry." Periphanes
—"Indeed it is, when it isn't encumbered with a wife."—Plautus,
Epidicus, act ii., scene i.

men, and slaves began to dominate the noisy city
now beginning to earn her title of Mistress of the
World. The visitor to Pompeii today, noting the
large and heavy paving blocks, the narrow side-
walks, the deep ruts made in these solid streets by
the heavy wagons, the open shops, the indecent
signs, sees Rome in miniature. All this cosmopoli-
tan disorder marked the greater town that had not
twenty thousand inhabitants but a million; the
noise and the congestion increased out of all
proportion to its size because of the character of
its dwellers, for Rome had a large foreign population. As in modern New York or London, it was
in the foreign quarters that were found the dis-
comforts, the loud misunderstandings, and the
noisy, tragic fights for small things.

The stranger arriving in Rome had hardly entered its gates when he was being jostled and
shoved. The narrow streets were filled with pedlars
calling their wares of all kinds, from matches (*sul-
phurata*), in exchange for broken glass where money
was scarce, to a dish of boiled peas for an *as*, or fine
smoking sausages for those who had more money.
Idlers filled the streets at all hours, but especially
at the lunch hour (the sixth) when business ceased
and those who patronized the cafés (*tabernæ*) were
hurrying to get to their accustomed tables.[1]

Around billboards (*programmata*) announcing

[1] Becker's *Gallus*, pp. 42 to 46; Suetonius, *Claudius*, p. 25;
Horace, Epistle, ii., 2, 27; Martial, xii., 57, 14; Plautus, *Merc.*,
iii., 4, 78; *Roman Life Under the Cæsars*, Emile Thomas, p. 59.

THE FINDING OF ROMULUS AND REMUS

(FROM AN OLD PRINT)

new plays or exhibitions, crowds gathered while other groups watched acrobats, who beat themselves for the comic effects produced; dancers, jugglers, snake charmers, and performers of every kind and nation abounded. Heavily loaded wagons rumbled noisily along while their drivers cursed and lashed the tired beasts of burden, or the appearance of a tamed bear threw an entire street into wild and joyous confusion. Or perhaps a new troupe of gladiators entered town, to the complete cessation of all business and pastimes.[1] Here and there in the streets, money-changers and others set up tables in convenient places where they were least apt to be driven away, and hawked loudly the bargains that they offered. Money from all the world was then flowing Romeward, and in nothing was this shown more than in expensive funerals, with their hired and vociferous mourners, blocking the streets and putting an end for the time being, to other business—and amusements.[2] Narrow as were the streets, they were made more so by the *tabernæ*, built up against the houses, this practice becoming so much of a nuisance (as in modern times) that the Emperor Domitian caused a decree to be issued against them, forcing the owners to remove the encroachments and confine themselves to the area of the house.[3]

[1] M. Dezobry, *Rome au Siècle d'Auguste*, Plautus, *Hecyra*, Prologue.

[2] "Those funerals with their horns and trumpets meeting in the Forum" was Horace's idea of the height of noise.

[3] Becker's *Gallus*, p. 46; Martial, vii., 61.

15

A drunken man taking the entire *via* in his navigation—to the amusement of the crowd; a member of the city guard hurrying some offender to the court; or, reclining in his *lectica*, a noble, carried by six uniformed slaves, his other numerous attendants clearing the way for him— all these added to the noise and confusion—while through it all children crowded the curb with their games.

Such was the Rome that Augustus found, its proud citizens masters of the world, luxurious, sensual, disdainful of the very idea of duty, idling days away while they scoffed at marriage. But the foreigners, the freedmen, and the slaves married, and when the burden of a new child was too much for the small income made by amusing or serving some Roman citizen, the little newcomer was thrown into the Tiber or left unmarked on a busy thoroughfare. One of the first undertakings of Augustus was to try to remedy these evil conditions by laws and fiscal measures, his principal endeavour being to put an end to the corruption of morals and the exhaustion of the legitimate population.

From the day of the battle of Actium (B.C. 31) when the Roman world practically lay at his feet, Octavius, or Augustus as he was afterward called, while gratifying his ambition in adding to his power, studiously and ostentatiously observed the forms of popular government. In this he was paying heed to the fate of his uncle and also

conciliating the people, though with every in-
gratiating move he increased his power.

One of the first laws he proposed was the *lex
Julia* (*de maritandis ordinibus*) which was rejected
by the *comitia tributa*, B.C. 18, but was adopted in
A.D. 4. To this was added as a supplement the
lex Papia Poppæa, the two being known as the
lex Julia et Papia or as *novæ leges*, or simply *leges*,
the latter reference indicating that they were
referred to as the laws *par excellence*. Not only
marriage, but everything connected with it was
treated in these two laws, which really constituted
a code, the most extensive after the laws of the
Twelve Tables.

These laws made a great impression on Roman
society. How completely customs had swung to
extremes since the days of Romulus is shown in
this *lex Papia*, as Gaius calls it. Instead of
securing the father in his right over the life of
children, as the stern head of the house who might
decide at will whether he should let his offspring
live, the law now decreed that it was through the
children that he gained a status in the community.
Persons who were not married and had no children
were unable to inherit; the unmarried person not
being able to take any part of what had been left
to him, and the married person without children
(*orbus*) being able to take only one half.[1] Among

---

[1] Gaius, ii., 286: "Unmarried persons who by the *lex Julia* are
debarred from taking inheritances and legacies were in olden
times considered capable of taking *fideicommissa*. Likewise

the provisions of the *lex Julia*, or the *leges*, were those entitling that candidate for office who had the greatest number of children to preference. Of the two consuls it was decreed that he should be the senior whose children were the most numerous; a relief from all personal taxes and burdens was granted to citizens who had three children if they lived in Rome, four if they lived in Italy, and five if they lived in the provinces.

With the establishment of the *caduca*, by which there was instituted a punishment for sterility and a reward for legitimate procreation, it can be seen that there would follow some diminution in the number of children exposed, though according to Tacitus,[1] "marriages and the rearing of children did not become more frequent, so powerful are the attractions of the childless state."

By giving the people, or the common treasury, the benefit of the clause forfeiting the inheritance on account of sterility, the law was recognizing the *populus* as the common father, a legal concept that is becoming more and more the attitude of the twentieth century, and was then first trenchantly expressed.

---

childless persons, who by the *lex Papia* lose half their inheritance and legacies because they have no children, were in the olden time considered capable of taking *fideicommissa* in full. But afterward by the *senatus consultum Pegasianum* they were forbidden to take *fideicommissa* as well as inheritances and legacies. And those were transferred to those persons named in the testament who had children, or if none of them had children, to the *populus*, just as the rule is regarding legacies and inheritances."   [1] Tacitus, *Ann.*, iii., p. 28.

Suppressed in part by the constitution of Caracalla as to the privileges of paternity to the claim upon the *caduca*, and by Constantine as to the penalties for celibacy, these laws were not completely and textually abrogated until Justinian. They were the beginning, however, of the new movement; out of the degeneration and degradation of the waning days of the Republic there had come at least this forward step, though the patricians complained that these provisions gave rise to despised informers and opportunities for tyrannical misuse of power.

The child now had some other than a future use; it had an immediate value. Occasionally, in times past, strangers had picked up children exposed by their parents and had reared them as slaves, or maimed and blinded them for the profession of begging. Augustus set aside a reward of two thousand sesterces (about $40.00) for the person who would rear an orphan. This was the seed of a growing humanity, the first intimation of an inclination to treat children with kindness, though it contrasts with Augustus's own personal conduct when his anger was aroused. Both his daughter and granddaughter were so profligate that he banished them; when his granddaughter Julia was delivered of a child after sentence, he ordered that the child be "neither owned as a relative nor brought up." [1]

From the death of Augustus, 14 A.D., to the

[1] Suetonius, *Octavius*, par. 65.

reign of Nerva, 96 A.D., the violent sway of the army and the tragic fate of successive emperors cloud the history of Roman law and progress.

The Emperor Claudius distinguished himself by ordering that Claudia, a child by his first wife, "who was in truth the daughter of his freedman Boter, be thrown naked at her mother's door."[1]

There were no successors to the great jurists of the type of Capito and Labeo, whose opinions in Augustan days were accepted by even the emperor himself. With the coming of Nerva there was a great change in the attitude toward children. Despite a short reign of two years and a reputation for a weak will, it was to his initiative that the State owed the movement to put an end to the practice of abandoning infants, by having the government subsidize poor parents.

Apparently there was no other way of stopping this ruinous custom in a degenerate day. It was useless to appeal to the rich to rear families, and the poor who were still producing children were becoming poorer. One of Nerva's noteworthy acts to alleviate conditions was the founding of colonies, and it was in accordance with the same general plan that, a few months before he died, he ordered that assistance should be given parents who found themselves without the means of bringing up their offspring.

This order was issued in the year 97, and so successful was the experiment under his successor,

[1] Suetonius, *Life of Claudius*, par. 27.

who accepted and enlarged the plan, that in the year 100, five thousand children were receiving aid from the State. Much credit is given to Trajan for following up the ideas of Nerva, but it was to Nerva that Rome owed Trajan, one of the most humane of her emperors.

Another evidence of the humanity of Nerva was the fact that he prohibited the making of eunuchs, a practice that had met with the disfavour of the Emperor Domitian years before, and a practice that led the Pope Clement XIV., to decree, centuries later, that no more *castrats* should sing in churches. And these things he did when the extravagance of his predecessors had made it necessary for him to sell the imperial furniture and jewels in order to replenish the treasury. One of his coins shows him seated in the *curule* chair, dispensing charity to a boy and girl, the mother standing near, with the legend "Tutela Italia."

One need only to read the gentle replies of the Emperor Trajan to the younger Pliny, to see that, in that reign at least, there was a great change and that the conception of duty in the modern sense was creeping into a military world. Pliny himself, in a letter to Cannius, describes how he settled five hundred thousand sesterces (about $20,000) on the city of Como for the maintenance of children, "who were born of good families"—an act as traceable to the growing protective tendency as to Pliny's patriotism and love of glory.

According to the tablet of Velia[1] to the Emperor
Trajan, the landed proprietors of the place received
on mortgage at five per cent.,[2] less than half the
usual rate of that time, what would be about $50,-
000 of our money, the interest of which was to go
to the maintenance of three hundred poor children.

The means employed to help parents and prevent them from exposing their children were
skilfully contrived. Through the municipality,
Trajan lent money to certain proprietors to improve their land, and the interest paid on this loan
constituted a benevolent fund by which the children were taken care of, or rather, by which their
parents were rewarded for not murdering them.
From the table of Velia we learn also that fifty-
one proprietors of that section received on land
twelve times the value of the loan, or 1,116,000
sesterces ($52,820) the annual interest of which,
55,800 sesterces ($2,650), constituted a fund for
the support of three hundred children, two hundred
and sixty-four boys and thirty-six girls. The boys
received annually 192 sesterces, and the girls 144
sesterces. Illegitimate children were given less,
the boys 144 sesterces, and the girls 120 sesterces,

[1] Velia was a town in Liguria destroyed by a mountain slide.
It was near the present town of Piacenza, about an hour's railway
ride from Milan. In 1747 the inscription was found, one of the
longest that has come down to us, containing six hundred and
thirty lines in seven columns.

[2] The usual rate in provinces was twelve per cent. Pliny, Epist.,
x., 62 (*duodenis assibus*). Later, Alex. Severus lent money to the
poor to enable them to buy land at three per cent.

although in the tablet there were only two illegitimate children, one boy and one girl. The fact that the number of girls assisted was only one-tenth the number of boys, goes to show, that this new institution was not due so much to the fact that the sentiment of charity had infiltrated through pagan society, as to the fact that pagan society was endeavouring to repair the ravages of degenerate and pauperistic days, shown in the diminution of the class of freedmen in Rome.[1]

Writing to Pliny at Bithynia, to which place he had been sent by Trajan as imperial legate, the Emperor mildly answers an inquiry as to what the law shall be in that province regarding deserted children. Trajan rules that deserted children, who are found and brought up, shall be allowed their freedom without being obliged to repay the money expended for their maintenance.

"The question concerning such children who were exposed by their parents," says Trajan, "and afterward preserved by others, and educated in a state of servitude, though born free, has been frequently discussed; but I do not find in the constitutions of the princes, my predecessors, any general regulation upon this head extending to all the provinces. There are, indeed, some rescripts of Domitian to Avidius Niguinus and Armenius Brocchus, which ought to be observed; but Bithynia is not comprehended in the provinces therein mentioned. I am of opinion, therefore, that the

[1] Tacitus, *Ann.*, iv., 27.

claims of those who assert their right of freedom upon this principle, should be allowed, without compelling them to purchase their liberty by repaying the money advanced for their maintenance."[1]

A new note this, for in order to encourage the saving of children who had been exposed, the custom had been rigidly followed that the person who saved a child was able to regard it as his slave, without regard to what its condition had been previous to exposure.

As shown in the correspondence of Pliny and Trajan, there is much truth, in the contention that the Emperor shows up better than the philosopher and poet.

The noteworthy thing about this remarkable exchange of letters is that a new spirit is revealed. It is a living, working philosophy that we discover, practical results of that philosophy bringing a kindlier treatment of slaves, a greater respect for women, a more thoughtful regard for the education of the young, and a gentler assistance of the helpless and distressed.

True, Cicero, a century and a half before had preached doctrines that paved the way, and for generations earlier there had been such a kindlier spirit in the air. But not until now do we find a man of Pliny's dominating prominence, or nearness to power, suggesting that he will pay a third of the expenses of the cost of founding a university

[1] *Pliny's Letters*, Letter 72, vol. ii.

in his own town. His reason, he says, is to save youths from going to Milan for their education and thereby getting away from the proper home influences.

Tracing the thin thread of child progress through these livid days we are brought in touch with the little known but better side of Roman life; for despite the general debauchery of the upper classes and the unwholesome pictures of Juvenal, there is evidence that there were Roman families untouched by the general immorality where women of the type of Marcia or Helvia, addressed in the letters of Seneca, presided over homes in which there was an atmosphere of virtue and self-restraint, and where tales of deeds of the Romans of the earlier days still had their charm and their influence.

CHAPTER XVI

REFORMS OF HADRIAN—PUNISHMENT OF FATHERS—
VALERIUS MAXIMUS—FAVOURITE STREETS IN
ROME FOR LEAVING ABANDONED CHILDREN—
MUTILATING CHILDREN FOR PROFIT.

NEVER, it has been said, had the human race enjoyed a state of prosperity equal to that under the reign of Hadrian, the successor to Trajan, and like him a philosopher among emperors. From Nerva to Marcus Aurelius—the five emperors, Nerva, Trajan, Hadrian, Antoninus Pius, and Marcus Aurelius—there was a reign of philosophy. Indeed they may also be called the emperors of the children for the reforms they accomplished and initiated—working as they did, contrary to the entire law and tradition of their country, and without the inspiration of complete knowledge of the intellectual and spiritual conditions that were governing them.

To appreciate all that Hadrian did, one must remember that he had Plutarch for a master, Suetonius for his secretary, and Phlegon, his freedman, as amanuensis to write the history of his reign. As a youth he had studied all the philosophic systems including that of Epictetus, and

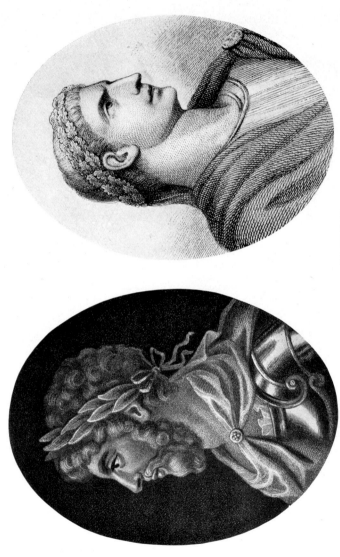

ANTONINUS PIUS, CONSECRATOR OF THE WORLD'S FIRST
PROTECTIVE FOUNDATION BENEFIT FOR GIRLS

CONSTANTINE THE GREAT, EMPEROR-PROTECTOR OF THE
ROMAN CHILD

showed an acquisitive spirit. Had he lived in our age of private railway cars probably he would have spent little time at the Capitol: in a time when travel was both disagreeable and dangerous he journeyed back and forth over his great domain, to the dissatisfaction of the Romans, but to his own greater knowledge of his people and consequent greater humanitarianism.

Out of that philosophy, that association, and that teaching, out of the character of Hadrian—for, despite the attempts of his biographers, Startianus and Dion Cassius, to make him a cruel and vain tyrant, his whole life shows an abhorrence of bloodshed—there was born a new rule.[1]

He closed the *ergastula*, or workhouses, where so many men, carried off by surprise, were detained and tortured; he protected slaves against the cruelty and murderous punishments of masters, prohibiting their sale to houses of prostitution or schools for gladiators, and also declaring against the indiscriminate torture of slaves whose masters had been assassinated. Up to that time even those who had not been within sight or hearing of a murder were liable to punishment. A woman who had ill-treated her female slaves he sentenced to five years' imprisonment—an unheard-of thing in those days.

Once before, during the reign of Tiberius, Carthaginian priests had been crucified by the Emperor for the sacrifice of children to their god

[1] Tertullian, *Epst.*, 9.

Moloch, but apparently the punishment had not acted as a deterrent, for we find a similar provision in the laws of Hadrian.

Going further and, as Duruy says, "employing logic in the service of humanity," he ruled that any woman who had been free at the time of pregnancy must naturally give birth to a free child, a ruling not important in itself but closely in touch with what we will come to see was the argument of the Christian Fathers in behalf of the lives of little children.

He ameliorated the condition of women, allowing them to make wills, and for the first time softened the law of the Twelve Tables which, according to Ulpian, had given a mother no rights in the property of a son dying intestate. Hadrian, however, following a *senatus consultum Tertullianum*, gave the mother, under the *jus trium liberorum*, the right to inherit when she had had three sons, and, if a freed woman, when she had had four.

But the great blow Hadrian struck at the theories that had hitherto held sway was the condemning to banishment a father who had killed his son. From time immemorial the boast of Rome had been fathers who, in the ardour of patriotism, and sometimes in the heat of anger or resentment, had sacrificed their sons, no matter how famous or important their sons were.

"Lucius Brutus," says Valerius Maximus, giving suitable incidents of the father's power, "who

THE SACRIFICING OF LIVING INFANTS TO THE GOD MOLOCH

equalled Romulus in honour, for he founded Rome and thus the Roman liberty, coming to the supreme power, and understanding that his sons endeavoured to restore Tarquin, caused them to be apprehended, and to be whipped with rods before the Tribuna; and, after that, caused them to be tied to a stake, and then ordered the sergeant to cut off their heads. He put off the relation of a father, that he might act like a consul; rather chose to live childless, than to be remiss in public duty.

"Cassius, following his example, though his son was a tribune of the people, and was the first that had promulgated the *Agrarian* law, and by many other popular acts had won the hearts of the people, when he had laid down his command, by advice of his kindred and friends, condemned him in his own house for affecting the kingdom; and after he was whipped, commanded him to be put to death; and consecrated his estate to Ceres.

"Titus Manlius Torquatus, famous for his many great dignities, and a person of rare experience in the civil law and the pontifical ceremonies, did not think it necessary to consult his friends in an act of the same nature. For when the Macedonians had by their ambassadors complained to the Senate of D. Silanus, his son, who was governor of that province, he besought the Senate that they would determine nothing in that affair till he had heard the difference betwixt his son and the Macedonians. Then, with the general consent of the conscript fathers, and of them that came to complain, he sat and heard the cause in his own house, wherein he spent two whole days alone, and the third day, after he had diligently examined the testimonies on both sides, he pronounced this sentence: 'Whereas it hath been proved that Silanus, my son, has taken money of our allies, I think him unworthy to live either in the commonwealth, or in my house, and I command him forthwith to get out of my sight.' Silanus, struck with the sharp and cruel sentence of his father, would not endure to live any longer, but the next night hanged himself.

"But M. Scaurus, the light and ornament of his country, when the Roman cavalry was worsted by the Cimbrians and deserting the proconsul, Catullus, took their flight toward the city, sent one to tell his son, who was one of those that fled, that he had rather meet with his carcass slain in the field, than see him guilty of such a shameful flight. And therefore if there were any shame remaining in his breast, degenerate as he was, he should shun the sight of his enraged father; for by the remembrance of his youth, he was admonished what kind of son was to be owned or contemned by such a father as Scaurus. Which message being delivered him, the young man was forced to make a more fatal use of his sword against himself, than against his enemies.

"No less imperiously did A. Fulvius, one of the Senatorian Order, keep back his son from going into the field, than Scaurus chid his for running away.   For he caused his son, eminent among his equals for his wit, learning, and beauty, to be put to death because he took part with Catiline, being seduced by ill-counsel; having brought him back by force, as he was going to Catiline's army, and uttering these words before his death, that he 'did not beget him to join with Catiline against his country, but to serve his country against Catiline.' He might have kept him till the heat of the war had been over, but that would have been only the act of a cautious, this was the deed of a severe father."

The father who was brought before Hadrian under the old conditions would have been honoured —he had killed a son who befouled his name. Nevertheless this man was ordered to be deported, "because he had killed as a thief rather than as one using the power (*jure*) of father; *nam patria potestas in pietate debet, non atrociate consistere.*"[1] Whatever the excuse given, he was punished. That he had not observed the forms in killing his son by calling a consultation of the members of his family, was the nominal reason for punishing him, but the unchecked power of the father over the life of his children, even when they had become adults, was ended.

Modern sensibility will be shocked at the thought that there had been sufficient social "advance" for distinct places to become estab-

[1] *Digest*, xlviii., 9, 5.

lished for the exposure of children. But advance it was when no longer were children left in unfrequented highways, no longer were they thrown into the Tiber.

There were two places where it was the custom to leave abandoned children. One was near the Velabrum, a street on the western slope of the Aventine Hill between the Vicus Tuscus and the Forum Boarium where the oil dealers and the cheese mongers made a practice of selling their wares; and the other, in the vegetable market, where there rose a column round which the children were placed. Because of this practice, according to Festus, the column was called the Lactaria.[1] It was said that courtesans favoured the Velabrum.

What happened to the children even in this "advanced" age was doubtless little different from the treatment they received when they were found on the highways. The elder Seneca has given a vivid account of the practice of the day in the "Thirty-third Controversy," book five, headed "Debilitans Expositos."[2]

Difficult as it is to believe that the people who eventually charged themselves with the rearing of the foundlings made a business of mutilating them, there is no doubt but that such was the case.

In the "Controversy" of Seneca the question is

---

[1] *De Verborum Significatione*, p. 188, edition Lipsiæ, 1880. Line six reads: "*Lactaria columna in foro olitorio dicta, quod ibi infantes lacte alendos deferebant.*"

[2] M. A. Seneca, *Opera*. Biponti, 1783.

whether those who mutilated exposed children have done a wrong toward the State. The debate is opened by Porcius Latro, who asks if after having suffered the misfortune of being exposed, it is not a piece of good luck to have, someone find them.

Cassius Severus then expresses his opinion.

"Look," he exclaims, "on the blind wandering about the streets leaning on their sticks, and on those with crushed feet, and still again look on those with broken limbs. This one is without arms, that one has had his shoulders pulled down out of shape in order that his grotesqueries may excite laughter. Let us view the entire miserable family shivering, trembling, blind, mutilated, perishing from hunger—in fact, already half dead. Let us go to the origin of all these ills—a laboratory for the manufacture of human wrecks—a cavern filled with the limbs torn from living children— each has a different profession, a different mutilation has given each a different occupation."

The conclusion is that inasmuch as the exposed children are slaves, being the property of those who rear them, they have no cause for complaint against the State.

"What wrong has been done to the Republic?" asks Gallio in reply to Severus. "On the contrary, have not these children been done a service inasmuch as their parents had cast them out?"

"Many individuals," adds F. Claudius, "rid themselves of misformed children defective in some part of their body or because the children are born under evil auspices. Someone else picks them up out of commiseration and, in order to defray the expenses of bringing the child up, cuts off one of its limbs. Today, when they are demanding charity, that life that they owe to the pity of one, they are sustaining at the expense and through the pity of all."

CHAPTER XVII

PROGRESS UNDER THE ANTONINES—FAUSTINA'S EF-
FORTS TO SAVE FEMALE CHILDREN—CHRISTIAN
SENTIMENT GROWS—PLEA OF LACTANTIUS—ITS
EFFECTS—CONSTANTINE.

FROM the strictly legal side the most interesting event of Hadrian's reign is the fact
that the opinions of the jurists, when they
were unanimous, were now recognized as written
law.[1] The constitutions or proclamations of law
of the emperors, although none were ascribed to
an earlier date, had probably been issued for a
century previously, but now what is called the
"Perpetual Edict" is finally arranged and authorized, and law proceeds from an intellectual and
philosophic source, instead of from an imperial
head.

In empowering Salvius Julianus, one of the
four greatest lawyers Rome ever produced, to
frame an edict, and by a *senatus consultum* em-
body this edict in the statute law of Rome, the
entire law of the Empire underwent a change in
spirit. What had hitherto been done by Augustus,
by Nerva, by Trajan, and by Hadrian himself,

[1] Hunter, *Spartianus*, part xvii., p. 67.

had furnished only the value of example or of an immediate law passed for the benefit of some particular condition. A succeeding emperor was at liberty to imitate or pass similar laws, or ignore the acts of his predecessors as he might choose. As we shall see, he usually ignored the noble examples of those who had gone before.

But by placing the making of the law in the hands of the jurists, men who were thinkers and scholars and under the influence of the spreading Stoic philosophy, many disciples of Zeno and Chrysippus, and some later to be under the influence of the Christian philosophy, Hadrian was laying a broad foundation for the complete passing of the Roman idea of the unimportance of the child as a child, and making way for the Christian idea which was to take its place.

By a *senatus consultum*, passed before the Edict of Julianus, the right of fathers to expose their children was for the first time taken away; *durante matrimonio* they were compelled to rear their children instead of exposing them, while later regulations made it necessary to maintain even those children born after divorce.[1]

This was the first attempt to prohibit the exposing of children.

As we have seen, the right of the father to reject his offspring was restricted in earliest times to weak and deformed children, and then only after there had been a conference with five neighbours,

[1] Julianus, 611; Walker, p. 77.

but the frequent reference to the exposure of children under the Republic and under the emperors
indicates that there was little regard for this legal
restraint.   Even Augustus himself did not hesitate
to expose the child of his granddaughter.

The law of Hadrian has not been placed by
scholars and commentators as the first law against
exposing children, partly no doubt because it was
too new to be really effective.   In an interesting
controversy[1] between Gerardus Noodt and Cornelius Van Binkershoek, as to whether there were
any prohibitory laws prior to those of Valentinian,
Valens, and Gratian (367 A.D.), Binkershoek maintains with great show of authority, what is undoubtedly true, that there were.   Interesting, too,
is the fact that we find in the Code of Justinian
(vii., 16, 1) reference to a rescript of Hadrian in
which the sale of children is referred to as "*res
illicita et inhonesta*," which is assumed by Walker
to refer to the sales not being properly conducted,[2]
but which, judging from the temper of the Emperor,
referred to the thing itself.

As the war-loving Trajan was succeeded by the
lover of peace, the nomadic Hadrian was succeeded
by the home-loving Antoninus Pius, who did not
leave Rome for almost a quarter of a century,
except for one rapid tour through Asia.   He made

[1] Gerardus Noodt, *Opera Omnia*, 1767.   Cornelius Van Binkershoek, *Opera Omnia*, 1761.

[2] Abdy and Walker, *Institutes of Justinian*, Appendix A.   Ortolan, p. 325.

it possible for children to inherit from their parents even though they had neglected to imitate a father in becoming a Roman citizen. He further showed his humanity by compelling cruel masters to sell slaves they had maltreated.

In the name of his wife, Faustina, for whom—despite the assaults on her character—he retained ever affection and respect, he consecrated a protective foundation for the benefit of girls, *puellæ alimentariæ Faustinianæ*—the first of its kind in the world, and the initial move to save female children other than the first-born. A medal of the time, showing the Empress, bears on the reverse side Antoninus surrounded by children, with the words *Puellæ Faustinianæ* in the exergue.[1] This, together with his continuous support of the *pueri alimentarii*, entitles him to the credit of saving more children from the "ancient and abominable" custom of being thrown out on the crossroads to die than any of his predecessors.

At the end of his reign it is evident from the inscriptions that endowments similar to those originated by Nerva had been made at Atina, Abellinum, Abella, Vibo, Caieta, Anagnia, Fundi, Cupra Montana, Industria, Brixia, Aquileia, Compsa, Æclanum, Allifæ, Aufidena, Cures, Auximum, and other places. What is more interesting than the point of view of E. E. Bryant, in his *Life of Antoninus Pius*, that these "endowments undoubtedly pauperized Italians and lightened

[1] Duruy, vol. v., p. 175.

unwisely the responsibility of parents for the maintenance of their children? But they *must certainly have been of assistance to farmers*, and have supplied them with the capital necessary for successful agriculture."[1]

The progress made in the matter of child history would be incomplete if one did not recall that in this reign appeared that bold and able defender of Christianity, Justin Martyr. The time had gone by for darkness and seclusion, and now, that which had been contemptuously but so well described as the religion of "slaves and women, of children and old men," strode abroad, proclaiming its right to be heard as a rational and uplifting doctrine. Pleading for the oppressed and the downtrodden, pleading for those the Roman world affected to despise, preaching a religion of humility —there is a fine, robust, masculine note in Justin's opening words of his apology, the challenging conviction of a man who knowingly throws down the gauntlet to the masters of the world.

To the Emperor Titus Ælius Antoninus, Pius, Augustus, Cæsar;
to his Son Verissimus, Philosopher;
to Lucius, Philosopher,
Son of Cæsar by Birth and of Antoninus by Adoption,
a Prince Friendly to Literature;
to the Sacred Senate and to the Entire Roman People,

[1] Cambridge University Press, p. 122.

In the Name of those who, among All Men,
Are unjustly Hated and Persecuted;
I, One of Them,
Justin . . . Have Written this Discourse.

It was during the reign of Antoninus that Tertullian was born.

Under Antoninus's philosophic successor the alimentary institution was further developed, Marcus Aurelius showing his interest by putting the supervision under a person of prætorian or consular rank.[1] He upheld the rights of children, going one step further in the direction of freedom by ending the tyrannical power of the father to oblige his son to put away his wife, if the latter were disagreeable to the head of the family.

With Marcus Aurelius vanished the humane emperors—they had reigned long. Culminating in his beneficent sway the Stoic philosophy, from Aristotle to Marcus Aurelius, kept developing, in the midst of surroundings the least encouraging. The Stoics, with their ideas of humanity, of mutual good will and moral equality, arrived at almost the same conclusions regarding religion and the same sentiment regarding humanity as did the followers of the Christian religion, although working from an entirely different source. The one reached its conclusion through the medium of patrician orators, philosophers, and emperors,

[1] Duruy, vol. v., p. 467. E. E. Bryant, *Life of Antoninus Pius*, p. 122, refers to the inscription at Aquileia of a "*præfectus alimentorum*" as indicative of what Pius had done.

the other through the slaves, the distressed, and those for whom life faced an unbroken wall.

From Aurelius to Septimus Severus there is little but bloodshed in Roman history. The selection of Papinian, the greatest of Roman jurists, as his adviser is in a way the greatest claim to fame that Severus has.[1] Among his many laws was one that permitted the sons of a condemned criminal to retain the rights the father had over freedmen, which was considered a great indulgence —*benignissime rescripsit.* He condemned to temporary exile the woman who, by practising abortion, had deprived her husband of the hope of children.

Of the bloody reign of Caracalla it is to be noted principally that he changed the *lex Julia* in such a way as to deprive paternity of its privileges. Those who were not married (*cœlebs*) and those who were married and had no children (*orbus*) suffered in regard to their inheritances as they had under the old law, but Caracalla filled his treasury by sweeping into the *fiscus* all the *caduca.*

While the barbarians are now beginning to press down on the northern frontiers of the Empire and the Christians beginning to rapidly and swiftly permeate the vast domain, there is little but a bloody chronicle of making and unmaking of emperors up to Diocletian. Even when persecuted and proscribed, says Ortolan, Christianity had a liberalizing and softening effect on the progress of

[1] Hunter, p. 68.

jurisprudence and legislation. The softening effect was also the effect of a new understanding. Trajan, one of the greatest of the humane emperors, had come from Spain, and Diocletian, who temporarily braced up the Roman legions, put energy into the government, and held the barbarians in check, was himself from a family of freedmen. The best of the patrician blood had become thoroughly impregnated with Stoic ideas, although it was true that the jurists who had obtained their philosophy from Greece and were given the task of defending existing law and institutions were still against the new religion. Though the persecutors under Diocletian were unusually severe, theirs was the final burst of oppression before the new religion was to triumph in having the head of the great Roman Empire, Diocletian's own successor, Constantine, accept the despised faith.

It matters little whether Constantine's conversion was a political move, based on a desire to absorb a growing and powerful organization. This was a century in which things were happening and his was a reign (306 or 313–337) that marked a long turn in the road in the attitude of the State toward the child. Despite the progress that had been made, the practice of murdering and exposing new-born children was becoming more and more frequent in the provinces, and especially in Italy.[1]

[1] Gibbon, vol. i., p. 497.

It was due to poverty, says Gibbon,[1] and the
principal causes of distress were the unendurable
taxes. The historian declares that "moved by
some recent and extraordinary instances of despair," Constantine addressed an edict[2] to all the
cities of Italy and afterward to those of Africa,
directing that immediate and sufficient aid be
given by magistrates to parents who produced
children that they were too poor to bring up.
Against the opinion of Gibbon is set that of Gode-
froy that it was not some unusual bit of misery,
some "Mary Ellen case," that moved the Emperor
to take this significant step.

The edict was published on May 12, 315 A.D.,
a few months before his victory over Licinius.
The Christians had prophesied to Constantine
that he would be victorious and he was more than
likely to be influenced by their point of view, especially that of Lactantius, the noted rhetorician
and teacher, to whom he had entrusted the education of his son, Crispus. Lactantius had just
written his work on *The Divine Institutes*, designed
to supersede the less complete treatises of Minucius Felix, Tertullian, and Cyprian. He had dedicated the work to Constantine, and perhaps had
conversed with him about it, discussing one particular chapter in which the Christian Father had
inveighed, with his accustomed grace but with

[1] Zosimus, book ii., says parents were obliged to sell their
children to pay the tax collectors.

[2] *Codex Theodosianus*, xi., 27, 1–2.

unusual force, against infanticide and the sale
and exposure of infants. A new day, indeed, had
come—the proud Emperor of the mighty Romans
sits high on his throne, listening to, and moved by
—a Christian Father!

This is Lactántius's plea for the new-born, from
the sixth book of his *Divine Institutes*[1]:

"Therefore let no one imagine that even this
is allowed, to strangle newly born children, which
is the greatest impiety; for God breathes into their
souls for life, and not for death. But men, that
there may be no crime with which they may not
pollute their hands, deprive souls, as yet innocent
and simple, of the light which they themselves
have not given. Any one truly may not expect
that they would abstain from the blood of others
who do not abstain even from their own. But
these are without any controversy wicked and
unjust. What are they whom a false piety com-
pels to expose their children? Can they be considered innocent who expose their own offspring
as a prey to dogs, and as far as it depends upon
themselves, kill them in a more cruel manner than
if they had strangled them?

"Who can doubt that he is impious who gives
occasion for the pity of others? For, although
that which he has wished should befall the child
—namely, that it should be brought up—he has
certainly consigned his own offspring either to
servitude or to the brothel? But who does not

[1] Chapter xx., p. 407, vol. i.

understand, who is ignorant what things may happen, or are accustomed to happen, in the case of each sex, even through error? For this is shown by the example of Œdipus alone, confused with twofold guilt. It is therefore as wicked to expose as it is to kill. But truly parricides complain of the scantiness of their means, and allege that they have not enough for bringing up more children; as though, in truth, their means were in the power of those who possess them, or God did not daily make the rich poor, and the poor rich. Wherefore, if any one on account of poverty shall be unable to bring up children, it is better to abstain from marriage than with wicked hands to mar the work of God."

As an additional protective measure Constantine withdrew the right of liberty that the Antonines had secured to foundling children, and in order to encourage strangers to pick up waifs cast away by parents, the Emperor made them the slaves of those who raised them. The father was punished for rejecting his infant by being no longer able to claim a right that had previously been his. Rather than that there should be murder, the Emperor went further; he gave poor parents the right to sell their new-born children.

One more step and the story of the Roman child ends. The Emperor Valentinian, a strange mixture of cruelty and sense—the same who kept two ferocious she-bears near him and saw that they had human food a-plenty,—is in the books as the author of the law condemning the exposition of new-born infants. It was in 374 that this edict was issued in the name of the Emperors Valentinian, Valens, and Gratian, declaring that whosoever should expose his children should be subject to punishment.[1]

[1] Justinian Code, viii., 52, 2. *Quod si exponendam putave.it; animadversoni, quæ constituta est, subjacebit.*

CHAPTER XVIII

PLEAS OF THE CHRISTIAN FATHERS.

IT has been said that the only way to understand the Middle Ages is to comprehend that the Roman Empire did not die down, or fade away; it remained, or continued to be the centre of civilized government, until comparatively recent times. In fact, nominally the Holy Roman Empire, the direct descendant of the Roman Empire, did not pass away as an idea until 1806, when the Emperor Joseph II. announced to the Germanic Diet his refusal to carry any longer the title of Emperor of the Romans.[1]

Even when the Roman Empire was at its greatest point of power and wealth, the actual founders of the Holy Roman Empire were at work in Rome itself, in the persons of the Christian Fathers; for, after all, it was the Church that was to rule the world once swayed by Roman legions. The men who, as representatives of Christ, were later to tame the barbarians, really laid the foundations for the future greatness of Christian Rome, amid

---

[1] Bryce, *Holy Roman Empire*, p. 1. E. A. Freeman, *Historical Studies.*

the very luxury and opulence of the pagan Rome
soon to pass away.

The struggles of these Christians among the
polished and cruel Romans was, in a way, a preparation for the struggle to come later with the
unpolished, but equally cruel, barbarians. In
their conquest of the Roman world, the Christian
founders saved their religion; in the conquest of the
barbarian hordes, they saved civilization; without
Christianity the German and Celtic races, with
their lustful, revengeful, and passionate natures,
either might have overwhelmed Roman civilization entirely, bringing on a night of barbarism, or
have been themselves "corrupted and destroyed by
the vices and sensuality which surrounded them."[1]

Amid all the differences of opinion and doctrine
that we find among the early founders of Christianity, there was one thing on which they were unanimous, and that was the attitude toward children.
It was a ceaseless war they waged in behalf of
children—those early and ofttimes eloquent founders. From Barnabas, contemporary of the Apostles, and by Luke even called one of them, to
Ambrosius and Augustine, they did not cease to
denounce those who, no matter what their reasons,
exposed or killed infants.

No distinction was made by the Fathers between
infanticide and exposure.[2] Both were murderous acts, particularly bitterly condemned by the

[1] Charles Loring Brace, *Gesta Christi*, p. 111.
[2] W. E. H. Lecky, *History of European Morals*, vol. ii., p. 27.

"SUFFER THE LITTLE CHILDREN TO COME UNTO ME"

(AFTER OVERBECK)

Christians because their enemies had charged them with murdering infants at secret rites. The letter attributed to Barnabas by Clement of Alexandria and Origen, and which in any case goes back to the earliest days of the religion, severely condemned infanticide. "Thou shalt not slay the child by procuring abortion, nor again shalt thou destroy it after it is born."[1] By such protests as these, made with one cannot tell what frequency, the Christians took their stand on the basic principles.

Justin, whose vigorous manner of addressing the Emperor is so attractive, succumbed, at the age of seventy-four, to the calumnies of the cynic Crescentius, and became a martyr; but his example and fervour left an indelible mark upon his time.

"As for us," he says, "we have been taught that to expose newly born children is the part of wicked men; and this we have been taught lest we should do any one an injury, and lest we should sin against God; first, because we see that almost all so exposed (not only the girls, but also the males) are brought up to prostitution. . . . Now we see you rear children only for this shameful use; and for this pollution a multitude of females and hermaphrodites, and those who commit unmentionable iniquities are found in every nation. And you receive the hire of these, and duty and taxes from them, whom you ought to exterminate from your realm."[2]

---

[1] Barnabas, Epistle, chapter xix.
[2] Justin, *Apol.*, i., chapter xxvii., p. 30.

And again he says: "We fear to expose children, lest some of them be not picked up, but die, and we become murderers. But whether we marry, it is only that we may bring up children; or whether we decline marriage, we live continently."[1]

Athanagoras,[2] the Athenian philosopher, who presented to Marcus Aurelius and to Commodus an apology for the Christians, in 166 A.D., asked the logical Romans to use their famous common sense in weighing false charges made against Christians.

"What man of sound mind," he said, "will affirm that we, who abhor murder, are murderers; we who condemn as murder the use of drugs for abortion, and declare that those who even expose a child are chargeable with murder."[3]

Tertullian, whose apology was written in the year 200, or 205, of our era, was equally bold.

"Rulers of the Roman Empire," he began, "seated for the administration of justice on your lofty tribunal"—and then made the charge direct: "You first of all expose your children, that they may be taken up by any compassionate passer-by, to whom they are quite unknown; or you give them away to be adopted by those who will act better to them the part of parents."[4]

[1] Justin, *Apol.*, i., chapter xxix., p. 31.
[2] Athanagoras, *Plea*, chapter xxxv., p. 419.
[3] A. J. Dogour, *Recherches sur les Enfants Trouvés*, p. 61.
[4] Tertullian, *Apologeticus*, par. 90.

Later, in another address, this time to the pagan people, he returns to the charges.

"Although you are forbidden by the laws to slay new-born infants, it so happens that no laws are evaded with more impunity or greater safety, with the deliberate knowledge of the public and the suffrages of this entire age, . . . You make away with them in a more cruel manner, because you expose them to cold and hunger, and to wild beasts, or else you get rid of them by the slower death of drowning [*sic*]."[1]

"Man is more cruel to his offspring than animals," said the learned Clement of Alexandria. "Orpheus tamed the tiger by his songs, but the God of the Christians, in calling men to their true religion, did more, since he tamed and softened the most ferocious of all animals—men themselves."[2]

No abler pleader for the new order of things was there than Minucius Felix, a Roman lawyer of education, who, on his conversion to the new faith, became one of the eloquent founders of Latin Christianity. A disciple of Cicero, he has been called the "precursor of Lactantius in the graces of style."

"How I should like to meet him," he exclaims, indignantly, "who says or believes that we are initiated by the slaughter and blood of an infant . . . no one can believe this except one who can

[1] Tertullian, *Ad Nationes*, chapter xv.
[2] Clement of Alexandria, *Pædagogus*, chapter iii., p. 3.

dare do it.   And I see that you at one time exposed your begotten children to wild beasts and
to birds; and another, that you crush them when
strangled with a miserable kind of death . . .
and these things assuredly come down from the
teachings of your gods.   For Saturn did not expose
his children, but devoured them.   With reason
were infants sacrificed to him by parents in some
part of Africa, caresses and kisses repressing their
crying, that a weeping victim might not be sacrificed.   Moreover, among the Tauri of Pontus,
and to the Egyptian Busiris, it was a sacred rite
to immolate their guests, and for the Galli to
slaughter to Mercury human, or rather inhuman,
sacrifices.   The Roman sacrificers buried living
a Greek man and a Greek woman, a Gallic man
and a Gallic woman; and to this day, Jupiter
Latiaris is worshipped by them with murder;
and, what is worthy of the son of Saturn, he is
gorged with the blood of an evil and criminal
man.''[1]

To drive home the awful character of a crime
that was so common we have the vision of Paul,
who sees the man and woman who have exposed
children, suffering in hell the terrible tortures of
the damned.

'''They [the parents] gave us for food to dogs
and to be turned out to swine. Some of us they
threw into the river,' exclaimed these children;
''and so now the guilty are condemned to eternal

[1] Minucius Felix, *Oct.*, chapters xxx. and xxxi.

punishment while the children are committed to the angels."[1]

We have quoted already the eloquent Lactantius. Basil the Great thundered against infanticide and the spectacle of free children being sold by avaricious creditors of their fathers. The same Ambrosius, who, although only a Christian Bishop, castigated the Emperor Theodosius for the massacre at Thessalonica, brought his force and courage to play against the law which permitted a debtor to satisfy his claim, at the cost of the liberty of his son, or the debauchery of his daughter, as the *fisc* was then authorized to sell infants to pay unsatisfied taxes.

A new religion in one of the least important provinces of the Roman Empire, Christianity, in three centuries, pushed its doctrines to the very end of the vast Roman domain, and even made the conquest of the imperial throne itself.

Its impassioned preachers and apostles vaunted the humanity of their new faith; for cast-out infants and the despised slaves the new priests fought such a battle of perseverance and martyrdom as the world had never seen before.

In the name of their new God, Jesus, himself admittedly a poor Jew and a carpenter, they took all the truth there was in the aristocratic philosophy of the Romans and their emperors, and made it live indeed—they applied it to the lowest, and the most humble—even to children. "No-

[1] Vision of Paul, par. 40.

thing human is alien"—this was a verity in the
lives of the men who fought the first battles of
Christianity.

Every human being had a soul—that was a
vital point in their fight. They asserted that
children had souls, to which religious doctrine
probably more is due in the way of checking the
practice of infanticide than any other single idea.
We have seen how Plutarch, the polished philosopher, had gone as far as the pagan mind could
under its philosophy, in directing thought as
to man's responsibility for actions toward the
child, by collecting opinions of the philosophers
as to when an unborn child became a human
being.

The Fathers won the battle in that they convinced the Roman world that children had souls
—but the economic battle was one not yet to be
won by preaching.   But it was not by orations and
preaching alone that they had won as much as
they had.

Constantine, in the year 315, as we have seen,
had put forth the proclamation:

"Let a law be at once promulgated in all the
towns of Italy, to turn parents from using a par-
ricidal hand on their new-born children, and to
dispose their hearts to the best sentiments. Watch
with care over this, that, if a father brings his
child, saying that he cannot support it, someone
should supply him without delay with food and
clothing; for the cares of the new-born suffer no

delay, and we order that our revenue, as well as our treasure, aid in this expense."[1]

To this he added, in 321, including the provinces:

"We have learned that the inhabitants of provinces, suffering from scarcity of food, sell and put in pledge their children. We command then that those found in this situation, without any personal resource, and being able only with great trouble to support their children, be succoured by our treasury before they fall under the blows of poverty; for it is repugnant to our morals that any one under our Empire should be pushed by hunger to commit a crime."[2]

Ten years later, Constantine had to modify the laws in relation to children—so acute were the sufferings in the Empire—by permitting those who "took up" children to have the right of property in them.[3]

"Whoever," said Constantine in his latest law, "has taken in a new-born boy or girl, exposed by the order and with the knowledge of its father or master, outside of the house of the one or the other, has the power to keep him as son or slave without fear that those who rejected him can reclaim him."

The conditions of the times, as Dugour points out, are well shown by the frequency with which these conditions are referred to. Julius Firmicus, an astrologer of the fourth century, devotes a

---

[1] *Codex Theodosianus*, xi., xxvii., 1.
[2] *Ibid.*, lib. ii., tit. 27.
[3] *Ibid.*, lib. v., tit. 7 and 8.

chapter of his work to revealing combinations of planets that will tell what will be the fate of the child that is exposed. Under certain signs the child will perish through lack of food; under others it will drown; under still another it will be eaten by dogs, and another combination indicated that it would find a saviour and a second father.

In 374, the Emperors Valentinian, Valens, and Gratian declared that the exposure of all infants was punishable, and ordered that parents see to it that their children were fed. The main question that seemed to agitate both the Empire of the East and the Empire of the West was that of the rights of the adoptive parent, as against those who owned the land where the child had been abandoned.

"Let men look to it that they nourish their children. If they expose them, they may be punished in conformity with the law. If other persons take the children up they cannot be reclaimed; as people cannot take again children they have wilfully permitted to perish."

In 391, Valentinian, Theodosius, and Arcadius permitted, by other law, the child sold by its father to become a free man after a short term of servitude, without reimbursing a master.[1]

In 409, Honorius and Theodosius issued an edict in favour of Romans sold to other Romans, limiting the period of slavery to five years. Nevertheless, in 412, Honorius and Theodosius confirmed

[1] *Codex Theodosianus*, chapter iii., title 3.

the law of Constantine concerning the sale of infants purchased or taken up with the knowledge of the bishop of the diocese.

An edict of the emperors maintained the rights of the adoptive parents. The right of the latter to their property was also confirmed in cases where the parent or master willingly and knowingly had allowed the child to be exposed.

Another imperial edict ordered that no newborn could be taken from the place where it had been found without the presence of witnesses. A form was drawn up which was to be signed by the bishop.

In 438, these regulations were collected by Theodosius the Second under the Code that bears his name.

In 451, Valentinian the Third declared that the *nutritor*, or person who had taken up the child, should receive an indemnity, independent of the years of service, and fixed the price to be paid him. The Emperor also declared that those who had sold children to barbarians, or who had purchased a free person for the purpose of transporting him across seas, should be compelled to pay to the *fisc*, six ounces of gold.[1]

Following the preachings of the Fathers, and supplementing and strengthening the laws of the Empire, the Church at various councils, called always for some other purpose, took action and frequently condemned the loose morals of the day.

[1] *Codex Theodosianus.*

Not orations, nor apologies and pleas alone, says Labourt, would have brought about the new point of view among people so hard pressed and so thoroughly imbued with the ideas of another civilization. At the Council of Ancyra, the modern city of Angora, in the year 314, it was decreed that the woman guilty of killing her offspring should be punished by being forbidden to enter a church for the rest of her life, a terrible punishment in those days.

At the Council of Elvira, the first one held in Spain, by some held to have met before 250, but by Tillemont placed in the year 300, a decree limited the period of retribution to ten years, of which two were to be passed in weeping, at the end of which time the recreant mother could receive the sacraments.

At a Council in 546, the period of penitence was reduced to seven years. At the Council of Constantinople, in 588, or 592, the crime was compared to homicide, and finally Sixtus Quintus and Gregory the Fourteenth stated that the culprits should suffer capital punishment.

At the Council of Nicaea, in 325,—the famous council at which a controversy between Bishop Arius and Bishop Athanasius was "settled," with the result that Arius was declared a heretic,—it was prescribed, in Article Seventy of its conclusions, that in each village of the Christian world there should be established an asylum, under the name of the *Xenodocheion*, the object of which was to assist voyageurs, the sick, and the poor. Without doubt, as Labourt suggests, these places became asylums for abandoned children.

The question of the property right was one that the Church had to face in the Council of Vaison, in 442. Frequently .after charitable strangers had taken children off the highways, educated them, and brought them up, their parents or their owners would demand their return. It was a vital question of the day: to whom did these children belong?

The Emperor Constantine had declared that those who received them had a right to them and the Emperor Honorius had added the restriction that the Church must know of the adoption. Many were the arguments and the legal battles that ensued, during which time people were little inclined to rescue the abandoned infants and many perished as victims of the voracity of dogs, many as the victims of hunger and cold.[1]

These conditions were presented to the Council, which ordered the following measures:

"Whoever takes up an abandoned child shall bring him to the Church where that fact will be certified. The following Sunday the priest will announce that a new-born child has been found and ten days will be allowed to the real parents to claim their infant. When these formalities have been complied with, if any one then claims a child or in any way calumniates those who have

[1] Terme et Monfalcon, p. 79.

received it, he will be punished according to the Church laws against homicide."[1]

Ten years later the act of the Council of Vaison was sanctioned at the Council of Arles and again in 505, by the Council of Agde.

It has been said that this was comparatively little when one thinks of this great union of bishops representing not only the interests of religion but "the moral needs of the epoch." On the other hand, any criticism would be unjust that did not take into consideration the fact that it was great progress in the face of great poverty and greater barbarity.[2]

Church and State united in the movement for the protection of the child in the laws of Justinian, who, raised to the throne in 527, published in 529, and with considerable changes in 534, a collection of laws that have immortalized his name, in which the great lawyer Tribonian remade the three other codes, the Gregorian, Hermogenian, and the Theodosian.

Justinian proclaimed absolute liberty for foundling children, declaring that they were not the property of either the parents who exposed them or of those who received them.

One of these laws, promulgated in 553, punished severely those who tried to hold as slaves, children who had been exposed. This law stated expressly

[1] *Acta Conciliorum Parisiis*, 1715. Tome i., p. 1789. Chapters Concilium Vasense, Anno Christi 442, chapters 9 and 10.
[2] Terme et Monfalcon, p. 80.

that all children left at churches or other places were absolutely free. It also stated that the act of exposing a child exceeded the cruelty of an ordinary murder, inasmuch as it struck at the most feeble and the most pitiable.

The imperial edict of 553 invited the Archbishop of Thessalonica and the prefect to give to the foundlings all the help possible and to punish those who disobeyed the injunction with a fine of five livres of gold. In addition, the Justinian Code contained a provision by which a father whose poverty was extreme was allowed to sell his son or his daughter at the moment of birth and to repurchase the infant later. The Emperor also ordered that some organized endeavour be made to take care of children for whom no other provision had been made. Unchanged and little modified, with the exception of those amendments made by the Emperor Leon, the philosopher, these laws and these conditions governed the Eastern Empire from now on until its fall before the arms of the Turks.

CHAPTER XIX

CONDITIONS AMONG THE PEOPLES WHO CONQUERED THE
ROMAN EMPIRE—IRISH SACRIFICED FIRST BORN
—THE WERGELD—THE SALIC LAW—CODE OF THE
VISIGOTHS ON EXPOSED CHILDREN—THEODORIC
AND CASSIODORUS.

WITH Church and State united in defence
of the child's right to live, we turn to
the barbaric hordes that were then en-
filading the Roman civilization. For the first
time in the history of man the religious law was
the same as the civil law, and for the first time in
the history of man both represented human law.

With Diocletian's division of the Empire into
four almost equal parts under two Augusti and
two Cæsars, there was frank acknowledgment that
the great Roman Empire was at an end. With
him, too, ended the fiction of a popular sovereignty.
The Roman Emperor became an Eastern despot.
He was no longer a man of the people easily to
be seen and showing his democracy in frequent
unofficial parade.

He was now a secluded person wearing the dress
of the Orientals, surrounded by servile officials;

THE HOLY FAMILY

(AFTER RUBENS)

(REPRODUCED BY PERMISSION OF MUSEUM OF ART, NEW YORK)

and the Orientalism of the government went further when Constantine, at the farthest limit of Europe, built a new city, Constantinople, named after himself. Nominally it was but to divide with Rome the honours of being the capital; in reality it was to dim the even now fading lustre of the Seven Hills.

From the frontiers of China to the Baltic there came pressing down on the fast disintegrating Roman Empire armies of barbarians. Amid all the disorder, the calamities without number, when civilization, science, and the arts were all obscured, the Church gained strength, its tenets held sway, its humanities were accepted as the conquerors in their turn became the conquered. The Christian religion slowly gripped them all as out of the convulsions of government there was born the modern Europe.

To the Romans and their adopted allies it was a world of terror—to the Christians it was a friendly world, for the barbarians were known to the Church long before they were known to the soldiers who tried to repulse them.

It has been the fashion to decry the value of the check that the Church put on the barbarous tribes in the early part of the Christian era.[1] Up to the very door of the Church there was, it is true, slaughter—there it stopped. Had it not been for the Church upholding what it did of civilization and humanity, it is difficult to say what would

[1] S. A. Dunham, *Europe in the Middle Ages*, p. 8.

18

have been the outcome of the hordes of Ostrogoths, Visigoths, Gephids, Longobards, Vandals,
Burgundians, Franks, and Saxons who, at one time
or another, fell upon Rome.

But from the third century these invaders in
their very triumph came face to face with a moral
force that checked them as no army could, softened
their manners, and uniting their rude strength with
the last remains of the glory of Rome, gave to the
world the civilized nations that now practically
control both hemispheres.

Of the first missionary efforts little is known.
Jesus himself had said, "Go ye therefore and teach
all nations. . . . Teach them to observe all things
whatsoever I have commanded you,"[1] and was
indeed himself the first missionary of the new faith.
Of his immediate followers only three undertook
missionary work.

After the death of Jesus, the Apostles scattered
over the whole world. "Thomas," says Eusebius,
"received Parthia as his alloted region; Andrew
received Scythia, and John, Asia. . . . Peter appears to have preached through Pontus, Galatia,
Bithynia, Cappadocia, and Asia . . . and Paul
spread the Gospel from Jerusalem to Illyricum."[2]

From another source we are told that Matthew
went into Æthiopia, but in the following century
there is little light as to who were the missionaries;
but that they were everywhere successful is shown

[1] Matthew xxviii., 19, 20.
[2] Eusebius, *Ecclesiastical History*, book iii., chapter i.

by the reports of the Roman governors to the emperors. Undisputed claims of Tertullian and Justin also show that the work of conversion, despite the proscriptions, was going on rapidly enough. Ulfilas, "the Apostle of the Goths," translated the Bible into their language in 325; Eusebius, Bishop of Vercelli in 370, made his cathedral the centre of missionary work. Chrysostom trained people in the Gothic language and in missionary work and sent them among the Goths according to Theodoretius.[1]

It was harder work in the West but it was more lasting. From Berins, an islet off the roadstead of Toulon where, in 410 A.D., a Roman patrician, Honoratus, had founded a monastic home, there were sent bishops to Arles, Avignon, Lyons, Troyes, Metz, and Nice, and many other places in southern and western Gaul, all to become the centres of missionary work.[2]

The proselyting spirit among these Frankish bishops gave rise to a great movement in the north. The preaching of Patrick was followed by what has been described as a marvellous burst of enthusiasm; and Celtic enthusiasm was from now to be counted on. Columba, the founder of Iona, was the missionary for the Northern Picts and the Albanian Scots; Aidan for the Northumbrian

---

[1] Theodoretius, *History of the Church*, book iv., chapter xxx.

[2] Smith and Chetam, *Dict. of Ch. Antiq. Missions* (see also Socrates, *Ecc. Hist.*, vii., 30; Ozanam, *Civilisation chez les Francs*, p. 51).

Saxons; Columbanus for the Burgundians of the Vosges; Callich or Gallus for north-eastern Switzerland and Germany; Kilian for Thuringia; Virgilius for Carinthia; Fridolin in Suabia and Alsace; Magnoald founded a monastery in Fingen; Trudpert penetrated as far as the Black Forest, where he was killed.

Among these people there had been a variety of conditions before the coming of, first the Romans, and secondly the Christians. Before the arrival of St. Patrick and the conversion of the natives there is very little doubt that part of the pagan worship included human sacrifice. On a plain in what is now the county of Leitrim which was then called the Magh-Sleacth, or Field of Slaughter, these primeval rites took place.

"There on the night of Samhin, the same dreadful tribute which the Carthaginians are known to have paid to Saturn in sacrificing to him their first-born, was by the Irish offered up to their chief idol, Crom-Cruach."[1]

Of the Gauls and the Germans we learn something from Cæsar and Tacitus, but both are vague enough when it comes to the subject of children. The two people, according to Strabo, were as much alike as brothers.

"The two races have much in common," said Martin, "in their social organization." In Gaul the power of the father was absolute—*viri in uxores sicut in liberos vitæ necisque habent potesta-*

[1] Thomas Moore, *History of Ireland*, vol. i., p. 49.

tem, wrote Cæsar, and Tacitus tells us in *Germanicus* that the husband had assisted in the execution of his adulterous wife by her nearest relatives— a condition that would lead one to believe that there was high regard for the mother of the family, although it has been said that Tacitus in painting the Germans as virtuous as he did[1] was following much along the lines of Fenimore Cooper in painting the Indians a holy pink—he wished to improve the morals of his own countrymen and sacrificed truth as a detaining cargo.

The Germans of the fourth century represented about the period of culture that our American Indians did when the English first arrived in this country.   Unlike the Indians, they had the power to learn, whereas the Indians seemed to be able to learn only the vices of civilization.   Their imagination stirred by the stories that came back to them of the glory of Rome, they were for pressing forward.   With the growing population that made migration necessary, and with the inimical forces pushing them from the rear, the "open road" beckoned them on to Rome.

Before the close of the fourth century the Gospel had been carried to them, especially to those near the Roman border.

We have seen the laws of old Rome become more humane—what were the laws of this later Rome?

Among some of the German tribes, notably

[1] Guizot, *Civilization*, vol. i., p. 429.

among the Frisians, we learn that the father had
the right to kill and expose his children when he
was unable to provide them with nourishment;
but once the child had taken of milk or eaten
honey it could not be killed. The Emperor Julian,
who loved literature more than he loved religion
and has been decorated with the title Apostate,
speaks of a custom of some of the barbarians who
lived on the banks of the Rhine, which consisted
of abandoning the new-born children on the waves
of the river, believing that adulterous children
would drown and legitimate children would
survive.

The Church was here able "to concord the es-
sentials of two bodies of law by discarding the
elements of formalism and egoism in the Roman
law and the hard and barbaric qualities of the
German law; and introduced as governing principles of social and communal life the grave moral
principles which Christ had proclaimed. The
New Testament was the great law, the legislative
ideal for all the Romano-Germanic peoples."[1]

In the semi-barbarian laws that came out as
the result of the blending of their own customs
with the Roman law, the combined product being
softened by the Christian teaching, there is evident always the Germanic idea of the *wergeld* by
which a man paid for a crime, from the smallest
to the greatest. And instead of the *patria potestas*

[1] La Boulaye, *Recherches sur la condition de la femme depuis
les Romains jusque au nos jours.*

we find the *mundium*, this word (hand) being used to describe all classes of protection.

Infanticide is not mentioned as frequently as is abortion.   To the belief that the infant had a soul was traceable this phase of semi-barbarian legislation.

The Franks were not spoken of in history until 240 A.D. (Aurelianus) and Salian Franks whose laws Montesquieu declared were much quoted and seldom read were subdued by Julianus.[1]

According to the Salic law[2] to "kill a child that did not as yet have a name, that is to say one under eight days of age, was to be subject to a fine or *wergeld* of 100 sous or 4000 deniers"[3] xxiii., 4. *Si utero in ventre matris sui occisus fuerit, aut ante quod nomen abait, malb anneando, sunt din. iiiM fac. sol. culp. iud.*

To kill a boy under ten, according to the early manuscripts, meant a fine of 24,000 deniers, while the later manuscripts raised the age to twelve, as there was greater *wergeld* for killing one who was then considered a man.   Oghlou suggests that while it cost but 200 sous to kill an ordinary free man, the price of an infant under twelve was 600

---

[1] Ammian. Marcell., xvii., 8.

[2] Codex, second edition of Hessels and Kern, xxviii., section 4, and the Wolfenbuttel edition as quoted by Garabed Artin Davoud-Oghlou, *Histoire de la législation des Anciens Germains,* vol. i., p. 496.

[3] A sou was worth about 1000 grains of silver and the denier had a weight of about 25 grains of silver. Davoud-Oghlou, vol. i., p. 465.

because "the cowardice of killing a child that had not arrived at the twelfth year appealed to the barbarians." Such an interpretation would be crediting the Salians with a most humanitarian and nineteenth-century point of view. As a matter of fact, the fine for the murder of a child is the same as for the killing of a *sagbaron* (*Dicuntur quosi senatores*).

The words *puer crintus* have been shown by Kern[1] to refer not to the fact that the boy was one of twelve years who had been allowed to wear his hair long, but one who "by right of birth is allowed to wear his hair long in contradistinction to slaves and serfs."[2]

To cut the hair of a boy or girl by force—and apparently against their will—meant a fine of forty-five sous. To kill a free girl before the age of twelve cost 200 sous, after the age of twelve, here given as the age of puberty, meant 600 sous. To kill a woman who was *enceinte* meant a *wergeld* of 700 sous; to strike a woman who was *enceinte* was 200 sous; if the child died, 600 sous, if the woman also died, 900 sous, and if the woman was *in verbo regis*, under the care of the king, 1200 sous.

The Salic law, which was put together by four chosen seigneurs and corrected by Clovis, Child-

---

[1] *Leys Salica*, column 491.

[2] J. F. A. Payre, *Lois des Francs*, pp. 82 and 83. The kings and the nobles wore their hair long, while the plain people wore their hair short, as did the Romans for whom these barbarians had a great contempt.

bert, and Lothair, is also interesting in that it put
a penalty on murders in such a way as to show
that even the unborn child was given a value. A
wergeld of 700 sous was declared against one who
killed a woman who was *enceinte*, and to kill an
unborn child entailed a *wergeld* of 200 sous.

The law of the Allemands, the people who have
passed away but who have left the name by which
the French designate the Germans, differed from
the Salic law in an interesting way.

The tendency and underlying idea of the laws
of the time is well shown in the law of the Angles
which punished the murder of a noble girl *non
nubile* with the same *wergeld* of 600 sous that it
punished the murder of a noble woman who was
no longer able to bear children. The murder of a
woman who was capable of bearing children was
punishable by a *wergeld* three times the size of
this. But the fine for a young girl or *non fecund*
woman of the plain people was only 160 sous.

The Burgundians in their law had no regulation
on either infanticide or abortion. The Ripurian
Francs declared strongly against both in a law
that imposed a fine of 100 sous on "any one
who killed a new-born child that had not been
named."

The code of the Visigoths which was arranged
after the middle of the fifth century is the severest
of all in its penalties as to abortion and those in
any way responsible for it.

In the matter of exposed children the law went

into details. Parents could not sell children, it states, nor put them in pawn.

"Whoever nourished a child that had been exposed, gained the value of a slave, which had to be paid by the parents of the exposed child when it was reclaimed by its parents. If the parents did not present themselves but they should be found out, they were forced to pay and might be sent into exile. If they did not have the means to pay, the one who had exposed the child became a slave in his place to the rescuer.

"If a slave expose a child unknown to the master and the master swear that he was ignorant of the act, the person who rescues and brings up the child can recover only one fourth of its value; but if the exposure has been with the master's knowledge, the rescuer can recover the full value of the child."[1]

Those to whom a child had been given away to bring up received an agreed price during the first ten years of the child. After that the law declared that the service of the child was sufficient compensation for its nurture—an interesting sidelight on the time when a child became amenable to the "laws of industry."

In these laws of the Visigoths it is easy to see the influence of *Codex Theodosianus*.

Among the Anglo-Saxons there was a law (*domas*) of Ina, King of Wessex, which declared

[1] Dugour, p. 93; Davoud-Oghlou, vol. i., p. 613; Lallemand, p. 91.

EVENING RECREATION CENTRE FOR BOYS, NEW YORK CITY

MEETING OF AN '' EVENING CENTRE,'' NEW YORK CITY

that the nourishment for a child exposed and recovered should be fixed at six sous for the first year, twelve sous for the second year, and thirty for the third. Another law of the same peoples, ascribed to Alfred, made it necessary for the person in charge of a foundling at the time of its death, to establish the fact that the death had occurred in a perfectly natural way, a sage precaution and one centuries ahead of the time.

Theodoric, or Dietrich as Charles Kingsley called him to the chagrin of Max Müller and others, as King of the Ostrogoths made an interesting ruling on the subject of the freedom of children in the year 500. We learn of this through his secretary, Cassiodorus, for, like other kings, the Ostrogoth was wise enough to have the cleverest literary man of his day to write his letters and leave behind his own approved account of his reign.

According to this law, when a father because of poverty was obliged to sell his child, the child did not therefore lose his liberty.[1]

Showing how nimble was not only the literary talent but the spirit of Cassiodorus, it is interesting to read in another part of the writings of the same author a rescript sent in the name of King Athalaric, the successor of Theodoric and his grandson, to Severus, the governor of Lucania. As a picture

---

[1] "*Parentes qui cogente necessitate filios suos alimentorum gratia vendiderint ingenuiati eorum non pare juicant. Homo enim liber pretio nullo æstimatur.*" Edictum Theodorici, art. 94.

of the times that we are accustomed to think of
as dark, as well as an example of the dexterous
literary skill of Cassiodorus, the letter is worth
printing, for while it takes a most reactionary
stand on the matter of the sale of children it suggests the epistle of Trajan to Pliny.

"KING ATHALARIC TO SEVERUS, Vir Spectabilis.

"We hear that the rustics are indulging in dis-
orderly practices, and robbing the market-people
who come down from all quarters to the chief fair
of Lucania on the day of St. Cyprian.   This must
by all means be suppressed, and your Respectabil-
ity should quietly collect a sufficient number of
the owners and tenants of the adjoining farms to
overpower these freebooters and bring them to
justice.   Any rustic or other person found guilty
of disturbing the fair should be at once punished
with the stick, and then exhibited with some mark
of infamy upon him.

"This fair, which according to the old superstition was named Leucothea (after the nymph)
from the extreme purity of the fountain at which
it is held, is the greatest fair in all the surrounding
country.   Everything that industrious Campania,
or opulent Bruittii, or cattle-breeding Calabria,
or strong Apulia produces, is there to be found exposed for sale, on such reasonable terms that no
buyer goes away dissatisfied.   It is a charming
sight to see the broad plains filled with suddenly
reared houses formed of leafy branches inter-

twined: all the beauty of the most leisurely built city, and yet not a wall to be seen. There stand ready boys and girls; with the attractions which belong to their respective sexes and ages, whom not captivity but freedom sets a price upon. These are with good reason sold by their parents, since they themselves gain by their servitude. For one cannot doubt that they are benefited even as slaves (or servants?), by being transferred from the toil of the fields to the service of the cities.

"What can I say of the bright and many coloured garments? what of the sleek well-fed cattle offered at such a price as to tempt any purchaser?

"The place itself is situated in a wide and pleasant plain, a suburb of the ancient city of Cosilinum, and has received the name of Marcilianum from the founder of these sacred springs.

"And this is in truth a marvellous fountain, full and fresh, and of such transparent clearness that when you look through it you think you are looking through air alone. Choice fishes swim about in the pool, perfectly tame, because if anyone presumes to capture them he soon feels the Divine vengeance. On the morning which precedes the holy night (of St. Cyprian), as soon as the priest begins to utter the baptismal prayer, the water begins to rise above its accustomed height. Generally it covers but five steps of the well, but the brute element, as if preparing itself for miracles, begins to swell, and at last covers two steps more, never reached at any other time of the year.   Truly a stupendous miracle, that streams of water should thus stand still or increase at the sound of the human voice, as if the fountain itself desired to listen to the sermon.

"Thus hath Lucania a river Jordan of her own. Wherefore, both for religion's sake and for the profit of the people, it behoves that good order should be kept among the frequenters of the fair, since in the judgment of all, that man must be deemed a villain who would sully the joys of such happy days."[1]

[1] Thomas Hodgkin, *The Letters of Cassiodorus*, book viii., letter 33.

CHAPTER XX

IN the Eastern Empire it was always a fight
with the Church on the one hand and barbarian customs on the other for the humanization of the rapidly developing peoples. We may
now look at the Dark Ages in a very different
spirit from that which animated our fathers. We
now know that whatever may have been the faults
of the priests or the rulers, the world was making
progress, and new and inherently strong peoples
were developing as fast as they could assimilate
a superior civilization.[1]

The Church, very early in the history of the
Christian era, became the avowed protector of the
parentless children and it soon became a custom
to confide infants to the Church when mothers felt
that they were unable to raise their offspring.

[1] Terme et Monfalcon, *Hist. des Enfants Trouvés*, p. 28.

The gain made by the Church by this step was immeasurable, for however much those opposed to Christianity might argue, the onward march was irresistible when religion rested itself on the mother instinct and, without accusation or attempted retribution, willingly assumed the ties that maternity was obliged to forego.

By the door of the churches it became the custom to have a marble receptacle in which mothers placed the children that they were forced to abandon. The newly born was received by the *matricularii* or by the priest, who, following the form prescribed, asked those who assisted at the adoption ceremonies if there was any known person who would consent to take charge of the infant. These formalities had to receive the sanction of the bishop. Not infrequently the priest succeeded in finding among the parishioners of his church someone who would adopt the infant, but if he did not, the church always assumed the responsibility and took care of the orphan. In some places the children that had been abandoned by their mothers were, by the order of the bishop, shown at the door of the church for ten days following their abandonment, and if any one recognized and was able to declare who the parents were, he made such a declaration to the ecclesiastical authorities—a dangerous custom as many unfortunate though innocent people discovered.

In the case where some person not officially connected with the church assumed the responsibility of bringing up the abandoned child, such a person (*nutricarii*) received with the charge, a document wherein the fact of adoption was set forth, the circumstances under which the child was found, and the right of the adoptive parent to hold the child henceforth as a slave. In this connection it must be remembered that the Code of Justinian, which had put an end to this custom in the East, had no force in the West. The result was that in the European States which succeeded to the Western Roman Empire it was an almost general custom that abandoned children grew up in slavery. Indeed, so general was this custom that even the Church placed the newly born as among its assets, the church of Seville in Spain enumerating the number of abandoned children taken in as among its revenues.

At the Council of Rouen, held in the seventh century, the priests of each diocese were enjoined to inform their congregations that women who were delivered in secret might leave their infants at the door of the church. The church thereby attended to the immediate care of the newly born, and while the fact that the children were brought up in slavery was bad, it was a great improvement over the conditions in Rome and Greece. At least, if brought up in slavery, they were brought up with no criminal purpose and as far as the ecclesiastical authorities were able to regulate their lives, they were not condemned to lives of immorality.

19

So bad, however, were the conditions in the seventh century, and so miserable and poor were the people, that despite the example and the preachings of the Church, thousands of children were thrown on the highways or left in deserted places to perish of starvation. Among the Gauls, before the domination of the Franks, the heads of families that lacked food, or the means to obtain it, took to the market their children and sold them as they would the veriest chattels.[1] This traffic was not only common but it took place publicly, and not only in ancient France but in Germany, in Flanders, in Italy, and in England. Northern Europe was colder, more swampy, and more desolate then than it is now and across the bleak and uncultivated country, country such as one finds nowhere in Europe today but on the professional and bleak battlefields of Bulgaria and Servia, the half-starved peasants tramped, each with his group of children to place on sale when the coasts of Italy or France were reached.

It was in this way that Saint Bathilde, afterward the wife of King Clovis II., became the slave of the mayor of the palace, Archambault. Bought by the latter, she was working as a slave in his household when the King saw her and fell in love with her.[2]

Moved by such great misery and such odious traffic, holy men went, purse in hand, to the places

[1] Terme et Monfalcon, p. 84.
[2] Lerousse, *Bathilde*.

where these infants were being sold and purchased the unfortunates, giving them later their liberty. In this manner, Saint Eunice was purchased by an Abbé du Berry and Saint Thean by Saint Eloi.

The poverty led to even worse crimes than the selling of their own children for when it was found by the shiftless and impoverished that they could sell their own children and the foundlings that they picked up, not infrequently they robbed more fortunate parents of children that were being well taken care of.

Similar distress and want had led to similar conditions in the fifth century. In 449 A.D., the times were so hard and the people were in such a famished condition in Italy and Gaul that parents sold their children to middlemen even though they knew the children were to be resold to the Vandals in Africa. Two years later Valentinian broke up this practice, declaring that the person who sold a free person for the purpose of having that person sold to the barbarians would be fined six ounces of gold. [1]

This traffic was carried to such an excess in the British Islands that it became the principal object of an apostolic mission of Gregory who became Pope in 590.

"Our Divine Redeemer," he wrote, "has delivered us from all servitude and has given unto us our original liberty. Let us imitate his example

[1] Lebeau, *Hist. du Bas Empire*, vol. vi., p. 179.

by freeing from slavery those men who are free by the laws of nature."

The attitude toward children in England under the Anglo-Saxon kings[1] is shown by the fact that a boy's accountability, his capability of bearing arms and of the management of his property began, according to the earlier laws, in his tenth, but according to the laws of Æthelstan, in his twelfth year.[2] "The accountability of children was extended even to the infant in the cradle, whereby, in the case of theft committed by the father, they, like those of mature age, were consigned to slavery, but this cruel practice was by a law of Cnut strictly forbidden.[3] This premature majority of the Anglo-Saxon youth accounts for the early accession to the throne of some of the kings, as Edward the Martyr, who was crowned in his thirteenth year. Majority at the age of ten is not mentioned in any other Germanic laws, excepting in favour of the young testator, or the son whose father could not or would not support him. The beginning of the thirteenth year as that of majority is strictly and universally Germanic."[4]

"The doctrines of the Church," say Terme and

[1] *The History of England under the Anglo-Saxon Kings*, vol. i., p. 414, translated by Benj. Thorpe.

[2] Laws of Hloth. and Ead., vi. Ine, vii. Æthels., v., i. By the Salic law also (tit. xxvi., art. 6) twelve was fixed as the age of responsibility.

[3] See Laws of Cnut, lxxvii.

[4] Thorpe, p. 414.

Monfalcon, "were indeed admirable—they breathed
the purest, the finest morality and the most ardent
love of humanity, but they were unable to prevail
against the ignorance of the people and the barbarity of their morals."

Coming to the first attempts at organized effort
to save children by the Church we find that Article
70 of the Council of Nicaea instructed the bishop
to establish in each city a place to which travellers,
the sick and the poor, might appeal for aid and
shelter. The *Xenodocheion*, as it was called, is
to this day the word for "hotel" in modern
Greece, where the traveller in Europe will conclude
there is little evidence of improvement since the
ecclesiastical foundation. These places were also
used as the asylums for children, a fact that led
them to be called *Brephotrophia.* [1]

In the West a similar movement sprang up, and
in the life of Saint Gour, contemporary of Childe-
bert, it is said that at Trèves there was something
like a systematic endeavour to protect children.
A great obscurity hangs around this foundation,
and it is equally difficult to determine positively
what is the exact character of the institution
ascribed to Saint Marmbœuf, who died in Angers
in 654.

Of the efforts of Datheus, however, there are
no doubts, though interesting is the fact that no
biographical encyclopædia contains even his name.
He was Archbishop of Milan, and the first insti-

[1] Gaillard, p. 83.

tution to take care of helpless children was founded
by him in 787.

"An enervating and sensual life," declared
Datheus in founding the asylum, "leads many
astray. They commit adultery and do not dare
show the fruits in public and therefore put them
to death. By depriving the children of baptism
they send them to hell. These horrors would not
take place if there existed an asylum where the
adulterer could hide her shame, but now they
throw the infants in the sewers or the rivers and
many are the murders committed on the new-born
children as the result of this illicit intercourse.

"Therefore, I, Datheus, for the welfare of my
soul and the souls of my associates, do hereby
establish in the house that I have bought next to
the church, a hospital for foundling children. My
wish is that as soon as a child is exposed at the
door of a church that it will be received in the
hospital and confided to the care of those who will
be paid to look after them. . . . These infants
will be taught a trade and my wish is that when
they arrive at the age of eight years they will be
free from the shackles of slavery and free to come
or go wherever they will."[1]

In 1380 a similar institution was opened in Venice,
and in Florence in 1421. There is no doubt that
similar institutions were most frequent in the
fifteenth century. Pontanus, a writer of that

[1] Muratori, *Antiquates italicæ medii ævi*, Mediolani, 1740,
vol. iii., p. 587.

age, speaks of having seen nine hundred children
in the one at Naples, and openly expresses his admiration for the liberal education that they received and the care bestowed on them by their
teachers. [1]

The most purely religious institute appears to
have been, according to the able Gaillard, that
of the Bourgognes [2] in imitation of the charity of
St. Marthe in her house in Bethany. An order,
that of the *chanoines réguliers du Saint Esprit*, was
founded, or at least encouraged by Guy of Montpellier about the end of the twelfth century for
the express purpose of caring for poor and abandoned children. The same institution is also
said to have had for its founder, Olivier de la
Crau in 1010.   In any case it was not until 1188,
eight years after the foundation of the order
ascribed to Guy of Montpellier, that the hospital
of Marseilles was established.

The historians of Languedoc [3] do not justify
the assumption that this same Guy was the son
of the Count of Montpellier, and all that we know
is that "Brother Guy" or "Master Guy," as he
was differently called, [4] apparently founded an
asylum for sick men and abandoned children.

The success of this order was immediate. In
1197, Bernard de Montlaur and his wife left a

[1] Pontani, *Opera*, Basil, 1566, t. i., chapter xix.
[2] Gaillard, vol. i., p. 85.
[3] *Histoire de Languedoc.*
[4] Ramcle, p. 34.

substantial donation to the Hospital of Saint Esprit at Montpellier, and to Guy, its founder.[1] Public approval was followed by official approval, for the Senate of Marseilles, or the Honourable Council, as it was called, held its meetings in the hospital founded there by Guy in 1188 and began its deliberations always with a discussion about the condition of the poor.[2]

Following the efforts of Guy of Montpellier, at Montpellier and at Marseilles, the movement, under the auspices of the *hospitaliers* of Saint Esprit, spread so rapidly that before the end of the century there were institutions at Rome,[3] one at Bergliac, and one at Troyes, and others in different places.[4] The order founded by Guy was given the approval of the Holy See, and its founder was called to Rome by Innocent III. and placed in charge of the house of Santa Maria in Sassia, where the Pope wished the same spirit that had marked Guy's own institution at Montpellier. Guy died in Rome, 1208.

The house of Santa Maria in Sassia to which Guy was called was attached to the church of that name which had been founded by Gna, king of the later Saxons, in 715. It had undergone many disastrous changes, but in 1198 Innocent III., at

[1] Ramcle, p. 360.
[2] Gaillard, vol. i., p. 85.   *Bulletin Ferussac, pact de la Geog.*, t. xvi., p. 66.
[3] Ramcle, p. 34.   *Bullarium Romanorum*, t. i., p. 74.
[4] See Bull of Innocent III., 28th of April, 1198.

FILLING CHRISTMAS BASKETS FOR POOR CHILDREN—MOTHERS' HELPING HAND CLUB, NEW YORK CITY

his own expense, had it renovated and repaired for the sick and poor of Rome. In 1204, moved by the frequency with which the fishermen of the Tiber found in their nets the bodies of children that had been thrown into the river, the Pope dedicated part of the hospital to the care of abandoned children, and it was to this institution that Guy of Montpellier was called.

The humane movement spread rapidly, generally under at least the nominal guidance of the Order of Saint Esprit. Many institutions, however, were founded in the name of Saint Esprit where little attention was paid to children.

The institution at Embeck[1] founded in 1274 made a special work of taking care of abandoned children in the name of Saint Esprit. We come now to the name of Enrad Fleinz,[2] that bourgeois of Nuremberg, who in 1331 founded in his natal town the first hospital where not only children might be left, but where women might go to be delivered, without regard to whether the offspring were legitimate or not. This, too, was in the name of Saint Esprit, and in the year 1362, a similar asylum for orphans was founded in Paris.

It was indeed under the auspices of this order that the movement which began with the imperial *Brephotrophia* in the sixth century grew, until the various institutions of one sort or another intended to prevent the outright murder of child-

[1] Beckmann, *Histoire des Inventions et Découvertes*, tome iv.
[2] *Dictionnaire des Sciences Medicales*, "Enfans Trouvés."

ren or their abandonment in deserted places were
dependent, not on the humanity of any one man
or group of men, but on the new-born spirit that
was then spreading throughout Europe and that
continued to spread even when individualism and
materialism as ruling forces had supplanted religion and asceticism.   The history of charity,
which, as Lecky says, is yet to be written, will
doubtless reveal, when it comes to be written, the
various unappreciated factors that went to produce
the humane movement.

Some idea of how rapidly these institutions had
multiplied may be obtained from a bull of Nicholas IV., containing a long enumeration of the various foundations, which includes places in Italy,
Sicily, Germany, England, France, and Spain.[1]

Besides those enumerated by the Pope, there
were however other institutions springing up
where, either as an adjunct to hospital work or as
an independent work itself, children were being
cared for.   As one of the original and most schol-
arly writers on this phase of the subject has pointed
out, it is difficult to make positive statements
about these foundations, for the men interested
were intent on their work rather than on leaving
a record of it behind.   Perhaps in this connection,
some future historian, in viewing the voluminous
charitable records of our day, will assume that
"social" egotism has been well saddled, and made

[1] Ramcle, 38.   *Bullarium Romanorum*, Nicholas IV.

SAINT VINCENT DE PAUL, FOUNDER OF THE FIRST PERMANENT ASYLUM
FOR CHILDREN IN FRANCE

to do more than the work of a timely charitable impulse.

The conditions that led to the crusade of Vincent of Paul antedated that philanthropist by several hundred years. Where the religious spirit had failed to arouse interest in the problem of the welfare of parentless children, the large cities of Europe were themselves forced to take some action. Milan, in 1168, on the prayer of the Cardinal Galdinus, founded a hospital (which would indicate that the institution founded by Datheus had either fallen into disuse or was inadequate) and Venice in 1380 followed the example of Milan, while the magnificent hospital for foundling children in Florence (Spidale degl' Innocenti) was founded, after a long deliberation in open council, on October 25, 1421.

Included in these governmental or municipal movements is that of St. Thomas of Villeneuve, Archbishop of Valence, who created an asylum in his own palace at the beginning of the fifteenth century, and gave orders that no children presented there should be turned away.

The Hotel-Dieu de Notre Dame de Pitié of Lyons, which by letters patent of 1720 was declared to be the oldest hospital of France, commenced in 1523 the same work, and in that year is recorded as having received nine children. On February 25, 1530, François the First recognized the right of the institution to take in these children.

In 1596 the city of Amsterdam began to make
provision for the abandoned children.

The beginning of the movement in Paris, we
learn, was the result of the terrible conditions
that followed the war in 1360, 1361, and 1362.[1]
Poverty and misery were everywhere, and a large
number of orphans practically lived and died in
the streets, says Breuil in his *Antiquités de Paris*.
Various charitable people took in some of these
unfortunates, the Hotel-Dieu being overrun; but,
as the conditions were but little ameliorated, on
February 7, 1362, a group of citizens went to the
"Reverend father in God, Messire Jean de Meu-
lant, 88th Bishop of Paris," and discussed with
him the frightful conditions of the poor boys and
girls of Paris. The evils attending the homeless
condition of the latter were especially considered.
We are told that the result of the conference was
that the Bishop gave them permission to institute
and erect a hospital of Saint Esprit and bestowed
on each one of the conferees forty days' indulgence.

The institution that arose as a result of this
conference has been criticized as being narrow in
its purpose, inasmuch as the rules declared that
only legitimate children, born of parents in Paris,
were to be admitted; but the restriction, it must
be understood, was necessary, in view of the small
funds in hand.

But humanitarian feeling was growing; and
people were beginning to be proud of being

[1] Ramcle, p. 40.

thoughtful and kind.   It was no longer a mark of superiority to be lustful of blood.   Botterays, in a Latin poem on Paris,[1] spoke of the splendid way in which the orphan children of Paris were brought up, referring to the Hospital of Saint Esprit and the House of the Enfants-Dieu. After long years of nominal acquiescence in its teachings, the barbarians of the North were really beginning to accept the Christianity of Christ.

[1] Cited by de Breuil.

CHAPTER XXI

CRUELTY TO CHILDREN IN THE SIXTEENTH AND SEVEN-
TEENTH CENTURY—ATTEMPT AT REGULATION
—DEFORMING CHILDREN FOR MOUNTEBANK PUR-
POSES—ANECDOTE OF VINCENT DE PAUL—HIS
WORK AND HIS SUCCESS.

FROM Datheus to Vincent de Paul the general
history of the child in Europe moves as
from one mountain peak to another with
a long valley of gloom in between. Datheus has
received no credit; Vincent de Paul has been justly
recognized as a deserving contemporary of that
list of brilliant men who went to make up the
Golden Age of France. Golden Age that it was,
with its highly polished manners, there, under the
reign of the elegant Mazarin and the delicate Anne
of Austria, it was no uncommon sight to see a
child lying dead on the pavements, while others
died of misery and hunger under the very eyes of
the passers-by. Not a day passed, say the chron-
iclers, when the men who had charge of the sewers
or the police did not draw out at least the body
of one child.

At the beginning of the seventeenth century
Europe, and France especially, was war-ridden.

During the sixteenth century, the religious and charitable impulses had suffered, first through the national war, then by the factional wars, and finally by religious wars.

"The religious war," said the historian of Languedoc,[1] "almost entirely destroyed the Hospital of Montpellier . . . and even the order of Saint Esprit was dying out throughout France."

It was a curious and disjointed society, that of the France of that day. Kingdoms there were within the royal domain; the laws of the large city frequently clashing with those of the province within which it was located; here and there provinces following their own laws rather than the laws of the kingdom itself. In some provinces the Church dominated; in others the nobles; elsewhere, the two classes were beginning to melt into the body of the nation which occasionally overrode both.[2]

At Aix, for instance, it was the custom to place the abandoned child in a religious home where, as in the rest of Provence, the unknown bastard was charged to the nearest hospital. Practically the same law was observed in Bretagne.

At Poitiers, a decree on September 15, 1579, "condemning the provision by which religious orders nourished infants found at their door," ordered that the monasteries and ecclesiastic chapters of the place should be called on to regu-

---

[1] *Histoire de Languedoc*, tome iii., p. 43.
[2] Ramcle, p. 63.

late their contributions to the support of the children.

But as a rule the great nobles were obliged to take care of the foundlings abandoned within their jurisdiction. In the origin of the fiefs, the bastards had been set down as *épaves* (waifs), and the interpreters of the law (*jurisconsults*) had decided that the lord had no right to refuse to take care of the *épaves*. The parliaments too took the view that, inasmuch as the *seigneur* profited by all deaths that occurred and succeeded to all titles in the case of disinheritance within his domain, he should accept the liability for the care of the unknown children found within their domain.

Of the many decrees which touch on this important point, the oldest is that of the Parliament of Paris in the year 1547. Many other *arrêts* followed, until on September 3, 1667, the following, in the interest of the special hospitals, declared that:

"All the *seigneurs* (*hauts jusiiciers*) will be held responsible for the expense and nourishment of all infants whose parents are unknown, and who are found exposed on their lands and taken to hospitals."

This regulation, as Ramcle says, failed in its purpose, for it was not possible to force what was considered charity on the none too generous nobles. The laws were evaded, and each community tried to send to its neighbours the unfortunate infants it should have guarded.

The mortality of infants increased, and as in Rome in the days of the Empire, mothers threw their children into the sewers or left them on the highways. Those less inhuman left them at the doors of the hospitals, where, during the winter, in the morning, they were frequently taken in more dead than alive.

Of course, the laws against these abandonments were promptly enforced—the unfortunate women were easily punished. A girl who killed her offspring was hung, and others who were caught leaving children in solitary places were whipped and disgraced in the cities and villages where they lived.

By an edict of Henry II., under penalty of punishment, a woman *enceinte* was obliged to declare her condition; and to add to this bungling legislative effort, she was obliged to tell who the guilty man was, the maxim *creditur virgini* being accepted everywhere. The attempts at curing the ills failed, for, while the intentions of the legislators were undoubtedly honest, they only exposed shameless conditions, made the unfortunate suffer even more, brought ruin to many honest families, and gain to shameless women only. The number of children abandoned and murdered in defiance of the regulations increased instead of decreasing.

At this time there came an individual effort to better things, by a woman whose name is not even known and whose efforts at a noble work have, owing to the actions of her servants, been much misinterpreted.

20

Living in a house in the Cité de Saint-Landry, Paris, with two servants, she received every morning the infants that the soldiers (or police) had collected during the night. So many were eventually turned over to her, that she was unable to feed them, and many died in her own house for lack of food. In the crowded conditions we are also told a selection[1] was made and some of the children were exposed again, or at least they were turned over to some charitable or interested person who would accept them. The care of the children devolving finally on the two servants, many of them are said to have perished from the drugs they were given to keep them quiet. The availability of children as beggars led the servants to look on them as a means of money making, and they were sold for various cruel and evil purposes, a condition that eventually led to the reform undertaken by Vincent de Paul.

The fact that they frequently fell into the hands of magicians, mountebanks, and pedlars, who deformed them in order to make them of assistance in earning a livelihood, is attested by the biographer of Vincent.

"Returning from one of his missions," says Maury, "Vincent de Paul, whom I have dared to call almost the visible angel of God, found under the walls of Paris one of these infants, in the hands of a beggar, who was engaged in deforming the

[1] *Rapport fait àl 'Académie Royale des Sciences.* Par MM. Dumeril et Coquebert-Monbret. Paris, 1825, p. x.

limbs of the child. Although almost overcome
with horror, he ran to the savage with that in-
trepidity with which the virtuous man always at-
tacks crime.

"'Barbarian,' he cried, 'how you deceive me—
from a distance I took you for a man!'

"He snatched the victim from its persecutor,
carried it in his arms across Paris, gathered a
crowd about him and called on them to witness
the brutality of the day and place in which they
lived. A few days later he had founded his first
institution for children, and the cause of children
had enrolled one of its noblest champions."

In order to thoroughly understand the situation,
a number of charitable women under the guidance
of Madame Legas, niece of the Lord Chancellor
Marillac,[1] went to the house in the Cité de Saint-
Landry and studied the question from the inside
of the house. Their horror at the things they
saw led them to declare that the children mas-
sacred by Herod were fortunate in comparison
with the condition of the orphans of Paris.[2] As
it was impossible to take charge of all the children
then in the Cité de Saint-Landry twelve children
were taken, and in 1638, under the care of Madame
Legas and some charitable women, a house was
opened for them in the Faubourg Saint-Victor.
As they were able to enlarge the scope of their

[1] *Considérations sur les Enfants Trouvés*, Benoiston de Chateauneuf, p. x.
[2] Gaillard, p. 90.

institution, more and more children were taken
care of; the enthusiasm of these women ran so
high under the glowing example of Vincent,
that even in the dead of night in the cold corners,
they would be found going about the streets of
Paris, into the worst and least lighted sections,
doing police duty, gathering the unfortunate
victims, and carrying them to the house in the
Faubourg Saint-Victor.[1]

In the course of time, sufficient interest had
developed in this work so that enough money was
forthcoming to enlarge the scope.   Vincent gathered together the pious women who had acted as
his assistants and addressed to them that *tou-
chante allocution*, sometimes quoted as a model of
eloquence.[2]   The house in the Faubourg Saint-
Victor was soon found to be too small, and
the Château de Bicêtre was obtained from the
king.

The place was not found suitable on account of
the *vivacité de l'air* and the children were transferred to the Faubourg Saint-Lazare, then in
1672 to the Cité, near Notre Dame, where they
remained up to the Revolution.   Then they were
assigned the ancient *abbaye* of Port Royal and the
maison de l'Oratoire, located in the southern part
of Paris.

The success of the new undertaking was so
great that even Louis XIII. became interested and

[1] Gaillard, p. 90.
[2] *Id.,,* p. 90.   Chateauneuf.

donated four thousand francs per year to the charity.   Inasmuch as in the long history of the child's fight for a place in the government, this was the first recognition by a government since the Roman emperors, it is interesting to read Louis's own statement in the preamble of the letters patent relating to this gift:

"Having been informed by persons of great piety, that the little attention which has been given up to the present to the nourishing and care of the parentless children exposed in the city and outskirts of Paris has been the cause of death, and even has it been known that they have been sold for evil purposes, and this having brought many ladies to take care of these children, who have worked with so much zeal and charitable affection that their zeal is spreading, and wishing so much to do what is possible under the present circumstances,[1] we have," etc.

The example of Louis was followed in 1641 by his widow, Anne of Austria, who made an annual gift of 8000 francs.   She had become regent and, speaking in the name of the young King, said that "imitating the piety and the charity of the late King, which are truly royal virtues, he adds to this first gift, another annual gift of 8000 francs. Thanks to what has already been given and the charity of individuals, the greater number of the

[1] At that time Louis was at war with Germany in the Pays-Bas and in Cologne, and the conspiracy of Cinq-Mars had just been discovered.

infants rescued have been raised, and there are now more than four hundred living."

In June, 1670, Louis XIV. made the children's hospital one of the institutions of Paris, and authorized it to discharge the functions and enjoy the privileges of such an institution.

"As there is no duty more natural," he declared, "and none that conforms more to the idea of Christian charity than to care for the unfortunate children who are exposed—their feebleness and their misfortune making them doubly worthy of our compassion . . . considering also that their protection and safeguarding is to our advantage inasmuch as some of them may become soldiers, others workmen, inhabitants of the colonies," etc.[1]

The edict declared that while the expenses of the institution had reached forty thousand francs a year, the royal donation could not exceed twelve thousand francs, and the King exhorted the women of charity who had done so much, to continue their notable work.

This royal recognition of the great institution at Paris was not without evil effect in the provinces. The nobles and the civic authorities of rural communities, wishing to get rid of the burden of the infants deserted within their jurisdiction, had the unfortunates taken to Paris.[2] They were usually carried there by men who were driving in on other business, and as many stops were

[1] Terme et Monfalcon, p. 100.
[2] Gaillard, p. 92.

made between the starting point and the destination, and as the drivers were more interested in other things than in the infant baggage, for which they were paid in advance, the mortality greatly increased.

"There was hardly a town in the kingdom," said Latyone,[1] "where abandoned children were admitted freely and without information being requested. In the towns that were not too far from Paris, they were carried thirty and forty leagues, at the risk of having them die on the way; and the hospital at Paris was overcrowded and in debt."

This condition of affairs led to a new law, after a report which declared that of two thousand infants carried to Paris from the provinces, in all sorts of weather, by public vehicles without care or protection, three quarters had died within three months. The new law decreed that any wagoner bringing an infant to Paris to expose it would be fined one thousand livres. Inasmuch as the rule was made in the interest of the children, it was also decreed that abandoned children must be brought to the nearest hospital, and if that hospital declared that it had not enough funds to support the foundlings, the royal treasury might be drawn on.

[1] Curzon, p. 11.

CHAPTER XXII

RISE OF FACTORY SYSTEM—THE CHILD A CHARGE ON
THE STATE—CHILDREN ACTUALLY SLAVES UNDER
FACTORY SYSTEM—REFORM OF 1833—OASTLER
AGAINST THE CHILD SLAVERY—"JUVENILE LABOUR
IN FACTORIES IS A NATIONAL BLESSING"

THE cannibalistic stage has passed and the
day of sacrifice has passed—no longer is
the child frankly a convenience nor is its
life, as a result of past economic stress, a lightly
considered trifle to be tossed into the cauldron of
religious ceremony. Philosophy, humanity, civilization, and religion have combined to make the
life of the child safe.

With what result?

The general belief that children were not regularly employed until the middle of the last century, when the factory system arose, had led to the
equally erroneous belief that it was in the factory
where the industrial abuse of children was first
practised. In France where there was little industrial use for children in the large centres of
population, where in other words children did not
pay, the problem of modern humanity was to
save infants from exposure and death. In Eng-

land where there was an industrial use for them from early times, and where from the earliest times there are records of their abuse, there was no necessity for measures to protect them from infanticidal tendencies. But it is in England that we must study the ill-treatment of children that was brought about by the desire to make them useful.

The industrial records of the Middle Ages contain but few references[1] to children, for the adults were busy with their own troubles. One of the first of these notices was an order issued by the famous Richard Whittington, in 1398, and, although it is mixed with other considerations, it shows the human spark. It reads:

"ORDINANCES OF THE HURERS.

"*22 Richard II., A.D. 1398. Letter-Book H., fol. cccxviii. (Norman French).*

"ON the 20th day of August, in the 22d year, etc., the following Articles of the trade of Hurers were by Richard Whityngtone, Mayor, and the Aldermen, ordered to be entered.—

"In the first place,—that no one of the said trade shall scour a *cappe* or *hure*, or anything pertaining to *scouryng*, belonging to the said trade, in any open place: but they must do this in their own houses; seeing that some persons in the said

---

[1] L. F. Salzman, *English Industries of the Middle Ages*, p. 229.

trade have of late sent their apprentices and journeymen as well as children of tender age and others, down to the water of Thames and other exposed places, and amid horrible tempests, frosts, and snows, to the very great scandal, as well of the good folks of the said trade, as of the City aforesaid. And also, because of that divers persons, and pages belonging to lords, when they take their horses down to the Thames, are oftentimes wrangling with their said apprentices and journeymen; and they are then on the point of killing one another, to the very great peril that seems likely to ensue therefrom."[1]

In the eleventh and twelfth centuries, when the peasants were the villeins of the owners of the land and held their small farms in return for the work done, the work of children was contracted for, "the lord very frequently demanding the labour of the whole family, with the exception of the housewife."[2]

Nearly all the trades and manufactures in the Middle Ages were under the control of the guilds, so that almost all of the children working, excepting those on farms or in domestic service, came under their supervision. The attitude of the guilds toward child labour is shown in the regulations of the apprenticeships, but this interest was mainly industrial, for in regulating the work of

[1] *Memorials of London and London Life*, ed. by H. T. Riley, p. 549.

[2] W. J. Ashley, *The English Economic History*, p. 9.

the children they protected their members from cheap labour and at the same time, by their supervision over the work of the rising generation, saw that the guild's reputation for the proper kind of labour was kept up and prices therefore held to a desirable level.[1]

At the same time there was a religious side to the guilds, a strong religious side, and while everything they did, such as the prohibition of night work (not out of consideration of the health of the workers but because it might lead to bad work),[2] had a purely industrial aspect, there is no doubt that this social and religious side developed in the guilds and their members an outlook on the broader and more humane aspects of their own place in society. The custom of not permitting a man to employ other than his own wedded wife and his own daughter was not humanitarian in its intention but its effect could not be other than beneficial.

"No one of the said trade," said the ordinances of the Braelers (makers of braces) in 1355, "shall be so daring as to work at his trade at night . . . also, that no one of the said trade shall be so daring as to set any woman to work in his trade, other than his wedded wife, or his daughter."[3]

In 1562 the Statute of Artificers was passed, regulating the system of apprenticeship which had

---

[1] O. J. Dunlop and R. D. Denman, *English Apprenticeship and Child Labour*, p. 29.

[2] *Id.*, p. 56.

[3] H. T. Riley, *Memorials of London and London Life*, p. 278.

hitherto been a matter of regulation only among the guilds themselves. The national sanction thereby given to the apprentice system meant much and had a great influence in the years to come. The chief features of the Act, binding by indenture, registration of the agreement, and a minimum term of seven years on the indoor system, led to the master's entire control of the boy and up to 1814 affected the relationships of the child employed or otherwise under the control of an employer.

Coincident with the development of the interest in the child as an industrial factor arose the interest in the child as a charge on the State, a phase of the child question that in the ancient civilizations had found its answer mainly in the toleration of infanticide. The Common Council of London on September 27, 1556, passed an Act, the following extract from which will go to show that there was then an attempt to go back of the child problem and an endeavour to regulate marriage.

"FORASMUCHE AS great pouertie, pernurye and lacke of lyvynge hathe of late yeres by dyverse and soundrye occasyons wayes and meanes arysen growen and encreased within this Cytye of London not onelye amongste the pore artyficers and handye craftes men of the same Cytie but also amongest other Cytezens of suche Companyes as in tymes paste have lyved and prosperouslye and in greate wealthe and one of the Chiefeste occasyons thereof (as it is thought and semeth to

all men who by longe tyme have knowne the same
Cytie and have had experyence of the state thereof)
is by reason of the ouer hastie mariages and ouer
soone setting vpp of howsholdes of and by the
youthe and yonge folkes of the saide Cytye whiche
have commenlye vsyd and yet do to marye them-
selues as soone as euer they comme out of their
Apprentycehood be they neuer so yonge and
unskyllfull. . . ."¹

In the time of Henry VIII. an attempt was
made to take care of the question of the growing
number of vagrant children by making all vagrant
children between the years of five and fourteen
liable to be bound out to some master as apprentices, the boys until they were twenty-four and
the girls until they were twenty.²

In 1601 a statute was passed which gave to
justices of the peace the power of apprenticing
not only the children of paupers and vagrants
but the children of those parents who were overburdened with children and who were unable to
support them.

"AND be it further enacted that it shalbe lawfull
for the saide churchwardens and overseers, or the
greater parte of them, by the assent of any two
justices of the peace aforesaid, to binde any suche

---

¹ Act of Henry VIII., passed by the Common Council of London, September 27, 1556. See *A Transcript of the Registers of
the Company of Stationers of London*, vol. i., ed. by Ed. Arber,
introduction, p. xli.

² H. de B. Gibbins, *Industry in England*, p. 341.

children as aforesaide to be apprentices, where they shall see convenient, till suche man child shall come to the age of fower and twentie yeares, and such woman child to the age of one and twenty yeares, or the tyme of her mariage; the same to be as effectuall to all purposes as if suche childe were of full age, and by indenture of covenant bounde hym or her selfe."[1]

In the seventeenth century, the practice of putting children prematurely to work prevailed to an extent which, when compared with the extent of the manufacturing system, "seems almost incredible," says Macaulay.[2]

A little creature of six years old was thought fit for labour in the town of Norwich, the chief seat of the clothing trade. Writers at that time, and among them some who were considered as eminently benevolent,[3] mention, "with exultation, the fact that in that single city boys and girls of tender age created wealth exceeding what was necessary for their own subsistence by twelve thousand pounds a year."

The industrial revolution of the eighteenth century was sudden and violent. All the great inventions of Watt, Arkwright, and Boulton were

[1] Rep., 7 and 8 Vict. c. 101, s. 13.

[2] Macaulay, *History of England*, vol. i., pp. 389 and 390.

[3] Chamberlayne's *State of England;* Petty's *Political Arithmetic*, chapter viii.; Dunning's *Plain and Easy Method;* Firmin's *Proposition for the Employing of the Poor*. "It ought to be observed that Firmin was an eminent philanthropist," Macaulay observes.

A HEALTHY PAIR OF INDIAN CHILDREN, WESTERN CANADA

INFANT TOILERS IN A SILK MILL, SYRIA

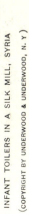

(COPYRIGHT BY UNDERWOOD & UNDERWOOD, N. Y.)

made within twenty years, steam was applied to the new looms, and the modern factory system had fairly begun.[1] With the demand for labourers and the fact that the division of labour brought about a call for low-priced workmen, some of the divisions really necessitating no greater intelligence than that of a child, the children were in great demand.

It was here that the Statute of Artificers assisted in the crushing industrial conditions, for the overseers of the poor became the agents of the mill-owners and arranged for days when the pauper children could be inspected and selected for the factory work. When the selections had been made, the children were conveyed by canal boats and wagons to the destination, and then their slavery began. Sometimes men who made a business of trafficking in children would transfer them to a factory district where they were kept in a dark cellar until the mill-owner, in want of hands, came to look them over and pick out those that he thought would be useful. Nominally the children were apprentices, but actually they were slaves and their treatment was most inhuman. The parish authorities, in order to get rid of the imbeciles, often bargained that the mill-owners take one idiot with every twenty children. What became of the idiots after they had passed into the hands of the capitalist is not known, but in

[1] H. de B. Gibbins, *Industry in England*, p. 388.

most cases they did not last long and mysteriously disappeared.

No matter what the conditions and no matter how ill the children, they were worked without any visible vestige of human feeling. Even as late as 1840 in the evidence given before the Select Committee investigating the conditions of factories after the passage of the Reform Act of 1833, these were the conditions that the inspectors reported:

Q. "Have you many lace-mills in your district?"

A. "I have about thirty mills."

Q. "What are the usual hours of work in these mills?"

A. "The usual hours are, about Nottingham, *twenty hours a day*, being from four o'clock in the morning till twelve o'clock at night; about Chesterfield, the report I have had from the superintendent is, that they work twenty-four hours, all through the night, in several mills there."

Q. "Are there many children and young persons in those mills?"

A. "The proportion is less in lace-mills than in others, but it is necessary to have some of them; the process of winding and preparing the bobbins and carriages requires children; those that I saw so employed were *from ten to fifteen years of age*."

Q. "Are the children detained in the mills during a considerable period of the day and night?"

A. "I can speak from information derived from two or three mill-owners, and also more extensively from reports by one of the superintendents in my district; and I should say that in most of the mills they do detain them at night; in some of them, the report states that they are detained all night, in order to be ready when wanted."

Q. "Are the children that are so detained liable to be detained throughout the day, and do they sometimes begin their work at twelve o'clock at night?"

A. "In the mills at Nottingham there are owners that make it a rule that they will not keep the children after eight, or nine, or ten o'clock, according to the inclination of the mill-occupier."

Q. "Where are those children during the time they are detained in the mill?"

A. *When detained at night, and not employed I am told they are lying about on the floor.*"

Q. "Is it customary to close at eight on Saturday evening in the lace-mills?"

A. "I think it is."

Q. "How then do they compensate for the loss of those four hours' work in those mills?"

A. *"By working all night on Friday;* those are the mills in which they pay so much for their power."

Q. "Must not there be a considerable wear and tear upon the physical constitution of children who are kept in this state?"

21

A. "I think it is self-evident."

Q. "Is there any possibility of their obtaining education under those circumstances?"

A. "None whatever, except on Sundays."

Q. "But, after one hundred and twenty hours' work in the week, is it possible that they can have much capacity for study on Sunday?"

A. "It is not always that the same children are kept twenty hours, because some mills have two complete sets of hands for their machinery, and they work the same set of hands only ten hours."

Q. "But, even under those circumstances, it must frequently happen that the same children are employed during the night twice or thrice in the course of a week?"

A. "The practice generally is that they take the night-work for one week, and then the next week the morning-work."

Q. "So that during one whole week they are employed in the night-work?"

A. "Yes."

Q. "At the end of a week, during which they have been employed in the night, do you think that they have much capacity left for study on Sunday?"

A. "No; my opinion is most decidedly that either turning out at four o'clock in the morning, or being kept out of bed at night, must be injurious to children, both to their physical constitution and their mental powers."

Q. "The law, as it stands, does not prevent the children from being employed even twenty hours?"

A. "It does not apply to lace-mills."

Q. "Therefore the period during which the child is employed depends upon the varying humanity of the individual proprietor of the mill?"

A. "Yes."

Q. "You say that it sometimes happens that the children come to the mill at five in the morning, and do not leave it till ten at night?"

A. "It is reported to me that it does so happen about Chesterfield."

Q. "If a child is kept in winter till twelve o'clock at night, and has then to go home and return to the factory in the morning, a distance of two miles, does not he undergo fearful hardships?"

A. "Certainly."[1]

The children who were apprenticed out to the mill-owners were fed on the coarsest kind of food and in the most disgusting way. They slept by turns, in relays, in beds that were never aired, for one set of children were turned into the beds as soon as another set had been driven out to their long and filthy toil. Some tried to run away and after that they were worked with chains around their ankles; many died and the little graves were unmarked in a desolate spot lest the number of the dead attract too much attention.

[1] *The Quarterly Review*, vol. lxvii., 1841, pp. 175 and 176.

Sixteen hours a day, six days a week, was no uncommon time for children, and on Sunday they worked to clean the machine.

"In stench, in heated rooms, amid the constant whirling of a thousand wheels, little fingers and little feet were kept in ceaseless action, forced into unnatural activity by blows from the heavy hands and feet of the merciless overlooker, and the infliction of bodily pain by instruments of punishment, invented by the sharpened ingenuity of insatiable selfishness."[1]

The agitation against these conditions led, in 1802, to an Act being passed by the influence of Sir Robert Peel for the preservation of the health and morals of apprentices and others employed in cotton and other mills.

The immediate cause of this was the fearful spread through the factories in the Manchester district of epidemic diseases due to overwork, scanty food, wretched clothing, long hours, bad ventilation, among the working people and especially among the children.

As far as reforming the conditions in which the children lived, the Act, however, was a dead letter, and in a debate introduced by Sir Robert Peel on June 6, 1815, one speaker, Horner, told of the sale of a gang of children with the effects of a bankrupt.

"A still more atrocious instance," continued the speaker, "had been brought before the Court

[1] Alfred, *History of the Factory Movement*, vol. i., pp. 21, 22.

of King's Bench two years ago, when a number of these boys apprenticed by a parish in London to one manufacturer had been transferred (*i. e.*, sold) to another and had been found by some benevolent persons in a state of absolute famine."[1]

No longer could people ignore conditions such as these and a Select Committee of the House of Commons was empowered to take evidence on the state of children working in the manufactories of Great Britain. Despite the horrible nature of the evidence, when the Act resulting from the investigation was passed, all that it did was to make nine years the limit to age employment and twelve hours a day the working day for those under sixteen years. But it was limited in effect to cotton factories only, leaving the woollen and worsted factories absolutely untouched, and even in the matter of the cotton factories these provisions were frequently avoided.

Conditions continued to become worse instead of better, children of both sexes being beaten and overworked to make profit for the rich capitalists until 1830, when Richard Oastler, who had led in the fight against black slavery, had his attention called to the conditions under which the children of England were practically enslaved.[2]

Oastler was talking one night about his slavery reforms to a friend near Bradford and the remark was made to him: "I wonder you never turned

[1] Quoted in Alfred's *History of the Factory Movement*, i., 43.
[2] H. de B. Gibbins, *Industry in England*, par. 226, p. 393.

your attention to the factory." "Why should I?" replied the young abolitionist, "I have nothing to do with factories." "Perhaps not," was the answer, "but you are very enthusiastic against slavery in the West Indies and I assure you that there are cruelties practised in our mills on little children which I am sure if you knew you would try to prevent."

The man who gave this suggestion, John Wood, was himself an owner of a mill and he admitted to Oastler that in his own mill the little children were worked from six in the morning until seven at night with a break of only forty minutes for lunch and that various devices, including beatings with sticks and straps and clubs, were employed to goad them on to renewed labour.

The very next day Oastler began a crusade which lasted for many weary years. He succeeded in interesting J. Hobhouse and M. T. Sadler, both members of the House of Commons, and the ten hours agitation began in and out of Parliament. In the course of a speech delivered in March, 1832, in favour of the ten hours bill, Sadler declared that so great was the demand in some districts for children's labour that "an indispensable condition of marriage among the working classes was the certainty of offspring whose wages, beginning at six years old, might keep their inhuman fathers and mothers in idleness."

"Our ancestors could not have supposed it possible," exclaimed Sadler, "posterity will not believe it true—that a generation of Englishmen could exist, or had existed, that would work lisping infancy a few summers old, regardless alike of its smiles or tears, and unmoved by its unresisting weakness, twelve, thirteen, fourteen, sixteen hours a day, and through the weary night also, till in the dewy morn of existence, the bud of youth was faded and fell ere it was unfolded."

But, to the nation's eternal disgrace, that generation of Englishmen did exist, and Mr. Sadler told the House, detail by detail, of the evils and outrages of the whole abominable system. Excessive hours, low wages, immorality, ill-health—all were enumerated, and then he continued:

"Then in order to keep them awake, to stimulate their exertions, means are made use of to which I shall now advert, as a last instance of the degradation to which this system has reduced the manufacturing operatives of this country. Children are beaten with thongs, prepared for the purpose. Yes, the females of this country, no matter whether children or grown up, and I hardly know which is the more disgusting outrage, are beaten, beaten in your free market of labour as you term it, like slaves. The poor wretch is flogged before its companions, flogged, I say, like a dog, by the tyrant overlooker. We speak with execration of the cartwhip of the West Indies, but let us see this night an equal feeling rise against the factory thong in England."[1]

[1] H. de B. Gibbins, *Industry in England*, p. 398.

Interesting too was the fact brought out at this time that while these were the conditions in England, in the colonies black labour was protected to the extent that nine hours a day was the legal day for adults and young persons and children were not allowed to work more than six, while night work was simply prohibited.

The investigation of the Sadler Committee evoked the interesting information from one witness that children were never employed if they were under five.

The attitude of the employers toward the agitation can be best judged from the following extracts:

"Every man acquainted with the political history of the last century must know, that the labour of children was actually pointed out to the manufacturers by Mr. William Pitt, as a new resource by which they might be enabled to bear the additional load of taxation which the necessities of the State compelled him to impose.   The necessity for labour created by this taxation has not yet abated; because the immense capital taken away by the enormous expenditure of the great wars arising out of the French Revolution, an expenditure which was mainly supported out of the industrial resources of the country, has not been replaced.   But even independent of these considerations, and irrespective of a past which can never be recalled, we mean to assert, as we have done elsewhere, in broad terms and the plainest language, that the infant labour, as it is erroneously called—or the juvenile labour, as it should be called—in factories, is in fact a national blessing, and absolutely necessary for the support of the manifold fiscal burthens which have been placed upon the industry of this country. It is quite sufficient to say that the children of the operatives have mouths, and must be fed; they have limbs, and must be clothed; they have minds, which ought to be instructed; and they have passions, which must be controlled. Now, if the parents are unable to provide these requisites, and their inability to do so is just as notorious as their existence, it becomes absolutely necessary that the children should aid in obtaining them for themselves. To abolish juvenile labour, is plainly nothing else than to abolish juvenile means of support; and to confine it within very narrow limits, is just to subtract a dinner or a supper from the unhappy objects of mistaken benevolence."[1]

The result of all this agitation and debate was the famous Act of 1833 introduced by Lord Shaftesbury which prohibited night work to persons under eighteen in cotton, woollen, and other factories, and provided that children from nine to thirteen years of age were not to work more than forty-eight hours a week and those from thirteen to eighteen not to work more than sixty-eight hours. Children under nine were not to be employed at all

[1] W. Cooke Taylor, *Factories and the Factory System*, pp. 20 and 21.

Even this much was not obtained until Oastler had succeeded in driving home to the British mind conditions such as are described in a speech delivered at Huddersfield, December 26, 1831, of which the following is an extract:

"I will not picture fiction to you," said Oastler, in the early days of the factory movement, "but I will tell you what I have seen. Take a little female captive, six or seven years old; she shall rise from her bed at four in the morning of a cold winter day, but before she rises she wakes perhaps half a dozen times, and says, 'Father, is it time? Father, is it time?' And at last, when she gets up and puts her little bits of rags upon her weary limbs—weary yet with the last day's work—she leaves her parents in their bed, for their labour (if they have any) is not required so early. She trudges alone through rain and snow, and mire and darkness, to the mill, and there for thirteen, fourteen, sixteen, seventeen, or even eighteen hours is she obliged to work with only thirty minutes' interval for meals and play. Homeward again at night she would go, when she was able, but many a time she hid herself in the wool in the mill, as she had not strength to go. And if she were one moment behind the appointed time; if the bell had ceased to ring when she arrived with trembling, shivering, weary limbs at the factory door, there stood a monster in human form, and as she passed he lashed her. This," he continued, holding up an over-looker's strap, "is no fiction. It was hard at work in this town last week.   The girl I am speaking of died; but she dragged on that dreadful existence for several years."[1]

While Oastler was delivering this speech and these conditions were rife, Malthus was revising the first edition of his *Essay on Population*.

[1] H. de B. Gibbins, *Industry in England*, p. 402.

CHAPTER XXIII

FOLLOWING the Civil War, there began in the United States a humanitarian movement, an aftermath well becoming a unique and heartrending struggle. In that period, humane endeavour, like so many creepers, overran ordinary activities, and philanthropic movements unprecedented sprang up over the country.

Labour conditions until this period were about the same in the United States as they were in England. The Puritan idea had been that sin was in idleness, even for small children; "Colonial records bear evidence that it was a matter of conscience to keep children at work."[1]

In the latter half of the eighteenth century the development of manufactures, especially the cloth-making industry, impressed on the American mind, as it had impressed the English mind, that

[1] Edith Abbott, *Journal of American Society*, 14, 37.

CHILDREN OF TWO FAMILIES—AS THE SOCIETY FOR THE PREVENTION OF CRUELTY
TO CHILDREN FOUND THEM

THE SAME FAMILIES—AFTER ATTENTION FROM THE SOCIETY

child labour was a national asset. When the first cotton factory was started at Beverly, Mass., it was stated that it would afford "employment to a great number of women and children many of whom will be otherwise useless, if not burdensome to society."[1]

A special report was made by a committee to the Massachusetts Legislature in 1866 in which it was stated that representatives of the factories went about systematically canvassing for small children: "Small help is scarce; a great deal of machinery has been stopped for want of small help, so that the overseers have been going around to draw the small children from schools into the mills; the same as a draft in the army."

Asked if there were "any limit on the part of the employers as to the age when they take children," a witness replied: "They'll take them at any age they can get them, if they are old enough to stand. . . ."[2]

The same year that this report was made there was founded in New York a Society for the Prevention of Cruelty to Animals, in imitation of a similar society that had been founded in England, in 1823. Out of that movement in America there grew, in 1874, a movement to look after the rights of children, the first enunciation in terms of modernity of the fact that society must not only punish crimes against children, but that it must prevent

[1] Edith Abbott, *Journal of American Society*, 14, 21.
[2] *Id.*, 14, 32.

them. Following the formation of this society, the first special laws "known in the world were enacted specifically to protect and punish wrongs to children."

The result of this development was that in 1880 Frederick A. Agnew visited America and after an examination of the work being done in New York and the methods employed, returned to Liverpool, his home, and there in conjunction with Samuel Smith, M. P., founded the Liverpool Society for the Prevention of Cruelty to Children, in 1883—the first society in Europe to prevent wrongs against children. Shortly after this the Earl of Shaftesbury organized a similar movement in London. Then, under the auspices of the late M. Jules Simon, whose work in behalf of children has not yet been fully appreciated, the movement was taken up in France, M. Paul Nourisson and M. Ernest Nusse aiding greatly in bringing about a comprehensive law in relation to the prevention of cruelty to children.

With Lieut.-Gen. D. von Pelet-Narbonne as chairman, the "Verein zum Schutz der Kinder vor Ausnutzung und Misshandlung" was formed in Berlin. In 1899 Fräulein Lydia von Wolfring aided in the organization of the "Wiener Kinder Schutz und Rettungs Verein" with von Krall, Privy Chancellor of Austria, as chairman. Count Borromeo inaugurated the movement at Milan in Italy where the padrone system flourished to such an extent as to indicate that the old Roman theory of the *patria potestas* was still alive, at least with the peasants. Through the other countries of Europe the interest in the new movement ran and the work was taken up; then into India, China, and South America, until today there is no quarter of the globe where there is not a society, organized for the purpose of assisting the law in preventing crimes against the helpless child.

Nothing indicates better the seeming accidental and casual beginnings of large movements than the formation of this first society in America. Like Vincent of Paul's recognition of the horrible crimes that were being perpetrated in Paris only when he came face to face with an ill-treated infant, so it was only when it was discovered that, with all the law, there was no legal way of protecting an American child, that the child-protection movement, with its many subsequent laws in behalf of children, sprang up.

A mission worker named Mrs. Etta A. Wheeler had found in what was then the slums of New York that a child, famous after as Mary Ellen, was being cruelly beaten and ill-treated by a man and woman who had taken it when it was less than two years of age from a charitable institution. Some idea of the condition among the slums of a large city of this time may be gained from the statement of a contemporary newspaper that "at least 10,000 young boys roamed the streets of New York by day and took shelter by night in any place that seemed to afford a safe retreat, while their older and more vicious confederates planned how they should succeed in pilfering and plundering the public. The crumbling and rotten wooden docks of the metropolis had been for years haunted by these young vagabonds, and as they were at that time inefficiently policed, they were excellent localities for the incubators of petty thievery."

Unless these youngsters actually committed a crime, or unless someone collected evidence that they were leading an immoral life, they were free to do what they willed.

Mrs. Wheeler was unable to gather the evidence necessary to remove the child in which she had become interested, and as the stories of the cruelties continued, she went to the Society for the Prevention of Cruelty to Animals, at the head of which was Henry Bergh, whose work in this direction was as notable in this country as was Richard Martin's in England.

After consultation with the counsel of the Society, Elbridge T. Gerry, it was decided that "the child being an animal" the Society would act. Mr. Gerry after a careful examination of the evidence, sued out a writ *de homine replegiando*, the child was taken to court, complaints were made against the so-called guardians, and the woman who had cruelly beaten the child was afterwards sent to the penitentiary for one year.

And so, for the first time by legal machinery, punishment was meted out for cruelty to children.

When it became known that the Animal Soci-

The "INSPIRATION," written by Mr. HENRY BERGH, on which The Society for the Prevention of Cruelty to Children was organized.

THE "INSPIRATION" OF HENRY BERGH ON WHICH THE SOCIETY FOR THE PREVENTION OF CRUELTY TO CHILDREN WAS ORGANIZED

THE JUVENILE COURT, NEW YORK CITY; JUSTICE WYATT ON THE BENCH

ety, as it was called, would interest itself in children who were being ill-treated, the complaints became numerous. It was decided that a separate society should be incorporated as a hand attached to the arm of the law.

Of the various movements that grew out of the protection movement, none was more interesting or attracted more controversy than the endeavours to protect children of the stage. We have seen in the account of the elder Seneca and in the treatment by the mountebanks of children in Paris in the seventeenth century, how easily the unprotected child lent itself to the calling of the vagabond entertainer. While no such barbarities were practised in modern times, it was difficult for many people to realize that the child of five, undergoing training as an acrobat for long hours, was not being brought up in accordance with the modern theory of the obligations of the State toward the helpless.

The importation of children that had been sold by their parents in Italy was also a matter that the Society took up, and in 1879, the white slave question, even now a live question, arose in an endeavour to stop the *padroni* from bringing into America the minors they had gathered abroad.

Probably the most important question that has come before the Society in recent years has been the proper treatment of those children who, for one reason or another, are brought into contact

with the police.   One of the first things that the
New York Society did was to insist that the children who had to be taken to court should not be
mixed with the really criminal.   In 1892 an amendment to the Penal Code made the separation imperative, and out of this movement has grown the
children's court movement and the proper study
of the so-called juvenile criminal.

Another important branch of the child-protection movement that had its beginning in New York
City, was placing laws on the statute book, and
then enforcing them, against the sale of injurious
liquors to children.   Laws tending to protect the
morality of children followed these, and in fact almost from the first year of its birth, every year
has seen the Protection Society enlarging its field
of action until today it hardly seems possible that
it was only a few hundred years ago that the very
life of a child itself was considered of no importance.

The general law laid down by Spencer, in virtue
of which everything passes "from the homogene-
ous to the heterogeneous, from the indefinite to
the definite, from the simple to the complex," is
evident in the history of the progress of the child
as a factor in society.

When in neolithic times there was no moral
instinct in man, the child's only hope of life was
the parental or rather the maternal instinct, of
beings not yet risen to the plain of reasoning
animals.   In a higher stage of civilization one

finds, where the matriarchal régime exists, children
have a value, the value of chattels and live stock,
though the maternal uncle has more rights over
them than their own father.[1]   The *patria potestas*
of the Romans was not so strange or unusual as
it seemed to Gibbon, for the power of life and
death (*jus vitæ ac necis*) is found among the
Apaches, the Botocodos, the Bedouins, and the
Samoyedes and is a stage in the development
and evolution of the family idea.

In the religious and philosophical stage the
child takes on an importance of its own; it is
humanely treated because it is now recognized as
a human being, or it is protected because it is
said to have, young and apparently unimportant
as it seems to be, a *soul* of its own.   From there
on to the time when the child, as the father of the
man, is a charge upon the State,—or on all men,—
until it is able to take care of and protect itself,
the murder of a child is theoretically as great a
crime as the murder of an adult.   In fact, the
conditions of the past hold long after each recognized step of progress, the most primitive habits
obtruding in the very midst of the most advanced knowledge and the most complete en-
lightenment.

It is for this that the story of the past is valuable.   That we may know and understand and

[1] Duprat, p. 200, and Steinmetz, "Das Verhaltniss zwischen
Eltern und Kindern bei den Naturvolken," *Zeitschrift für
Socielwissenschaft*, vol. i.

value rightly what is past, past for all time so far
as intelligent and self-governing humanity is able
to will—that is one of the surest steps to knowledge and truth.

APPENDIX A

NAPOLEONIC DECREE OF 1811.

IMPERIAL DECREE CONCERNING FOUNDLINGS, ABANDONED CHILDREN, AND POOR ORPHANS OF JANUARY 19, 1811.

1ST TITLE.

ARTICLE 1. The children whose education is entrusted to public charity are:

1st. Foundlings.

2d. Abandoned children.

3d. Poor orphans.

2D TITLE.

2. Foundlings are those born of unknown parents, who have been found exposed in any place, or those taken to the hospitals intended to receive them.

3. In each hospital intended to receive foundlings there shall be a place where they may be left.

4. There will be at most in each district (*arrondissement*) an institution where the foundlings may be received. Registers shall state day by day, their arrival, their sex, their apparent age, and shall describe the natural marks and the swaddling clothes which may serve for their identification.

3D TITLE.

Of Abandoned Children and Poor Orphans

5.   Abandoned children are those born of known parents and at first raised by them, or by other persons for them, and are abandoned by them, the whereabouts of the parents being unknown or there being no means of discovering them.

6.   Orphans are those who, not having either father or mother, have no means of subsistence.

4TH TITLE.

Of the Education of Foundlings, Abandoned Children, and Orphans.

7.   Newly born foundlings will be placed with a wet nurse as soon as possible; up to that they will be nourished by the bottle or even by means of wet nurses resident in the establishment.   If they are weaned or susceptible of being weaned, they will either be put to nurse or weaned.

8.   These children will receive a layette.   They will remain to the age of six years.

9.   At six years, all the children will be, or as many as can, put to board with farmers.   The price of the board will increase each year up to the age of twelve, at which period the infant males in a state to serve will be placed at the disposition of the Minister of the Marine.

10.   The infants who cannot be put to board, the crippled and the infirm, will be raised in the hospitals.   They will be occupied in the workshops at those employments that are not below their age.

5TH TITLE.

On the Expenses of Foundlings, Abandoned Children, and Orphans.

11. Hospitals designated to receive foundlings are directed to furnish the layettes and all the inside expenses pertaining to the nourishment and education of the children.

12. We herewith set aside the sum of 4,000,000 francs annually to contribute to the monthly payment of wet nurses and the boarding of the foundlings and abandoned children.

If it should turn out after the division of this sum that it is inadequate, the difference will be provided by the hospitals from their revenues or by drawing on the funds of the community.

13. The monthly payments of the nurses and their board shall not be made except on the certificate of the mayors of the communities where the children are. The mayors must attest each month that they have seen the children.

14. The administrative commissioners of the hospitals will visit at least twice in the year each infant, either a special commission, or by physicians or surgeons, vaccinators or others.

6TH TITLE.

Of the Guardianship and of Foundling Children and Abandoned Children

15. Foundling and abandoned children are under the guardianship of the hospital, in conformance with existing regulations. A member of this commission is especially charged with this guardianship.

16. The aforesaid children, brought up at the cost of the State, are entirely at its disposition, and when the Minister of Marine so decides, the guardianship of the Commission ceases.

17. When the infants have reached the age of twelve years, those whom the State has made no disposition of will, as soon as it is possible to do so, be apprenticed out, the boys with the workmen, the girls with housewives, seamstresses, and other workwomen in the factories or manufacturing establishments.

18. The contracts of apprenticeship shall not stipulate in favour of either the master or the apprentice, but they will guarantee the master the free services of the apprentice up to an age which shall not exceed the twenty-fifth year, and the apprentice food, shelter and clothing.

19. At the call of the army, or a conscription, the obligations of the apprentice will cease.

20. Those of the infants who cannot be put out as apprentices, the crippled and the infirm, who cannot find places outside of the hospitals will remain there as a charge to each hospital.

Workshops will be established in order to provide them with employment.

7TH TITLE.

*On the Recognition and Announcement (Reclamation)
of Foundlings and Abandoned Children.*

21. No charge is made in the rules relative to the recognition and advertising of foundling and abandoned children, but before exercising any right, the

parents must, if they have the means, reimburse the authorities for all expenses made either by the State or by the hospitals, and in no case, can an infant of which the State has made disposition, be released until those obligations are met.

8TH TITLE.

General *"Dispositions"*

22.   The Minister of the Interior will propose to us before January 1, 1812, the rules of administration, which will be discussed in our Council of State.   These rules will determine, for each department, the number of hospitals where foundlings will be received and all that relates to their administration concerning principally the disposition of the infants now in charge and the payment for nurses and boarding.

23.   Individuals who are convicted of having exposed children and those who make it a practice of transporting them to hospitals will be punished in accordance with the law.

24.   Our Minister of Marine will present to us a plan dealing with: 1st. An organization relative to those clauses in which his powers are defined in this decree. 2d. For the regulation of the employment without delay of those who, on the 1st of January, will become twelve years of age.

25.   Our Minister of the Interior is directed to see to the execution of the present decree and will have it inserted in the bulletin of laws.

APPENDIX B

CERTIFICATE OF INCORPORATION

OF

THE NEW YORK SOCIETY FOR THE PREVENTION OF CRUELTY TO CHILDREN.

The undersigned persons all being of full age and a 'majority of whom are citizens of the United States of America and citizens of and residents within the State of New York, and who desire to associate themselves together for the purpose of preventing cruelty to children, have this day associated themselves together pursuant to Chapter One Hundred and Thirty of the Laws of eighteen hundred and seventy-five and hereby adopt the following:

ARTICLES OF ASSOCIATION.

ARTICLE FIRST: This society shall be known in law by the name and title of "The New York Society for the Prevention of Cruelty to Children."

ARTICLE SECOND: The particular business and objects of this Society are, the prevention of cruelty to children and the enforcement by all lawful means of the laws relating to or in any wise affecting children.

ARTICLE THIRD: The number of directors to manage this Society shall be fifteen.

346

ARTICLE FOURTH: The names of such directors for the first year of the existence of this society are:

Benjamin H. Field	Charles Haight
Henry Bergh	Adrian Iselin, Jr.
John Howard Wright	B. B. Sherman
Thomas C. Acton	Richard R. Haines
Ferdinand De Luca	James Stokes
Sinclair Tousey	William H. Webb
William M. Vermilye	Frederic DePeyster

Harmon Hendricks

In Witness Whereof we have hereunto severally subscribed our names this Twenty-fourth day of April in the year Eighteen hundred and seventy-five.

John D. Wright	Thos. C. Acton
Henry Bergh	Chas. Haight
Elbridge T. Gerry	Adrian Iselin, Jr.
Benj. H. Field	Benj. B. Sherman
Wm. L. Jenkins	Richd. R. Haines
John Howard Wright	James Stokes
Ferd. De Luca	W. H. Webb
Sinclair Tousey	Frederic DePeyster
W. M. Vermilye	Harmon Hendricks

In the presence of

AMBROSE MONELL.

STATE OF NEW YORK
CITY AND COUNTY OF NEW YORK } *ss.*

On this Twenty-fourth day of April, 1875, personally appeared before me John D. Wright, Henry Bergh, Elbridge T. Gerry, Benjamin H. Field, William L.

Jenkins, John Howard Wright, Ferdinand De Luca, Sinclair Tousey, William M. Vermilye, Thomas C. Acton, Charles Haight, Adrian Iselin, Jr., Benjamin B. Sherman, Richard R. Haines, James Stokes, William H. Webb, Frederic DePeyster, and Harmon Hendricks, known to me to be the persons above named, and each severally acknowledged the foregoing to be his signature to the before mentioned Certificate and Articles of Incorporation.

(*Seal*)   AMBROSE MONELL,
                                    Notary Public,
                              COUNTY OF NEW YORK.

(*Endorsed*)

I hereby approve of the within organization and its purposes and consent to and authorize the filing of this Certificate and Articles of Incorporation.

Dated, NEW YORK, April 26, 1875.

                              GEO. C. BARRETT,
                              Justice Supreme Court.

(*Endorsed*)

CERTIFICATE OF INCORPORATION
            OF

THE NEW YORK SOCIETY FOR THE PREVENTION OF
            CRUELTY TO CHILDREN.

Under Chapter 130, Laws of 1875.

Filed, April 27, 1875.

    GEORGE FRANKLIN,
        Dep. Secy. of State.

APPENDIX C

AMERICAN CONSULATE,
ALEPPO, SYRIA, December 15, 1913.

Subject: TREATMENT OF CHILDREN.
(*Consul*, JESSE B. JACKSON, ALEPPO, SYRIA.)

THE HONOURABLE,
  THE SECRETARY OF STATE,
    WASHINGTON.

SIR:

I have the honour to report as follows concerning the treatment of children by the various races and sects in Aleppo Consular District, viz.:

In many ways the treatment of children by the various races and sects inhabiting Northern Syria differs vastly from that practised in other countries. Strangely similar in one particular to the custom of the American Indian, immediately after birth the child is wrapped in cloths until it resembles the form of a mummy of ancient Egyptian times, in which state it is kept and carried about by nurses and small children until it is considered old enough to learn to walk, when it is given the freedom of its limbs. Very young babies must suffer considerably by this treatment, evidenced by their constant restlessness and crying, no doubt preventing the baby from attaining to its natural strength and activity until after it has been free for some months. During cold weather a ball of a certain kind of clay about the capacity of a quart is heated and kept wrapped at the feet of the infant to prevent it catching cold. Among certain of the lower classes the illness of a girl baby does not cause the anxiety that it does in the case of a boy, consequently causing a much higher rate of mortality among the female than the male children.

Among the Arabs, as soon as the children of the tribesmen are six or seven years old they are put to herding sheep and goats, which vocation they generally follow during their lives, never going to school or having any kind of instruction. The sons of the sheiks (chiefs) of the tribes are either sent to school in the cities, or a private tutor, usually a "hodja" (Mohammedan teacher or priest), is engaged, while the girls are given no education whatever.

The position of a girl varies greatly as between the different races and sects of the country. For instance, among the Arab and Kurdish tribes, and the Fellaheen (non-Christian farmers), a girl is a source of revenue to the father who, when she is of marriageable age, trades or sells her to her prospective husband, obtaining live stock or money to the equivalent of eight to twenty "chees," or $176 to $440 (a "chees" equals $22.00), the selling price depending upon the beauty of the girl and the prominence of her family from the standpoint of wealth and influence. Among these races the really fat girl commands the highest admiration. The heavier she is the more she is desired and the better price she brings.

Formerly the Christian and Hebrew families gave their girls little schooling, but instead taught them to do embroidery and crochet work. Among even relatively poor families there exists a certain pride that causes housework to be regarded as degrading, and only those will become servants who are forced to do so by straitened circumstances. In late years there is a tendency to give the girls some education, which the Christians and Jews receive at the mission establishments of the Americans, French, English, Italians, Germans, Swiss, etc., while a very limited number of Mohammedan girls attend local public schools conducted exclusively for them.

Contrary to the custom prevailing among the Arabs, Kurds, and Fellaheen, the Christians and Jews greatly prefer to have boy babies, and it is considered a great misfortune if most or all of the children of a family are girls. The boys are sent to the respective community and foreign mission schools, and some of the more enlightened and progressive families afterwards send their boys to the colleges at Beyrouth, Syria, to complete their education.

It is the main object of every such family to marry off the girls as soon as possible, for it is considered a great shame to the girl if she is left unmarried until after twenty or twenty-two years of age. Marriage is the most important event, and the only one in which she is in any way prominent in all her life. Her great object in life is to become a wife and be the mother of a boy, the latter event always raising her in the estimation of her acquaintances and friends, and giving her considerable importance for the time being, whereas it is the contrary if the baby is a girl. In many families the young wife is not permitted to speak aloud in the presence of strangers or of the father-in-law until a boy is born to her.

Parents generally engage their children at very

early ages, in which little attention is paid to the wishes
or dislikes of the prospective bride and groom.   In
fact, unborn children are sometimes provisionally
engaged to each other by their parents, either for
sentimental or financial reasons.   Perhaps three-
fourths of the girls of the country are married before
they reach the age of sixteen, and many are married
between twelve and fourteen.

The consideration paid on the occasion of the
marriage of non-Mohammedan, or Christian and
Jewish girls, goes the other way from that paid at the
marriage of an Arab girl, it being the desire of the
groom to have as large a dowry as possible for his
wife, and which goes to help make up the family
exchequer.   It consequently results that if a family
that is not well to do has many girls it is very difficult
to marry them well.

A certain brutality of parents towards their children
exists among the lower classes, a condition that is
probably due more to inferior intelligence caused by
lack of education than to anything else.   As but a very
small minority of the population of this part of the
country, say twenty per cent., and a much smaller
proportion of the tribes of the interior read and write,
this attitude is readily understood.

The prevalence of crippled begging children in the
cities leads to the supposition that they are not all
deformed by accident or disease, but that in many
instances they have been purposely so rendered in
order to more profitably ply their trade by creating
sympathy in the minds of the persons addressed in
their appeals for succour.   During the summer months
a considerable number of such pitiable creatures
between four and eight years old may be seen in the

streets of Aleppo, some with deformed legs, some with spinal afflictions, and others blind or otherwise maimed, many unable to walk and hutching from place to place, collecting coppers from those whom their condition touches. As the hour grows late in the night these unfortunates gradually disappear one by one, and if a person is interested in their destination they may be seen to be gathered up in some obscure corner by an apparent relative or guardian, lifted to the shoulder and carried away into the maze of various Oriental residential quarters, where their scanty collection is spent in support of a family, or for the poisonous rakee, a strong alcoholic drink much relished by the lower element. It was suspected that a sort of society existed whereby such children were produced and let out to certain parties to be exploited for their personal benefit, but no serious investigation has ever been made, and the nefarious traffic continues.

I have the honour to be, Sir,

Your obedient servant,

(*Signed*) JESSE B. JACKSON,

American Consul.

AMERICAN CONSULATE,
ALEPPO, SYRIA, December 15, 1913.

Subject: REPORT: TREATMENT OF CHILDREN.

(*Consul*, JESSE B. JACKSON, ALEPPO, SYRIA).

THE HONOURABLE,
THE SECRETARY OF STATE,
WASHINGTON.

SIR:

I have the honour to transmit herewith a report in

23

triplicate,[1] of today's date, subject, "Treatment of Children," which is in reply to an inquiry addressed to this Consulate by Mr. George Henry Payne, New York City, to whom the triplicate copy is hereby requested to be forwarded.

Copies thereof are being sent to the Embassy and Consulate-General, respectively, Constantinople.

I have the honour to be, Sir,

Your obedient servant,

JESSE B. JACKSON,
American Consul.

Enclosure:

[1] Copy of triplicate report, as above indicated.

AMERICAN CONSULAR SERVICE,
SIERRA LEONE, AFRICA, April 7, 1914.

GEORGE HENRY PAYNE, ESQ.,
NEW YORK.

SIR:

Yours dated November 1, 1913, has been in my hands some time. The information you request is rather broad, and would require much investigation to be of any real service to you. Certainly I have some information, in a general way, but to write it would take much more space than a letter could contain. But in short, the attitude of the natives of Sierra Leon at present toward children is all of that of a primitive people emerging into European civilization. Children are regarded very much as a financial asset, especially by the mothers, and are kept much under the influence and control of the mothers so long as they live. Those emerging out of tribal customs into European customs have pretty much the same relations as exist between parents and children in Europe or America. However, there is little love between the child and father, generally speaking, but much between mother and child. Boys usually remain in the care of the mothers until they reach the age of puberty, at which time they leave the association of their mothers and sisters and have that of their older brothers and fathers, almost exclusively. Upon leaving their mothers' care and training they are usually, among those who cling to tribal customs, turned over to the "medicine man," or doctor, who claims to know much. They are taken into the "Poro Society" where they are circumcised, and taught the duties of a man, the use of certain native medicines, etc. The girls remain in the care of the mothers, but at the age of puberty, or a little while before, are placed into the care of one or more old women who conduct a female school, the "bundoo" society, where the girls have an operation performed upon them similar to circumcision, and are taught the duties of a mother and wife, how to care for themselves, and the use of certain native medicines. The rule is that the girls are not eligible for marriage until they have been through the "bundoo," and boys or young men not until they have been circumcised; but in addition boys must earn their wives by the payment of dowries —presents to the girls' mothers and fathers. Children are usually required to perform such work or labor as they are physically able to perform, strict obedience to their parents and great respect for their seniors, even for older brothers and sisters, though they be not grown. Children are expected to care for and to provide for their parents in their old age. Etc.

I regret that I am unable to give you fuller information.

Very sincerely,
W. J. YERBY,
American Consul at Sierra Leone.

———

EMBASSY OF THE UNITED STATES OF AMERICA,
TOKYO, March 26, 1914.

GEORGE HENRY PAYNE, ESQUIRE,
NEW YORK CITY.

DEAR SIR:

In reply to your inquiry regarding the attitude of the people of Japan toward children and the practice of infanticide, I have the following, which is the result of interviews with representative Japanese and of my own observations.

As a rule, Japanese are very kind to children and very fond of them; usually they are allowed their own way a good deal when small and spoiled so that very severe discipline is administered later in an effort to correct this. Among the lower classes children are very often looked upon as a sort of insurance or investment against old age; also the system of ancestor worship makes it a highly desirable thing to have children, particularly sons. For these reasons children are looked upon with great favour and large families are the rule.

Infanticide is now a crime and is so strictly and severely punished that it cannot be said to be common, although it does exist to some extent. However, up to about fifty years ago this was not the case; it was not a crime and was very common. The father of a family had supreme power over the family, even including the power of life and death, and was free to do with his children almost as he chose. In regions where the people were poor, infanticide was the regularly recognized means of preventing large families. The following incident illustrates this very well: In a certain section in northern Japan was a district where so little could be produced that the people were very poor and no family had more than one or two children, infanticide being regularly practised. The feudal lord of the district, being a wise man, decided to remedy this condition, which he proceeded to do by a system of irrigation which made the district quite fertile; immediately the size of the families rose to eight and ten and infanticide disappeared.

With regret for my long delay in answering, which has been due to an effort to find some books on this subject, and trusting that this may be of some slight use to you,

I am,
Yours very truly,
J. K. CALDWELL,
Assistant Japanese Secretary.

AMERICAN CONSULATE-GENERAL,
SANTO DOMINGO, D. R., December 16, 1913.

MR. GEORGE HENRY PAYNE,
NEW YORK, N. Y.

SIR:

In reply to yours of November 1, 1913, I have not been able to find any material of interest in regard to the attitude of the natives before the landing of

Columbus. The ruthless attitude of the Spaniards toward the natives is well known, and apparently neither women nor children were spared. The treatment of the natives resulted in their rapid decrease in number, and as early as 1510 the traffic in African slaves was begun and long continued.

Statistics as to the present condition of the child are few. During a typical quarterly period there were registered 8288 births (4269 males and 4019 females) but this probably represents only a portion of the actual births; of this number 3290 were legitimate and 4998 illegitimate. This does not, however, represent the extreme state of immorality that it might indicate, as mating lasting through years and clung to with fidelity and accompanied by a tender care for the offspring is frequently not preceded by a marriage ceremony, which is regarded as more or less of a useless expense. The population of the Republic is not known but is estimated as approximating 600,000.

As among the Spanish races in general, great affection is shown to children. Fathers and mothers, brothers and sisters lavish caresses upon them continually and in public.

There being few factories in the Dominican Republic, child labour, as we know it, does not exist. Children early begin to earn their living, but the work is mostly in the open air or open shops and labour conditions are far from strenuous. The clothing worn by children is scant, and youngsters of the lower classes up to the age of five or six years usually run nude, decorated only by a necklace or a pair of earrings

School facilities, though provided by the State, are inadequate. The reported annual attendance at all schools in the country is only 20,000.

Health conditions in the island are good. The total deaths registered in one quarter (again short of the real figures) is 1770, of which 318 deaths were of children less than a year old, and 336 of children between one and five years. The number of persons reported guilty of crimes or disorders in one quarter totaled 1910, of which 301 were between fourteen and twenty-one years of age.

I am, Sir,

Very respectfully yours,

CHARLES H. ALLRECHT,

Vice and Deputy Consul-General.

AMERICAN CONSULAR SERVICE,
PORT ELIZABETH, UNION OF SOUTH AFRICA, Mar. 7, 1914.

MR. GEORGE HENRY PAYNE,
NEW YORK, N. Y., U. S. A.

SIR:

Your letter requesting information for your book on the history of the attitude of states and tribes toward children received. Such information as has been obta'ned would indicate that the South African natives in this section are universally kind to children.

The only "natives" in this district, using the words in a strict sense, are the "Bantus" otherwise the Kaffirs. These people are specially fond of children and use them well.

If a child is left an orphan, any relative, no matter how distant, is willing to adopt the child. Indeed the services of the magistrate are frequently required in deciding disputes between claimants.

Love of, and kindness to, children are undoubted characteristics of the Kaffir.

South Africa has a considerable population of mixed races, but, so far as known, the colored people are kind to their children.

Trusting this may meet requirements.

         I am, Sir,

              Very respectfully yours,

                 E. A. WAKEFIELD,

                     American Consul.

BIBLIOGRAPHY

ABBOTT, JOHN S. C., *The Empire of Russia.* New York, 1860.

ACOSTA, JOSÉ DE, *The Natural and Moral History of the Indies.* London, 1880.

ACTON, BARON JOHN, *Lectures on Modern History.* London, 1906.

ADAM, ALEXANDER, *Roman Antiquities.* New York, 1826.

ADAMS, BROOKS, *The New Empire.* New York, 1902.

ADAMS, I. W., *Shibusawa; or The Passing of Old Japan.* New York, 1906.

ÆLIANUS, CLAUDIUS, *De Natura Animalium.* Jena, 1832.

ALEXANDER, GEORGE G., *Confucius the Great Teacher.* London, 1890.

ALLARD, PAUL, *Les Esclaves Chrétiens.* Paris, 1900.

AMIR ALI, MAULAWI SAYYID, *A Critical Examination of the Life and Teachings of Mahommed.* London, 1873.

—— *Student's Handbook of Mahommedan Law.* Calcutta, 1906.

—— *Islam.* London, 1906.

—— *Personal Law of the Mahommedans.* London, 1880.

—— *A Short History of the Saracens.* London, 1899.

ANDERSON, RASMUS B., *Norse Mythology.* Chicago, 1876.

ANDREE, RICHARD, *Die Anthropophagie.* Leipzig, 1887.

Anthropological Institute Journal. Vol. xxv. London, 1896.

APULEIUS. London (Bohn), 1853.

ARBOIS DE JUBAINVILLE, HENRI D'. *The Irish Mythological Cycle.* Dublin, 1903.

ARBUTHNOT, FOSTER F., *Persian Portraits.* London, 1887.

ARISTOPHANES, *Comedies of.* (Translated by W. J. Hickie.) Vols. i. and ii. London, 1874.

ARISTOTLE. *The Ethics.* (Transl. by Taylor, Thos.) London, 1811.

—— *The Politics.* (Translated by W. L. Newman). Vols. i. and ii. Oxford, 1887.

ARNOLD, SIR EDWIN, *Japonica*. London, 1892.

ARNOLD, MATTHEW, *Culture and Anarchy*. New York, 1889.

ARNOLD, THOMAS, *Introductory Lectures on Modern History*. New York, 1845.

ARVINE, REV. A. HAZLITT, *Cyclopedia of Moral and Religious Anecdotes*. New York, 1890.

ASAKAWA, KANICHI, *The Early Institutional Life of Japan*. Tokyo, 1903.

ASHLEY, WM. J., *An Introduction to English Economic History and Theory*. New York, 1888.

ATHENÆUS, *The Deipnosophists*. (Translated by C. D. Yonge.) Vols. i., ii., and iii. London, 1854.

ATTERBURY, ANSON P., *Islam in Africa*. New York, 1899.

AUBRY, JEAN B., *Les Chinois Chez Eux*. Lille, 1889.

AUGUSTINE, AURELIUS. (Translated by Rev. Marcus Dods.) Edinburgh, 1871.

AVEBURY, SIR JOHN LUBBOCK (BARON), *Marriage, Totemism, and Religion*. London, 1911.

—— *The Origin of Civilization and the Primitive Condition of Man. Mental and Social Condition of Savages*. London, 1882.

AZARA, FÉLIX DE, *Voyages dans l'Amérique Méridionale*. Vol. ii. Paris, 1809.

BACON, DAVID F., *Pious Women*. New Haven, 1833.

BADEN-POWELL, "Japanese Village Communities." *Quarterly Review*. Vol. i. Woking, 1896.

BAERLEIN, HENRY, *On the Forgotten Road*. London, 1909.

BAILEY, WM. B., *Modern Social Conditions*. New York, 1906.

BALFOUR, FREDERIC H., "Court and Society in Tokyo." *Transactions and Proceedings of the Japan Society*. London, 1897.

BALL, JAMES DYER, *Things Chinese*. London, 1904.

BAUDISSIN, W. W. G., *Adonis und Esmun*. Leipzig, 1911.

BAYLEY, HAROLD, *The Lost Language of Symbolism*. 2 vols. London, 1912.

BECKER, W. A., *Gallus*, or *Roman Scenes of the Time of Augustus*. (Translated by Rev. F. Metcalfe.) London, 1866.

BENJAMIN, SAMUEL G. W., *Persia*. New York, 1901.

BERGSON, HENRI L., *The Introduction to a New Philosophy*. Boston, 1912.

—— *An Introduction to Metaphysics*. London, 1913.

—— *Matter and Memory*. London, 1912.

BETTANY, G. T., *The World's Religions.* New York, 1891.
—— *The Teeming Millions of the East.* London, 1889.
BETTS, LILLIAN W., *The Leaven in a Great City.* New York, 1903.
BHATTÁCHAŔYYA, KRISHNA KAMAL, *Tagore Law Lectures.* Calcutta, 1885.
BIOT, ÉDOUARD, "Recherches sur les Mœurs des Anciens Chinc:s, d'après le Chi-king." *Journal Asiatique.* 4 ser., vol. ii. Paris, 1843.
BISHOP, ISABELLA B., *Korea and her Neighbours.* New York, 1898.
BJERREGAARD, CARL H. A., *The Inner Life and the Tao-Teh-King.* New York, 1912.
BOAS, FRANZ, *The Mind of Primitive Man.* New York, 1911.
BOOTH, CHARLES, *The Aged Poor in England and Wales.* London, 1894.
BOOTH, GENERAL WM., *In Darkest England and the Way Out.* London, 1890.
BOULGER, DEMETRIUS C., *History of China.* 3 vols. London, 1881.
BOYD, WM. K., *The Ecclesiastical Edicts of the Theodosian Code.* New York, 1905.
BRACE, CHAS. L., *Gesta Christi: or A History of Humane Progress under Christianity.* New York, 1882.
BRAUN, JOSEPH, *Die Liturgische Gewandung im Occident und Orient.* Freiburg, 1907.
BRAUN, LILY, *Die Frauenfrage.* Leipzig, 1901.
BREASTED, FRANCES H. (Translator), *Songs of an Egyptian Peasant.* Leipzig, 1904.
BREASTED, J. H., *Ancient Records of Egypt.* 5 vols. Chicago, 1906–7.
—— *A History of Egypt.* New York, 1905.
BREHM, DR. A. E., *Bird Life.* London, 1874.
—— *Illustrirtes Thierleben.* 4 vols. Hildburghausen, 1868.
BRINTON, DANIEL G., *The Cradle of the Semites.* 2 vols. Philadelphia, 1889.
—— *Races and Peoples.* Lectures on the Science of Ethnology. New York, 1890.
—— *Religions of Primitive Peoples.* New York, 1897.
BRODA, RODOLPHE, *Le Prolétariat International.* Paris, 1912.
BROWN, ARTHUR J., *New Forces in Old China.* New York, 1904.

BROWNING, OSCAR, *A History of the Modern World.* **2 vols.** London, New York, 1912.

BRYANT, ERNEST E., *Reign of Antoninus Pius.* Cambridge, 1895.

BRYANT, JACOB, *A New System; or, An Analysis of Ancient Mythology.* 6 vols. London, 1807.

BUCKLE, HENRY THOS., *History of Civilization in England.* New York, 1903.

BUDGE, ERNEST A. W., *Osiris and the Egyptian Resurrection.* London, 1911.

—— *Egyptian Reading Book.* London, 1896.

—— *The Gods of the Egyptians.* London, 1904.

—— *Egyptian Magic.* London, 1899.

—— *The Mummy.* Cambridge, 1893.

BUISSON, FERDINAND, *Dictionnaire de Pédagogie.* **2 vols.** Paris, 1887.

BULFINCH, THOS., *The Age of Fable.* Boston, 1881.

BURNETT, FRANK, *Through Polynesia and Papua.* London, 1911.

CADBURY, E., and Others, *Women's Work and Wages.* London, 1909.

CAIN, REV. JOHN, " The Bhadrachellam and Rekapalli Taluqas." *Indian Antiquary.* Vol. viii. Bombay, 1879.

CAIRD, EDWARD, *The Evolution of Religion.* 2 vols. Boston, 1882.

CALDECOTT, ALFRED, *The Philosophy of Religion in England and America.* New York, 1901.

Callimachus and Theognis. (Translated by J. Banks.) London, 1893.

CARROLL, HENRY K., *The Religious Forces of the United States.* New York, 1912.

CENSORINUS, *De Die Natale.* (Translated by Wm. Maude.) New York, 1900.

CHABAS, FRANÇOIS J., *Œuvres Diverses.* Vols. i., ii., and iii. Paris, 1899.

CHANCELLOR, WM. E., *A Theory of Motives, Ideals, and Values in Education.* Boston, 1907.

CHASLES, V. PHILARÈTE, *Le Moyen Âge.* Paris, 1847.

CHAVANNES, ÉDOUARD, *Les Mémoires Historiques de Se-Ma Ts'ien.* 4 vols. Paris, 1897.

CHATELAIN, ÉMILE, *Mélanges*. Paris, 1910.

CHIGNELL, ARTHUR KENT, *Twenty-one Years in Papua*. London, 1913.

CHURCH, RICHARD W., *The Beginnings of the Middle Ages*. New York, 1893.

CHURCHWARD, ALBERT, *The Signs and Symbols of Primordial Man*. London, 1910.

CHWOLSON, DANIEL A., *Die Ssabier und der Ssabismus*. St. Petersburg, 1856.

—— *The Semitic Nations*. Washington, 1874.

CLARK, SUE AINSLIE, and WYATT, EDITH, *Making Both Ends Meet*. New York, 1911.

CLARKE, JAMES F., *Ten Great Religions*. Boston, 1896.

CLAY, ALBERT T., *Amurru: The Home of the Northern Semites*. Philadelphia, 1909.

COHEN, HENRY, *Description Historique des Monnaies Frappées sous l'Empire Romain*. 8 vols. Paris, 1859.

COMPARETTI, DOMENICO, *Le leggi di Gortyna e le altre iscrizioni arcaiche cretesi*. Vols. ii., iii. Milan, 1893.

COMPTON, HERBERT, *Indian Life in Town and Country*. New York, 1904.

CONFUCIUS. (Translated by James Legge.) New York, 1875.

CONGER, SARAH PIKE, *Letters from China*. Chicago, 1909.

COOK, STANLEY A., *The Laws of Moses and the Code of Hammurabi*. London, 1903.

COOKE-TAYLOR, R. WHATELY, *Factories and the Factory System*. London, 1886.

COOPER, WILLIAM R., *An Archaic Dictionary*. London, 1876.

COOTE, H. C., "A Building Superstition." *Folk-lore Journal*. Vol. i. London, 1883.

CORNABY, W. A., "The Chinese Maiden at Home." *East of Asia Magazine*. Vol. iii. Paris, 1843.

CORY, ISAAC PRESTON, *Ancient Fragments*. London, 1832.

COX, GEORGE W., *The Mythology of the Aryan Nations*. 2 vols. London, 1870.

—— *An Introduction to the Science of Comparative Mythology and Folk-lore*. London, 1883.

CROOKE, W., "The Hill Tribes of the Central Indian Hills." *Jour. Asiatic Society*. Vol. i.

CROOKE, W. (*Cont'd*). *The Popular Religion and Folk-lore of Northern India.* 2 vols. London, 1896.

CRUISE, C. F. (Translator). *The Greek Ecclesiastical Historians of the First Six Centuries.* 6 vols. London, 1847.

CURR, EDWARD M., *The Australian Race.* 2 vols. Melbourne, 1887.

CURTISS, SAMUEL I., *Primitive Semitic Religion Today.* Chicago, 1902.

DAPPER, OLFERT, *Description de l'Afrique.* Amsterdam, 1686.

DAREMBERG, CHARLES, and SAGLIO, E., *Dictionnaire des Antiquités.* Paris, 1896.

DARWIN, CHARLES, *The Descent of Man.* New York, 1875.

—— *The Origin of Species.* New York, 1873.

DASENT, SIR GEORGE W., *Popular Tales from the Norse.* Edinburgh, 1888.

D'AVENNES, E. PRISSE, *Monuments Égyptiens.* Paris, 1847.

DAVIES, WILLIAM H., *Beggars.* London, 1909.

DAVOUD-OGHLOU, GARABED A., *Histoire de la Législation des Anciens Germains.* 2 vols. Berlin, 1845.

DAWSON, JAMES, *Australian Aborigines.* Melbourne, 1881.

DE CURZON, E. *Études sur les Enfants Trouvés.*

DE GENOUILLAC, HENRI, *Tablettes de Dréhem.* Paris, 1911.

—— *Tablettes Sumériennes Archaïques.* Paris, 1909.

DEISSMANN, GUSTAVE ADOLF. (Translated by L. R. M. Strachan.) *Light from the Ancient East.* New York, 1911.

DELAPORTE, LOUIS J., "Tablettes de Dréhem." *Revue d'Assyriologie et d'Archéologie Orientale.* Vol. viii. Paris, 1911.

DENBY, CHARLES, *China and Her People.* Boston, 1906.

DENIS, JACQUES, *Histoire des Théories et des Idées Morales dans l'Antiquité.* 2 vols. Paris, 1856.

DEWE, JUHL A., *Medieval and Modern History.* New York, 1907.

D'HORME, O. P., "Tablette rituelle néo-babylonienne." *Revue Assyriologie et d'Archéologie Orientale.* Vol. viii. Paris, 1911.

DILL, SAMUEL, *Roman Society from Nero to Marcus Aurelius.* New York, 1905.

DIMASHQI, ABU ABD ALLAH MUHAMMAD AL-. *Cosmographie.* St. Petersburg, 1866.

DIONYSIUS HALICARNASSENSIS. 4 vols. Leipzig, 1691.

DOUGLAS, SIR ROBERT K., *Confucianism and Taoism.* London, 1889.

DOUGLAS, SIR ROBERT K. (*Cont'd*).   *Society in China.*   London, 1894.

DRAPER, JOHN WM., *History of the Intellectual Development of Europe.*   New York, 1876.

DRIVER, SAMUEL R., *Modern Research as Illustrating the Bible.*   London, 1909.

DUNCAN, J. GARROW, *The Exploration of Egypt and the Old Testament.*   New York, 1909.

DUNCKER, MAX, *History of Antiquity.*   6 vols.   London, 1877.

DUNCOMBE, JOHN, *Select Works of the Emperor Julian.*   2 vols.   London, 1784.

DUNHAM, S. A., *History of Europe during the Middle Ages.*   4 vols.   London, 1833.

DUNLOP, O. JOCELYN, *English Apprenticeship and Child Labour.*   London, 1912.

DUPRAT, G. L. (Translated by W. J. Greenstreet.)   *Morals: A Treatise on the Psycho-sociological Bases of Ethics.*   New York, 1903.

DURUY, VICTOR, *Histoire du Moyen Âge.*   Paris, 1882.

DUTT, R. CHUNDER, *A Brief History of Ancient and Modern India.*   Calcutta, 1907.

DWIGHT, MARY A., *Grecian and Roman Mythology.*   New York, 1860.

EARL, GEORGE W., *The Native Races of the Indian Archipelago.*   London, 1853.

ELKINGTON, E. WAY, *The Savage South Seas.*   London, 1907.

ELLIS, WM., *Narrative of a Tour through Hawaii.*   London, 1826.

—— *Polynesian Researches.*   4 vols.   London, 1853.

EMERSON, EDWIN, JR., *A History of the Nineteenth Century Year by Year.*   3 vols.   New York, 1902.

EMERTON, EPHRAIM, *Introduction to the Story of the Middle Ages.*   Boston, 1903.

ERMAN, ADOLF, *A Handbook of Egyptian Religion.*   London, 1907.

—— *Life in Ancient Egypt.*   London, 1894.

ESPINAS, ALFRED, *Des Sociétés Animales.*   Paris, 1878.

EURIPIDES. *Tragedies.* (Translated by T. W. Buckley.)   2 vols.   London, 1850.

EVANS, D. DELTA, *The Ancient Bards of Britain.*   Merthyr-Tydfil, 1906.

EWALD, GEORG HEINRICH VON, *The History of Israel.* 4 vols. London, 1869.

FALCKENBERG, RICHARD, *History of Modern Philosophy.* New York, 1893.

FARNELL, LEWIS R., *The Cults of the Greek States.* 5 vols. Oxford, 1896.

FAUST, ALLEN K., *Christianity as a Social Factor in Modern Japan.* Philadelphia, 1909.

FEATHERMAN, AMERICUS, *Social History of the Races of Mankind.* 7 vols. London, 1885.

FERGUSON, CHARLES, "In the World of Religious Thought." *Current Literature.* Vol. xxx.

FESTUS, SEXTUS POMPEIUS, *De Verborum Significatione.* Leipzig, 1839.

FIGUIER, LOUIS, *The Human Race.* New York, 1872.

FIRISHTAH, MUHAMMAD K., *History of the Rise of the Mahomedan Power in India.* 4 vols. London, 1829.

FISKE, JOHN, *A Century of Science.* Boston, 1899.
—— *The Destiny of Man.* Boston, 1886.

FISON, LORIMER, and HOWITT, A. W., *Kamilaroi and Kŭrnai.* Melbourne, 1880.

FLORENCE and LACASSAGNE, "La Tunique d'Argenteuil." *Bibliothèque de Criminologie.* Lyons, 1895.

FLYNT, JOSIAH, *Tramping with Tramps.* New York, 1899.

FOREMAN, JOHN, *The Philippine Islands.* New York, 1899.

FORLONG, JAMES G. R., *Faiths of Man.* 3 vols. London, 1906.

FORREST, J. DORSEY, *The Development of Western Civilization.* Chicago, 1897.

FOX, JOHN, JR., *Following the Sun-Flag.* New York, 1905.

FRAZER, JAMES G., *The Golden Bough.* Vols. iii. and iv. London, 1900.

FRASER, JOHN, *The Aborigines of New South Wales.* Sydney, 1892.

FRASER, MRS. MARY C., *The Custom of the Country.* New York, 1899.

FREEMAN, EDWARD A., *Historical Essays.* London, 1896.

FRIEDLAENDER, LUDWIG, *Roman Life and Manners under the Early Empire.* Vol. i. London, 1909.

FRIEDMAN, I. KAHN, *The Autobiography of a Beggar.* Boston, 1903.

FROBENIUS, LEO, *The Childhood of Man.* Philadelphia, 1909.

FUERST, DR. JULIUS, *Der Orient.* Leipzig, 1843.

FUSTEL DE COULANGES, N. DENIS, *The Ancient City.* Boston, 1874.

GAILLARD, A. H., *Recherches sur les Enfants Trouvés en France.* Paris, 1837.

GALLICHAN, MRS. WALTER M., *The Age of Mother-Power.* New York, 1914.

GALLOWAY, GEORGE, *The Philosophy of Religion.* New York, 1914.

GASCOYNE-CECIL, REV. WM., *Changing China.* London, 1910.

GAYLEY, CHARLES M., *The Classic Myths in English Literature.* Boston, 1894.

GEIL, WM. EDGAR, *Eighteen Capitals of China.* Philadelphia, 1911.

GELLION-DANGLAR, EUGÈNE, *Les Sémites et le Sémitisme.* Paris, 1882.

GERLAND, DR. GEORGE, *Über das Aussterben der Naturvölker.* Leipzig, 1868.

GHILLANY, F. W., *Die Menschenopfer der alten Hebräer.* Nürnberg, 1884.

GIBBINS, HENRY DE B., *Industry in England.* London, 1896.

GIBBON, EDWARD, *Decline and Fall of the Roman Empire.* 5 vols. New York, 1880.

GIDDINGS, FRANKLIN H., *The Principles of Sociology.* New York, 1911.

GILES, HERBERT A., *A Chinese Biographical Dictionary.* London, 1897.

—— *China and the Manchus.* Cambridge, 1912.

—— *The Civilization of China.* London, 1911.

GILES, JOHN A., *Six Old English Chronicles.* London, 1848.

GLADSTONE, WM. E., *Juventus mundi.* Boston, 1869.

GOMME, GEORGE L., " Some Traditions and Superstitions Connected with Buildings." *Antiquary.* vol. iii. London, New York, 1881.

GOODRICH, JOSEPH K., *Our Neighbours: The Japanese.* Chicago, 1913.

GOODSPEED, GEORGE STEPHEN, *A History of the Ancient World.* New York, 1904.

—— *A History of the Babylonians and Assyrians.* New York, 1902.

24

GOUROFF, ANTOINE J., *Recherches sur les Enfants Trouvés*. Paris, 1839.

GRAY, B. KIRKMAN, *Philanthropy and the State*. London, 1908.

GRAY, G. Z., *The Children's Crusade*. Boston, 1872.

GRIFFIS, WM. ELIOT, *The Mikado's Empire*. New York, 1906.

—— *The Religions of Japan*. New York, 1895.

GRIMM, JACOB L. K., *Teutonic Mythology*. 4 vols. London, 1880.

—— *Deutsche Rechtsalterthümer*. Göttingen, 1854.

GROOT, JOHANNES J. M., *The Religious System of China*. Leyden, 1892.

GUERBER, HÉLÈNE A., *Myths of the Norsemen*. London, 1908.

GUPPY, HENRY B., *The Solomon Islands and their Natives*. London, 1887.

HABERLANDT, DR. M., *Ethnology*. (Translation by J. H. Loewe.) London, 1900.

HALL, HARRY R., *The Ancient History of the Near East*. New York, 1913.

—— and KING, L. W., *Egypt and Western Asia in the Light of Recent Discoveries*. London, 1907.

HALLAM, HENRY, *View of the State of Europe during the Middle Ages*. 3 vols. London, 1872.

HAMILTON, CHAS., *The Hedaya, or Guide*. 4 vols. London, 1791.

HAMMER-PURGSTALL, JOSEPH VON, "Extraits du Fihrist." *Journal Asiatique*. Vol. xii. Paris, 1841.

HARADA (JIRO), "The Five Festivals of the Seasons in Japan." *Jap. Soc. Trans. and Proc.* Vol. xi. London, 1912.

HARDY, E. G., *Studies in Roman History*. London, 1910.

HARLEZ, CHARLES DE, *L'Infanticide en Chine*. Louvain, 1885.

—— "San-li-tdu." *Journal Asiatique*. Ser. 8, vol. xv. Paris, 1890.

HARPER, ROBT. F., *The Code of Hammurabi*. Chicago, 1904.

HARRIS, GEORGE, *Civilization Considered as a Science*. London, 1872.

HARRISON, E. J., *The Fighting Spirit of Japan*. New York, 1913.

HARRISON, JANE E., *Prolegomena to the Study of Greek Religion*. Cambridge, 1903.

—— *Themis*. Cambridge, 1912.

HAUSSONVILLE, COMTE GABRIEL D', *Misère et Remèdes*. Paris, 1886.

HEDLEY, JOHN, "The Chinese Mandarin." *East of Asia Magazine*. Vol. iii. Shanghai, 1904.

HIGGINS, MRS. NAPIER, *Women of Europe in the Fifteenth and Sixteenth Centuries*. 2 vols. London, 1885.

HILPRECHT, H. V., *The Babylonian Expedition of the University of Pennsylvania*. Philadelphia, 1910.

—— *Explorations in Bible Lands during the 19th Century*. Philadelphia, 1903.

HIRTH, FRIEDRICH, *Ancient History of China*. New York, 1908.

HOBHOUSE, L. T., *Morals in Evolution*. 2 vols. London, 1906.

HOLMAN, HENRY, *Education*. London, 1896.

HORNE, HERMAN H., *The Psychological Principles of Education*. New York, 1906.

HUNTER, ROBERT, *Poverty*. New York, 1904.

HUNTER, WM. A., *Roman Law*.

HUNTER, SIR WM. WILSON, *The Indian Empire*. London, 1893.

HUNZICKER, I., *Poetarum Comicorum Græcorum Fragmenta Post Augustum*. Meineke, Paris, 1865.

IAMBLICHUS, *Life of Pythagoras*, etc. (Transl. Thos. Taylor.) London, 1818.

IHERING, RUDOLPH, *Geist des Römischen Rechts*. 4 vols. Leipzig, 1866.

INMAN, THOMAS, *Ancient Faiths Embodied in Ancient Names*. 2 vols. New York, 1874.

Japan Society, London, Transactions and Proceedings. London, 1893–1915.

JASTROW, MORRIS, *Religion of Babylonia and Assyria*. Boston, 1898.

JEREZ, FRANCISCO, *Conquista del Peru*. Madrid, 1853.

JEVONS, FRANK BYRON, *An Introduction to the History of Religion*. London, 1896.

JOHNS, CLAUDE H. W., *Babylonian and Assyrian Laws, Contracts, and Letters*. New York, 1904.

JORDAN, LOUIS H., *Comparative Religion*. Edinburgh, 1905.

JUSTIN MARTYR and ATHENAGORAS. (Translated by Rev. M. Dods and others.) Edinburgh, 1867.

JUSTINIAN. *Institutes*. (Translated by T. C. Sandars.) London, 1853.

JUVENAL. *Satires*. (Translated by Lewis Evans.) New York, 1860.

KADONO, CHOKURO, "The Bringing-up of Japanese Girls." *Transactions and Proceedings Japan Society*. Vol. vi. London, 1906.

KEANE, AUGUSTUS H., *Man—Past and Present*. Cambridge, 1899.

KEENE, HENRY G., *History of India*. Edinburgh, 1906.

KEIGHTLEY, THOMAS, *The Mythology of Ancient Greece and Italy*. London, 1836.

KEMP, E. G., *The Face of China*. London, 1909.

KIDD, BENJAMIN, *Principles of Western Civilization*. New York, 1902.

KIDD, DUDLEY, *The Essential Kafir*. London, 1904.

KIDDLE, HENRY, *The Cyclopedia of Education*. New York, 1877.

KING, LEONARD W., *A History of Babylonia and Assyria. History of Sumer and Akkad*. London, 1910.

—— *Letters and Inscriptions of Hammurabi*. 3 vols. London, 1898.

—— and HALL, H. R., *Egypt and Western Asia in the Light of Recent Discoveries*. London, 1907.

KINGSLEY, REV. CHARLES, *The Roman and the Teuton*. London, 1875.

KINGSLEY, MARY H., *Travels in West Africa*. London, 1897.

KODA, N., "The Pastimes of Modern Japan." *Japanese Magazine*. Vol. iii. Tokyo, 1913.

KOIKE, CHOZO, "A Glimpse of Japanese Home Life." *Transaction and Proceedings Japan Society*. Vol. v. London, 1902.

KOTZEBUE, OTTO VON, *A Voyage of Discovery into the South Sea*, etc. London, 1821.

KRACHENINNIKOW, STEFAN, *Histoire et description du Kamtchatka*. 2 vols. Amsterdam, 1770.

KRAPF, JOHANN L., *Travels, Researches, and Missionary Labours in East Africa*. London, 1860.

KRAUSSE, ALEXIS, *The Story of the Chinese Crisis*. London, 1900.

KUENEN, ABRAHAM, *The Religion of Israel*. 3 vols. London, 1875.

LADD, GEO. T., *Rare Days in Japan*. New York, 1910.

LAFITAU, JOSEPH F., *Mœurs des Sauvages Amériquains*, etc. Vol. i. Paris, 1724.

LALLEMAND, LÉON, *Histoire de la Charité*. 4 vols. Paris, 1903.

—— *Histoire des Enfants Abandonnés et Délaissés*. Paris, 1885.

LANCIANI,——, "A Building Superstition." *Folk-lore Journal.* Vol. i., p. 23. London, 1883.

LANE, EDWARD WM., *Arabian Society in the Middle Ages.* London, 1883.

LANE-POOLE, STANLEY, *A History of Egypt.* 6 vols. London, 1901.

LASELLE, MARY A., and WILEY, K. E., *Vocations for Girls.* Boston, 1913.

LAURENT, FRANÇOIS, *Histoire du Droit des Gens: Études sur l'Histoire de l'Humanité.* Tome v. ("Les barbares et le catholicisme.") Paris, 1857.

—— Same. Tome vi. "La papauté et l'empire." Paris, 1860.

—— Same. Tome vii. "La féodalité et l'église." Paris, 1865.

LEBEAU, CHARLES, *Histoire du Bas-Empire.* 10 vols. Paris, 1824.

LECKY, WM. ED H., *History of England in the 18th Century.* 8 vols. London, 1887.

—— *History of European Morals.* 2 vols. New York, 1877.

LE CONTE, JOSEPH, *Elements of Geology.* New York, 1878.

LEGENDRE, AIMÉ F., *Le Far-west Chinois.* Paris, 1910.

LEGGE, JAMES, *The Chinese Classics.* 7 vols. Oxford, 1893.

LELAND, CHARLES GODFREY, and PRINCE, JOHN DYNELEY (Translators). *Kuloskap the Master.* New York, 1902.

LENORMANT, FRANÇOIS, *The Beginnings of History.* New York, 1882.

LEONARD, E. M., *The Early History of English Poor Relief.* Cambridge, 1900.

LESCURE, MATHURIN, *De les Grandes Épouses.* Paris, 1884.

LETOURNEAU, CHAS., *La Condition de la Femme.* Paris, 1903.

—— *L'évolution du mariage et de la famille.* Paris, 1888.

—— *La Psychologie Ethnique.* Paris, 1901.

LEVÉE, JÉRÔME B., and L'ABBÉ LE MONNIER. (Editors.) *Théâtre Complet des Latins.* 15 vols. Paris, 1820.

LINCOLN, JONATHAN T., *The Factory.* Boston, 1912.

LITTLE, ARCHIBALD, *Gleanings from China.* London, 1911.

LITTLE, REV. HENRY W., *Madagascar: Its History and People.* London-Edinburgh, 1887.

LIVINGSTONE, DAVID, *Missionary Travels and Researches in South Africa.* New York, 1858.

LOOMIS, REV. A. W., *Confucius and the Chinese Classics.* San Francisco, 1867.

LORD, JOHN, *Ancient States and Empires*.   New York, 1869.

LUBBOCK, SIR JOHN (BARON AVEBURY), *Marriage, Totemism, and Religion*.   London, 1911.

—— *The Origin of Civilization and the Primitive Condition of Man. Mental and Social Condition of Savages*.   London, 1882.

LUNDY, JOHN P., *Monumental Christianity*.   New York, 1876.

LYON, D. G., and MOORE, G. F., ed., *Studies in the History of Religions*.   New York, 1912.

MACAULAY, THOMAS BABINGTON, *History of England*.   New York, 1882.

McCARTHY, JUSTIN, *A History of Our Own Times*.   2 vols. New York.

McKENZIE, F. A., *The Unveiled East*.   London, 1907.

MACLAGAN, ROBT. C., *Religio Scotica*.   Edinburgh, 1909.

MAHAFFY, J. P., *Empire of the Ptolemies*.   London, 1895.

—— *A Survey of Greek Civilization*.   New York, 1896.

—— *Twelve Lectures on Primitive Civilizations*.   London, 1869.

MAIMONIDES, MOSES, *The Guide for the Perplexed*.   (Translated by M. Friedlander.) London, 1904.

MAINE, SIR HENRY SUMNER, *Early History of Institutions*.   New York, 1890.

MALCOLM, SIR JOHN, *The History of Persia*.   2 vols. London, 1815.

MALINOWSKI, B., *The Family among the Australian Aborigines*.   London, 1913.

MALLESON, COLONEL C. S. I., "Famous Women of India." *Asiatic Quarterly Review*.   Vol. iii. London, 1887.

MANTOUX, PAUL, *La Révolution Industrielle*.   Paris, 1906.

MARCAIS, W., and HOUDAS, O., *Les Traditions Islamiques*.   Vols. i.–iii. Paris, 1906.

MARIAGER, PETER, *Pictures of Hellas*.   New York, 1888.

MARINER, WM., *An Account of the Natives of the Tonga Islands*.   2 vols. London, 1817.

MARKHAM, CLEMENTS R., *Cuzco and Lima*.   London, 1856.

MASON, AMELIA GERE, *Women in the Golden Ages*.   New York, 1901.

MASPERO, GASTON, *The Dawn of Civilization*.   London, 1894.

—— *Histoire Ancienne*.   Paris, 1878.

—— *The Passing of the Empires*.   New York, 1900.

—— *The Struggle of the Nations*.   London, 1896.

MAYNARD, MICHEL (L'ABBÉ), *Saint Vincent de Paul.* 4 vols. Paris, 1860.

MELMOTH, WM., *The Letters of Pliny the Consul.* 2 vols. London, 1810.

MEYER, E. H., *Mythologie der Germanen.* Strasburg, 1903.

MEYER, RICHARD M., *Altgermanische Religionsgeschichte.* Leipzig, 1910.

MILAN, HENRY H., *History of Latin Christianity.* Vol. i. London, 1854.

MITRA, RAJENDRALALA, *Indo-Aryans.* 2 vols. London-Calcutta, 1881.

MOMMSEN, THEODOR, *Romisches Strafrecht.* Leipzig, Duncker and Humbolt, 1899.

MOORE, GEORGE F., *History of Religions.* New York, 1913.

MORGAN, C. LLOYD, *Essays by George John Romanes.* London, New York, and Bombay, 1897.

MOVERS, DR. F. C., *Phönizische Terte.* 2 vols. Breslau, 1845.

MULLERUS, CAROLUS, *Fragmenta Historicorum Græcorum.* Paris, 1851.

MURATORIO, A. LUDOVICO, *Antiquitates Italicæ Medii Ævi.* 6 vols. Mediolani, 1734–1742.

MURRAY, J., *The Quarterly Review.* Vol. LXVII. London, 1841.

MURRAY, J. H. P., *Papua,* or *British New Guinea.* New York, 1912.

National Review, The. Vol. lx. London, November, 1913.

NITOBE, INAZO, *The Japanese Nation.* New York, 1912.

NOODT, GERARDI, *Opera Omnia.* Lugduni Batavorum, 1767.

NORDAU, MAX, *Interpretation of History.* New York, 1911.

NORTHROP, W. B., *Wealth and Want.* London, 1909.

O'BRIEN, HENRY, *The Round Towers of Ireland.* London, 1898.

OCELLUS, LUCANUS, *On the Nature of the Universe.* (Translated by Thomas Taylor.) London, 1831.

OLMSTEAD, A. T., *Western Asia in the Days of Sargon of Assyria.* New York, 1908.

O'NEILL, JOHN, *The Nights of the Gods.* 2 vols. London, 1893.

Orientaux Mélanges. *Publications de l'École des Langues Orientales Vivantes.* 2 series. Paris, September, 1883.

ORTOLAN, JOSEPH L. E., *The History of Roman Law.* (Translated by J. T. Pritchard and D. Nasmith.) London, 1871.

O'SHEA, M. V., *Social Development and Education.* Boston, 1909.

PALATRE, P. GABRIEL, *L'Infanticide et l'Œuvre de la Sainte-Enfance en Chine.* Shanghai, 1878.

PARKER, EDWARD HARPER, *China—Past and Present.* London, 1903.

PARKER, M. A., *Studies in Chinese Religion.* London, 1910.

PAUSANIAS, *The Description of Greece.* 3 vols. London, 1794.

PAYTON, L. B., PH. D.,*The Early History of Syria and Palestine.* New York, 1901.

PERRY, WALTER COPLAND, *The Women of Homer.* New York, 1898.

PHILLIMORE, JOHN GEORGE, Q. C.,*Private Law among the Romans.* London and Cambridge, 1863.

PIEGNOT, G., *Dictionnaire Critique, Littéraire, et Bibliographique.* 2 vols. Paris, 1806.

PIERCE, B. K., *A Half Century with Juvenile Delinquents.* New York, 1869.

PLACUCCI, MICHELE, *Usi e Pregiudizi dei Contadine della Romagna.* Vol. I. Palermo, 1885.

PLAUTUS. (Translated by H. T. Riley.) 2 vols. London, 1881.

PLOSS, H. H., *Das Kind in Brauch und Sitte der Völker.* Stuttgart, 1876.

PLUTARCH, *Œuvres Complet.* 25 vols. (Translated by J. Amyot.) Paris, 1783.

Polynesian Society. Journal containing transactions and proc. Vols. i., ii., iii. Leipzig, 1909.

POSECK, VON H., *East of Asia Magazine.* Vols. ii., iii., and iv. Shanghai, 1903.

Punjab Notes and Queries. A monthly periodical. Vol. ii. Allahabad, 1884–1885.

PUTNAM, GEORGE H., *The Censorship of the Church of Rome.* 2 vols. New York and London, 1906.

PUTZ, W., *Handbook of Mediæval Geography and History.* (Translated by Rev. R. B. Paul.) New York, 1850.

RALSTON, W. R. S., *Songs of the Russian People.* London, 1872.

RAWLINSON, GEORGE, *Ancient History.* New York, 1900.

—— *History of Herodotus.* 4 vols. London, 1888.

—— *The Five Great Monarchies of the Ancient Eastern World.* 3 vols. London, 1862.

—— *The Sixth Great Oriental Monarchy.* London, 1873.

Rawlinson, George (*Cont'd*). *The Seventh Great Oriental Monarchy.* London-New York, 1876.

—— *The Story of the Nations.* New York, 1893.

Reich, Emil, *Select Document.* London, 1905.

Reichardt, Noel, *The Significance of Ancient Religions.* London, 1912.

Renan, Ernest, *Histoire des Origines du Chrétienisme.* 8 vols. Paris, 1883.

—— *Histoire du Peuple d'Israël.* 5 vols. Paris, 1887.

Rengger, J. R., *Näturgeschichte der Säugethiere von Paraguay.* Aarau, 1835.

Report on Condition of Woman and Child Earners in the United States. 19 vols. Washington, 1910.

Revillout, M. D., "La Femme dans l'Antiquité." *Journal Asiatique.* Paris, 1906.

Revue Philosophique. Vol. xlix. Paris, 1900.

Rhys, John, *Lectures on the Origin and Growth of Religion.* Edinburgh, 1888.

Riis, Jacob A., *The Battle with the Slum.* New York, 1902.

—— *Children of the Tenement.* New York, 1903.

Riley, Henry Thos., B.A., *The Comedies of Plautus.* 2 vols. London, 1852.

—— *The Comedies of Terence.* London, 1853.

—— *Memorials of London and London Life.* London, 1868.

Robertson, William, *History of America.* 4 vols. London, 1817.

Rogers, Robt. W., *Cuneiform Parallels to the Old Testament.* New York, 1912.

—— *Outlines of the History of Early Babylonia.* Leipzig, 1895.

Rollin, Charles, *The Ancient History.* 4 vols. Philadelphia, 1876.

Romanes, George J., M.A., LL.D., F.R.S., *Animal Intelligence.* New York, 1886.

—— *Mental Evolution in Animals.* London, 1883.

Romilly, H. H., *The Western Pacific and New Guinea.* London, 1887.

Rosières, Raoul, *Histoire de la Société Française au Moyen-âge.* 2 vols. Paris, 1882.

Rosoy, de Ch., *Œuvres de Macrobe.* 2 vols. Paris, 1827.

Roth, H. Ling, *Great Benin.* Halifax, 1903.

Rusden, G. W., *History of Australia.*

RYDBERG, VIKTOR, *Teutonic Mythology.* 3 vols. London-Berlin, 1906.

SALT, HENRY S., *Animals' Rights.* New York and London, 1894.

—— and others, *Cruelties of Civilization.* 3 vols. London, 1893.

SARZEC, ERNEST DE, *Découvertes en Chaldée.* 2 vols. Paris, 1884.

SAYCE, A. H., *The Ancient Empires of the East.* London, 1884.

—— *The Egypt of the Hebrews and Herodotus.* London, 1902.

SCHAFF, P., D.D., and WACE, H., D.D., *The Nicene and Post-Nicene Fathers.* 7 vols. New York, 1896.

SCHLEGEL, FREDERICK, *A Course of Lectures on Modern History.* London, 1849.

SCHOEMANN, G. F., *Griechische Alterthumer.* Vols. i. and ii. Berlin, 1897.

SELLIN, DR. ERNST, *Denkschriften der Kaiserlichen Akademie der Wissenschaften.* Vols. l.–li. 1904–1906.

SEYMOUR, T. D., *Life in the Homeric Age.*

SHOOTER, REV. JOSEPH, *The Kafirs of Natal.* London, 1857.

SHUKBURGH, EVELYN S., *The Histories of Polybius.* 2 vols. London, 1889.

SIDGWICK, HENRY, *The Methods of Ethics.* London, 1893.

SILBERNAGEL, DR. ALFRED, *Bekampfung des Verbrechertums durch Rettung jugendlicher Delinquenten.* Bern, 1911.

SLAUGHTER, CHAS. W., "The Aboriginal Natives of North-Western Australia." *Westminster Review,* vol. clvi., pp. 411–426. London, 1901.

SLAWEY, C. M., *Imperial and Asiatic Quarterly Review.* Vols. ii., iv., and vi. Woking, 1896–8.

SLEEMAN, LIEUT.-COL. W. H., *Rambles and Recollections of an Indian Official.* 2 vols. London, 1844.

SMITH, M., *Rapport Fait au Conseil-Général de la Loire. Au Nom de la Commission.* Clermont-Ferrand, 1839.

SMITH, PHILIP, *A History of the Ancient World.* 3 vols. London, 1873.

SMITH, SAML. GEO., PH.D., LL.D., *Social Pathology.* New York, 1911.

SMITH, WM., *The Old Testament History.* New York, 1866.

SMITH, W. ROBERTSON, *Kinship and Marriage in Early Arabia.* London, 1903.

—— *Religions of the East.*

SMYTH, R. BROUGH, *The Aborigines of Victoria.* 2 vols. London, 1878.

SPARTIANUS, ÆLIUS, *Didius Julianus.* Lugduni Batav., 1671.

SPENCER, B., and GILLEN, F. J., *Native Tribes of Central Australia.* London, 1899.

SPENCER, HERBERT, *The Data of Ethics.* New York, 1886.

—— *Education.* New York, 1861.

—— *Essays: Scientific, Political, and Speculative.* 3 vols. London and Edinburgh, 1891.

—— *Facts and Comments.* New York, 1902.

—— *Justice.* New York, 1891.

—— *Negative Beneficence and Positive Beneficence.* New York, 1893.

—— *The Principles of Biology.* 2 vols. New York, 1898.

—— *The Principles of Psychology.* 2 vols. New York, 1877.

—— *Principles of Sociology.* 3 vols. New York, 1897.

—— *Recent Discussions in Science, Philosophy, and Morals.* New York, 1873.

—— *Social Statics.* New York, 1893.

—— *Northern Tribes of Central Australia.* London, 1904.

SPRENGER, ALOYS, *Das Leben und die Lehre des Moḥammad.* 3 vols. Berlin, 1869.

SQUIRE, CH., *The Mythology of the British Islands.* Glasgow and Dublin, 1905.

STEINMETZ, DR. S. R., *Ethnologische Studien zur ersten Entwicklung der Strafe. Mittheilungen der Anthropologischen Gesellschaft in Wien.* Vienna, 1895.

STENGEL, DR. PAUL, *Die Griechischen Kultursalterthumer.* München, 1898.

STEVENSON, ROBERT LOUIS, *In the South Seas.* New York, 1896.

STRACHEY, WM., *The Historie of Travaile into Virginia Britannia.* London, 1849.

STRACK, HERMANN L., D.D., PH.D., *The Jew and Human Sacrifice.* New York, 1909.

SUTHERLAND, A., *The Origin and Growth of the Moral Instinct.* 2 vols. New York-Bombay, 1898.

SYED, AMEER ALI, *A Short History of the Saracens.* London, 1899.

TACITUS. (Oxford translation.) 2 vols. London, 1854.

TAY, C. H., *Introduction to the History of Religions.* Boston, New York, Chicago, and London, 1913.

TAYLOR, ISAAC, M.A., *Etruscan Researches.* London, 1874.
—— *Greeks and Goths: A Study on the Runes.* London, 1879.
—— *Leaves of an Egyptian Note-Book.* London, 1888.
—— *Names and their Histories.* London, 1896.
—— *Words and Places.* London, 1873.
TAYLOR, THOS., *Select Works of Porphyry.* London, 1823.
TAYLOR, W. COOKE, *The Natural History of Society.* 2 vols. New York, 1841.
TERME, J. F., and MONFALCON, J. B., *Histoire Statistique et Morale des Enfants Trouvés.* Paris-Lyon, 1837.
—— *Nouvelles Considérations sur les Enfants Trouvés.* Paris, 1838.
THEODORET and EVAGRIUS, *History of the Church.* London, 1854.
THOMAS, ÉMILE, *Roman Life under the Cæsars.* London, 1899.
THOMPSON, R. C., *Semitic Magic.* London, 1908.
THUREAU-DANGIN, F., "Un Jugement sous Ammi-ditana." *Revue d'Assyriologie et d'Archéologie Orientale.* Vol. vii. Paris, 1910.
TIELE, F. P., *Outlines of the History of Religion.* London, 1877.
TOCQUEVILLE, M. ÉDOUARD DE, *Des Enfants Trouvés et des Orphelins Pauvres comme moyen de Colonisation de l'Algérie.* Paris.
TROPLONG, M., *De l'Influence du Christianisme sur le droit Civil des Romains.* Paris, 1855.
TRUMBULL, H. CLAY, *The Threshold Covenant.* New York, 1896.
TURNER, GEORGE, *Nineteen Years in Polynesia.* London, 1861.
—— *Samoa.* London, 1884.
VALDRUCHE, M., *Rapport au Conseil Général des Hospices sur le Service des Enfants-Trouvés dans le Département de la Seine.* Paris, 1838.
VERNON, EUGENE, *Mythologie dans l'Art Ancien et Moderne.* Paris, 1878.
VILLENEUVE-BARGEMONT (VISCOUNT), JEAN DE, *Économie Politique Chrétienne.* 3 vols. Paris, 1834.
VON KOTZEBUE, OTTO, *A Voyage of Discovery into the South Sea,* etc. London, 1821.
VON RANKE, LEOPOLD, *Universal History.* New York, 1885.
VOSKAMP, C. F., "The Story Teller in China." *East of Asia Magazine.* Vol. i. Shanghai, 1902.

WACHSMUTH, CURT, *Einleitung in das Studium der Alten Geschichte.*
  Leipzig, 1895.

WADE, MARY HAZELTON, *Our Little Japanese Cousin.* Boston,
  1901.

WAITZ, THEODORE, *Anthropology.*

WALLACE, ALFRED RUSSEL, *The Malay Archipelago.* 2 vols.
  London, 1869.

—— *The Wonderful Century.* New York, 1898.

WALLON, H., *Histoire de l'Esclavage dans l'Antiquité.* 3 vols.
  Paris, 1847.

WALSH, JAMES J., *The Thirteenth, Greatest of Centuries.* New
  York, 1910.

WALTER, FERDINAND, *Geschichte des Romischen Rechts bis auf
  Justinian.* Bonn, 1866.

WARE, J., *East of Asia Magazine.* Vol. ii. Shanghai, 1903.

WATSON, REV. J. S., *Justin, Cornelius Nepos, and Eutropius.*
  London, 1853.

WAUGH, ROSA, *Life of Benjamin Waugh.* London, 1913.

WEDGWOOD, JULIA, *The Moral Ideal.* London, 1907.

WELLES, FRANCIS CHANNING, *Principles of Social Development.*
  London, 1912.

WELSCKER, F. G., *Griechische Götterlehre.* 3 vols. Göttingen,
  1857.

WESTERMARCK, EDWARD, *The History of Human Marriage.*
  London, 1891.

—— *The Origin and Development of Moral Ideas.* 2 vols. London, 1906.

WHITNEY, A. D., *A Sanskrit Grammar.* Leipzig-Boston, 1889.

WHITON, JAMES M., PH.D., *Select Orations of Lysias.* Boston,
  1876.

WILCOX, DELOS F., *Great Cities in America.* New York,
  1910.

WILLARD, J. F. (JOSIAH FLYNT), *Tramping with Tramps.* New
  York, 1899.

WILLIAMS, MONIER, *Religious Thought and Life in India.* London,
  1883.

WINCKLER, HUGO, *The History of Babylonia and Assyria.* New
  York, 1907.

WOODFORD, CHARLES MORRIS, *A Naturalist among the Head-
  Hunters.* New York, 1890.

Woods, Erville Bartlett, *Progress as a Sociological Concept.* Chicago, 1907.

Worcester, Dean C., *The Philippine Islands and their People.* New York, 1898.

Wright, Hamilton M., *A Hand-Book of the Philippines.* Chicago.

Wulffen, Erich, *Das Kind.* Berlin, 1913.

Wyatt, Edith, and Clark, S. A., *Making Both Ends Meet.* New York, 1911.

Young, Lucien, *The Real Hawaii: Its History and Present Condition.* New York, 1899.

INDEX

The names of authors from whose works quotations have been made are printed in heavy-faced type.

A

Aaron, 162
Ab-ba-gi-na, 98
Abbott, Edith, 332
Abgal, 94
Abipones, 42
Abortion, 26, 259, 260, 279
Abraham, 158
Abu Tamman, 177
Abyssinians, 17
Accouchements, god of, 98
Achilles, 186
Acts of Parliament, 1802, 1833, 324, 329
Adelphi, 196
Adoption, 102, 288, 289; among the Greeks, 204; enjoined by Mohammed, 180; of orphans, China, 49
Adventures of Sanehat, 112
Ægean culture, 91
Ælian, 9, 207
Æsculapius, 187
Æthelstan, laws of, 292
Æthiopia, 274
Africa, 17, 23, 34, 106, 262
Agathocles, 8
Aghani, 173, 174, 175
Agis, 193
Agnew, Frederick A., 334
Agrarian Law, 215
Aha, island of, 74
Ahaz, 166
Aidan, 275
Ainu race, 71
Aix, 303

Akkado-Sumerians, 90, 92, 107
Albanian Scots, 275
Alexander the Great, 127–8
Al-Farazdac, 174, 175
Alfred, King, 283
Al Hidaya, 180
Allahabad, 137
Al Mostatraf, 172
Alsace, 276
Al Siyar, 182
Altar, infants buried at, 151
Ambrosius, 258, 263
Amenemhat I., 112
Ammianus Marcellinus, 177, 279
Ammonites, 164
Amosis, 113
Amphidromia, 193
Amphion, 187
Amraphael, 100
Amsterdam provides for children, 300
Amulius, 210
Amva, 124
Anacharsis, 196
Andromache, 185
Andromeda, 193
Angora (Ancyra), 268
Animal, care of young, 20; marriage, 3, 23; protection of child, 52, 186
Annales de la Sainte Enfance, 61
Antankarana tribes, 35
Antiphili, 197
Antiphon, 184
Antiquates italicæ medii ævi, 294

Index

INEQUALITY

OF THE

HUMAN

RACES

By Count Arthur de Gobineau
Author of "The Renaissance"

◎

Edited by Dr. Oscar Levy
Translated by Adrian Collins, M.A.

8vo. $2.00 net

The author shows the philosophical foundations upon which his brilliant studies of the Renaissance are based, and provides the historical student with a totally new standpoint from which to view his subject.

G. P. PUTNAM'S SONS
New York ∴ London

Social Progress and the Darwinian Theory

A Study of Force as a Factor in Human Relations

By George W. Nasmyth, Ph.D.

With an Introduction by Norman Angell

The philosophy of force, according to the author, is the real cause of the breakdown of civilization in Europe. This philosophy claims to find a scientific foundation in the application to human society of Darwin's theory of "the struggle for existence" and the "survival of the fittest." A critical study of this so-called "Social Darwinism," which upon analysis is found to consist in a belief that collective homicide is the cause of human progress, shows it to be entirely false. Moreover it is in direct contradiction to the ideas of Darwin himself, who bases his whole theory of social progress upon justice and the moral law.

G. P. PUTNAM'S SONS

New York ∴ London